HANDBOOK OF ANGER
MANAGEMENT AND DOMESTIC
VIOLENCE OFFENDER TREATMENT

In the *Handbook of Anger Management and Domestic Violence Offender Treatment*, Ronald T. Potter-Efron consciously connects anger management and domestic violence, two long separated fields, and addresses treatment options and intervention methods that meet the needs of individual clients, couples, families, and groups. Therapists, counselors, social workers, and other treatment specialists will find this book a useful overview and reference for anger and anger management techniques as well as domestic violence approaches.

This new edition is split into three distinct sections:

- A description of anger and domestic violence focused upon helping clients use the principles of neuroplasticity to dramatically alter their behavior.
- Assessment for anger problems and/or domestic violence.
- Group treatment or individual, couples, and family treatment for anger problems and/or domestic violence.

Woven through this book is a fair and balanced treatment of gender issues, reflected in the diversity of case examples that address jealousy, chronic anger, behavioral problems, group and individual counseling, and more. Readers are also shown how anger develops and can lead to verbal and physical outbursts, the five types of rage reactions, and how to treat anger turned inward. Potter-Efron also details four different approaches to treating anger: behavioral, cognitive, affective, and existential/spiritual. Mental health professionals are provided numerous questionnaires and worksheets to utilize with their clients. The *Handbook of Anger Management and Domestic Violence Offender Treatment* is an essential guidebook that illustrates effective theory and practice.

Ronald T. Potter-Efron, MSW, PhD, is Director of the Anger Management and Domestic Violence Center at First Things First Counseling in Eau Claire, Wisconsin. He is author of over fifteen books on anger management and related topics. His books for the general public include *Angry All the Time* (2004) and *Healing the Angry Brain* (2012).

HANDBOOK OF ANGER MANAGEMENT AND DOMESTIC VIOLENCE OFFENDER TREATMENT

Second Edition

Ronald T. Potter-Efron

Routledge
Taylor & Francis Group

NEW YORK AND LONDON

Second edition published 2015
by Routledge
711 Third Avenue, New York, NY 10017

and by Routledge
27 Church Road, Hove, East Sussex BN3 2FA

Routledge is an imprint of the Taylor & Francis Group, an informa business

© 2015 Taylor & Francis

The right of Ronald T. Potter-Efron to be identified as author of this work has been asserted by him in accordance with sections 77 and 78 of the Copyright, Designs and Patents Act 1988.

First edition published by Routledge 2005

Library of Congress Cataloging in Publication Data
Potter-Efron, Ronald T.
    Handbook of anger management and domestic violence offender treatment / Ronald T. Potter-Efron.
       pages cm
    Includes bibliographical references and index.
    1. Anger—Treatment.   2. Family violence—Treatment.   I. Title.
    RC569.5.A53P67 2015
    362.82'92—dc23   2014030929

ISBN: 978-0-415-71717-5 (hbk)
ISBN: 978-0-415-71718-2 (pbk)
ISBN: 978-1-315-87147-9 (ebk)

Typeset in Sabon
by Keystroke, Station Road, Codsall, Wolverhampton

This book is dedicated to the newest member of the family, Cédric Alexandre Bertrand.

CONTENTS

Preface   xi
Acknowledgements   xiii

PART I
Anger, Domestic Violence, and the Brain   1

1 **The Angry Brain**   3

   What is an "Angry Brain"? 4
   Emotions 6
   The Limbic System 8
   Neuroplasticity 11
   Ten Things to Know about the Angry Brain 17
   Healing the Angry Brain 24
   Summary 25

2 **Anger, Threat, Feeling Unsafe, and Domestic Violence**   27

   The Stressed and Traumatized Brain: Fear
      and Anger 27
   The Anger and Aggression Connection with
      the Stressed Brain 30
   Attachment Theory 32
   Anger, Domestic Violence, and Attachment Styles 36
   Romantic Jealousy, Fragile Self-Esteem, and
      Attachment 38
   Case Study: Excerpts from an Interview with
      a Jealous Man 40
   Attachment Theory Related Treatment
      Strategies for Romantic Jealousy Concerns 42

Polyvagal Theory 44
Helping Clients Develop a Relatively Safe Sense
of Themselves and the World 46
Summary 49

3 **Rage: Predictor of Out of Control Anger, Aggression,**
and Domestic Violence   50

What is Rage? 50
Varieties of Rage 52
Five Types of Rage 58
Summary 62

PART II
Assessment   63

4 **Assessment for Anger and Aggression**   65

General Concerns about Anger Assessment 65
Client Assessment 66
The Anger Styles Questionnaire 77
Anger Assessment as a Bridge to Treatment 82
Anger, Alcoholism, and Addiction 83
Case Study: Assessment of a Chronically Angry
Client with Multiple Problems 87
Summary 90

5 **Domestic Violence: Core Information and Assessment**   91

What is Domestic Violence? 91
How Common is Domestic Violence? 93
Which Gender Commits Acts of Domestic Violence? 94
Is Domestic Violence Unidirectional or Bidirectional? 94
Reasons People Use to Explain or Justify Acts of
Domestic Violence 94
Risk Factors 95
Anger's Relationship with Domestic Violence 96
Theoretical Models of Domestic Violence 97
Assessment of Participants 106
Summary 110

CONTENTS

PART III
Treatment 113

6 Intervention Approaches in Anger Management 115

Intervention Philosophies and Approaches 115
Treatment Intervention Areas in Anger
  and Aggression Management 118
Behavioral Approach: Introducing Clients to an
  Objective Change Focus 119
Cognitive Aspects of Anger Management 126
Affective Anger Management Approaches 131
Existential/Spiritual Anger Management Approaches 134
Effectiveness of Anger Management Counseling 137
Case Study: A Woman Angry at the Universe 138
Summary 141

7 The Anger and Aggression Cycle: A Therapeutic Model 142

Phase One: Activation 142
Phase Two: Modulation 144
Phase Three: Preparation 146
Phase Four: Action 147
Phase Five: Feedback (Including Empathy Training) 148
Phase Six: Deactivation (Including Forgiveness) 153
Case Study: How to Go Through the Anger
  Cycle Very Badly 167
Summary 169

8 Group Treatment for Domestic Violence Offenders 170

Domestic Violence Offender Treatment Program:
  Educational Focus 171
Extended Domestic Violence Offender Treatment Program 174
Women's Domestic Violence Offender Treatment Groups 179
Cultural Diversity: LGBT and Ethnic Minority
  Groups 181
Brain-Change Model for Domestic Violence
  Offender Treatment 182
Case Study: Domestic Violence Offender Brain-
  Change Program 192
Summary 195

CONTENTS

9 Alternatives to Group Therapy for Angry and
Domestically Violent People: Individual, Group,
and Family Therapy   196

Individual Anger and Domestic Violence Counseling 196
Case Study: A Man Who Benefited from Both
  Group and Individual Counseling 202
Couples Counseling with Angry or Violent Couples 203
Family Therapy Addressing Anger and Violence 211
Summary 217

10 Anger and Aggression Turned Inward   218

What is "Anger Turned Inward"? 218
Domestic Violence and Anger Turned Inward 220
Suppressed Anger 222
Case Study: The Lady Who Quit Smiling 228
Passive Aggression 229
Anger Directed at Self 232
What if Clients are High on Both Anger Turned
  Inward and Outward? 237
Summary 239

References   240
Index   250

PREFACE

This book is designed for treatment specialists in the areas of anger management and domestic violence offender treatment. There has been an unnecessary divide between these two fields for the last several decades. Unfortunately, that has often meant that anger management counselors were insufficiently trained to recognize or treat angry clients who were also domestic violence offenders, while domestic violence counselors were literally mandated in many states not to include anger management materials in their work with offenders. (The reason for this mandate will be discussed in chapter 5.) This artificial barrier is in the process of being broken down now and this volume hopefully will help connect these two long separated fields.

A note on terminology. I avoid terms that I believe are judgmental in the area of domestic violence. For that reason I have avoided the term "perpetrator," which casts one individual as chronically and seriously impaired and morally suspect. I also seldom use the terms "abuser," as this term fails to take into account the great frequency of mutual domestic violence. Instead, I write about "domestic violence offenders," a somewhat awkward phrase, but one I believe is less prejudicial than the others.

This book is divided into three major sections. The first part is on anger, domestic violence, and the brain. Here I present the research on what happens when people become immediately or chronically angry, how a central lack of physical and/or psychological safety makes people susceptible to anger and domestic violence, and how rage differs from anger and greatly increases someone's propensity toward violence. The second part consists of two chapters on assessment, one for anger management and one for domestic violence offenders. I strongly urge readers to consume both chapters regardless of your specialty. Finally, the third part is about treatment. Two of these chapters provide guidelines for group treatment of anger management and domestic violence offenders groups respectively. The domestic violence chapter includes information about a brain-change focused program for domestic violence offenders that we have been running at my clinic in Eau Claire, WI. The remaining chapters describe a typical anger/aggression cycle and its implications for treatment; alternative treatments including individual, couples and family therapy; and anger/aggression turned inward that is either suppressed or directed against the self.

Some of this material was provided previously in the forerunner to this book, which was entitled the *Handbook of Anger Management*. I retained the material from that volume I thought most useful.

ACKNOWLEDGEMENTS

I would like to begin by acknowledging two colleagues who have helped me gain enough information to write a book of this nature. The first is Lou Cozolino, who mentored me as I began learning about the human brain, the concept of neuroplasticity, and translation of pure scientific knowledge into practical ways to help people change their brains. The second is John Hamel, because of both his personal work with domestic offenders (*Gender-Inclusive Treatment of Intimate Partner Abuse*, 2014) as well as his ability to gather many scholars together to review the research literature on domestic violence (the PASK – Partner Abuse State of Knowledge Project). My understanding of the strengths and limitations of the domestic violence field has been greatly increased due to his steadfast effort.

Rich Pfeiffer, founder and director of the National Anger Management Association (NAMA), has been another source of inspiration. Rich has encouraged me to write and also to become a trainer in the domestic abuse arena (I've trained in the area of anger management for many years). He's also challenged me to think about anger management and domestic violence in a broad evolutionary manner. I also wish to thank another very active NAMA member, Lynette Hoy, as well as her husband David Hoy, both for their gracious hospitality when I come to Chicago and for Lynette's utilization of my anger management tools in her anger management counselor training programs.

My wife and frequent co-author Patricia Potter-Efron foresaw my entering the domestic violence area years before me. She has regularly steadied my resolve when I experience doubts about my insights and/ or knowledge. I doubt I would or could have completed this volume without her.

I am grateful for the professional illustration work created by Kelsey Temanson, recent graduate of the University Wisconsin–Eau Claire. Her excellent work is evident in chapter 1. Finally, I respect the highly professional work done by my editors at Routledge, including Katharine Atherton, Alison Foskett, and Elizabeth Lotto.

Part I

ANGER, DOMESTIC VIOLENCE, AND THE BRAIN

1

THE ANGRY BRAIN

In the first edition of this book (published as the *Handbook of Anger Management*, Potter-Efron, 2005) I included a small chapter on the emotional brain as somewhat of an afterthought at the end of the edition. This time I'm beginning the book with that topic. Let me explain why with this simple statement: angry people have angry brains. Now, because everybody becomes angry from time to time, let me revise that statement to a more accurate one: "chronically angry people have angry brains." Here's what I mean: a) anger can take over the emotional life of a person; b) as that happens the individual's entire way of perceiving and reacting to the universe is altered to justify his or her anger and hostility; c) these perceptual and behavioral reactions reflect real and long-lasting changes in the neural networks within the brain of this person; d) considerable conscious effort must be undertaken by the chronically angry individual to change this overdeveloped brain pattern; e) anger management and domestic violence counselors can both help their chronically angry clients (partially) disassemble these anger-directed brain patterns and also help them develop and reinforce positive brain networks. Presumably a therapist can do so without specific knowledge of how the brain works. However, I believe such information is quite valuable to both client and counselor.

Knowledge about the brain has expanded greatly in the last couple decades due to the availability of instruments like functional magnetic resonance imaging (fMRI) machines and other devices that track magnetic pulses, blood flow, water flow, and other aspects of brain activity. These important devices allow researchers to discover how the brain works without destroying it. Before they were developed, research could only be done on animals and deceased humans. Still, most of the material I present here is based on animal studies, particularly research utilizing rats, mice, and cats (Siegel, 2005). Readers should be aware that almost every year new information casts into doubt older ideas about what is occurring within the brain. Indeed, if you take a quick glance at articles in such leading journals as *Neuron*, you will discover they contain a large number of sentences beginning with the word "surprisingly." It is possible that by the time you read this book some of the information presented here might be outdated. However, I will concentrate on the core postulates that have stood up well over time.

What is an "Angry Brain"?

I will use the term "angry brain" in this book both metaphorically and more literally. Metaphorically, I mean that people with angry brains are individuals who have become so used to anger that they wake up mad, go through the day looking for things to get upset about, go to sleep angry, have mean dreams, and wake up angry again. It's as if anger had become that individual's default option. If so they respond to almost any stimulus with anger. They are also usually hindered in recognizing or utilizing other emotions because they are too focused upon anger. More literally, I use this term to describe people who have developed extensive neural networks consisting of hundreds of thousands or millions of neurons that fire together to bring about an angry word or action. These chronically angry people often lead unhappy lives. Their anger severely hinders them in day-to-day functioning. They often become clients seeking a better life. As I will elaborate upon soon, I believe many of these clients feel quite unsafe and that anger can be a way to defend against chronic feelings of danger and threat.

What causes someone to develop an angry brain? There is no single answer, of course. Here are some possibilities.

Deeply experienced feelings of danger, insecurity, and anxiety

I will emphasize this aspect of chronic anger throughout this volume. I believe that people who feel unsafe tend to develop chronic defensive anger patterns. Helping them feel safer both externally with regard to the world and internally with regard to an inner sense of safety will lessen the strength of their anger.

Family and cultural training

Angry clients often grew up in angry families. That's where they learned norms such as "An angry person gets what he wants," "When in doubt get mad," and "It's normal to say really mean things when you're upset." Modeling like this encourages anger to become habitual and desensitizes people from recognizing the harm their anger causes themselves and others. Later, when these children have families of their own, they will train their partners and children to abide by these same norms.

Families exist in larger cultures. Some nationalities are more volatile than others, such as Eastern European vs Scandinavian cultures. Volatile cultures are more likely to encourage the outward expression of anger, while less volatile ones may encourage their members to "stuff" their anger or to deny it completely. Membership in groups such as gangs can also create circumstances that create anger-dominant brain patterns.

Faulty neurochemical function

Neurotransmitters such as glutamate and GABA are critical for optimal brain functioning. Some neurotransmitters (glutamate, norepinephrine, acetylcholine, and dopamine) are generally excitatory; an excess of these chemicals might cause a person to feel agitated and thus become more defensively irritated and angry over time. As Niehoff (1998) pointed out, excess dopamine increases a person's sense of danger and therefore is likely to increase their irritability, anxiety, and degree of agitation. Other transmitters (GABA, serotonin) are generally inhibitory. Lack of these neurochemicals has been associated with impulsive aggression and suicidality. Anyone coming for anger management should be assessed for depression and suicidality as they have a common denominator in serotonin.

Hormonal influences

Testosterone and estrogen both have modest correlations with anger and aggression, but not enough for them to be considered major contributors to most people's chronic anger (Sapolsky, 2005).

"Bad genes"

No single anger gene has ever been identified. However, genes that increase someone's tendencies toward anxiety, impulsivity, and socio-pathy could contribute to the likelihood of someone developing chronic anger. The major research focus in the last decade, though, is the interplay between nature and nurture, a phenomenon called epigenesis. One well-studied example is the MAOA allele (variant) of the MAO gene. Men with this allele do have a tendency toward violent behavior, but only if they were raised in a violent home (Sapolsky, 2005).

Brain damage

Controlling one's angry impulses is a difficult task that needs a well-functioning brain. Some forms of brain damage definitely affect this capability. For example, frontal lobe damage impedes executive control over the urge to attack, while damage to the temporal lobes at the side of the head, where the amygdala and other limbic system regions reside, has been associated with rage attacks. These clients should be assessed by a neuropsychologist or psychiatrist to protect themselves and others. It is also the case that some angry clients may have difficult-to-diagnose minimal brain damage in several areas of their brains.

Emotions

A capacity to feel emotions is an ancient part of the human repertoire. Emotions precede thought in the sense that they are primarily experienced in relatively older parts of the brain that were functioning well before the cortex and neocortex (the newest and farthest front region of the brain) existed (Panksepp and Biven, 2012). The amygdala, a subcortical structure, is critical for the experience of many emotions, most strongly fear and anger (LeDoux and Damasio, 2013), but also positive emotions. Perhaps even more critical to most emotional experiences is the even more ancient PAG (periaqueductal gray) region of the midbrain (Panksepp and Biven, 2012). However, parts of the cortex and neocortex do play a role in our emotional experience and particularly in the conscious awareness of emotion. Indeed, some researchers distinguish between the unconscious sensation they call emotions and the conscious experience labeled feelings (Damasio, 2000, 2003).

There are at least six "primary" emotions, so labeled because they appear to be hard-wired and available from birth: anger, fear, sadness, joy, surprise, and disgust. These emotions all have immediate physical survival value. They are complemented by at least four "social" or "self-conscious" emotions: shame, guilt, embarrassment, and pride (Tracy, Robins, and Tangney, 2007). The social emotions are useful for social survival, in other words our ability to meet social demands and expectations.

The words "affect," "mood," "emotion," and "feeling" are so interwoven in both common and scientific discussion that it is difficult to distinguish meaningfully between them. In general, the word "affect" is used to refer to specific body sensation states, while "emotions" refer to a more complex state that has multiple components that are activated in response to some real or imagined object, person, or situation (Kring, 2001). LeDoux (1996, 2002) emphasizes the point that emotional processes are primarily unconscious or preconscious as the brain responds to certain situations by activating a cascade of physiological processes. Damasio (2000, 2003) distinguishes between three classes of emotions: background emotions that reflect a person's general sense of well-being or discomfort of being; primary emotions such as anger and fear that are hard-wired in the brain for rapid response; and social emotions such as

6

shame, guilt, and pride that regulate more sophisticated interpersonal processes. Although Damasio appears to agree with LeDoux that emotions are primarily preconscious, he adds that their full impact is only realized when they are sensed consciously, at which point he designates them as "feelings."

Panksepp (2009; Panksepp and Biven, 2012) offers a somewhat different explanation of emotions. He discusses prepropositional affective processes common to mammals. By this term he means that all basic emotional operating systems are organized in precognitive subcortical regions so that raw emotional tools for feeling and living are not created by lived experiences but are available at birth. He describes seven of these basic systems, of which two closely related ones are FEAR and RAGE. He names a number of brain areas associated with these systems, including the amygdala, but stresses that no single area should be considered the center of emotionality. Rather, emotionality involves interactions among many subcortical and cortical regions.

But what good are emotions? Here is my list of their value:

Survival. The ultimate purpose of emotions is to help us survive in a physically and socially dangerous world. Anger is no exception. It is important to remember that anger is necessary for survival. Anger is a messenger that warns of impending danger. Emotions inform us about the present and predict the future (Panksepp and Biven, 2012; Dispenza, 2007).

Intensification. Emotions place an exclamation point on experiences. They tell us to pay attention, that whatever is happening right now is important. Furthermore, they place these important experiences into our emotional memory banks (located, unconsciously, in the amygdala) so we will react emotionally whenever those events are triggered.

Preparation and Action. Emotions cannot be separated from actions. Each primary emotion carries with it an immediate action tendency. Fear makes us flee; surprise stops us in our tracks with a startle reaction; sadness draws us toward those who might comfort and nurture us. Meanwhile, anger's action tendency is to move toward an offending object, person, or situation with the intent of dislodging the obstacle or overcoming the threat.

Communication. Emotions, especially primary emotions, come with built-in, universally recognizable facial expressions (Ekman, 2003). Presumably a member of a tribe in unexplored jungle would recognize a Westerner's smile as a sign of happiness and a scowl as that of anger. With regard to anger, then, your scowling face tells others that you are angry and they need to be careful around you.

Truth Claim. Emotions feel right. We tend to trust our "gut feelings" because they emerge from deep within us. Indeed, some authors

(Gladwell, 2005) believe we are quite good at assessing another person's personality and credibility within seconds of meeting them. However, it turns out that emotions are not particularly trustworthy informants. The last thing I want to tell my chronically angry clients is to trust their gut. That's because their gut instincts can become just as distorted from chronic anger as their conscious thoughts. Still, it is important to assess one's emotions and they do normally provide essential information to us.

The Limbic System

Emotions have developed, mostly from brain structures originally utilized to detect smell (Ratey, 2002), to help individuals quickly and effectively respond to significant situations, especially those situations that could threaten survival. Thus, emotions can be conceived as a chain of loosely connected brain pathways and behavioral sequences that are activated whenever physical or social survival is potentially threatened. Plutchik (2001) describes two of these sequences in which an external stimulus event creates physiological arousal that in turn triggers overt behavior. With fear, the sequence goes from: a) the immediate perception (not necessarily conscious) of a threat; to b) an inferred cognition of danger; to c) a physiological feeling state of fear; to d) escape behavior; so as to e) restore safety. With anger the sequence becomes a) an awareness of an obstacle; b) creates an inferred cognition of there being an enemy; c) that produces the physiological state of anger; d) which in turn leads to attack behavior with the goal of destroying the obstacle. Note, though, that safety is important with anger as well as fear. A sense of threat may as easily trigger the "fight" part of the "fight or flight" reaction as the "flight" component.

Before continuing, let me add a note of caution. It is important to recognize that actually very little is known about how the brain functions at this time since only recently has it been possible to gather systematic information about it from living individuals. Furthermore, the brain is a very complex organ, composed of approximately 100 billion neurons, each of which might make as many as 10,000 connections with other neurons (Ratey, 2002). Also, the brain's development is never complete. One reason is that parts of the brain continue to develop well past childhood, including, for instance, cells in the hippocampus that contribute to impulse inhibition (Cozolino, 2002). Another equally significant fact is that new brain circuitry is continuously created as new pathways are developed as the result of new learning and experiences. A very thorough review of brain structures and mechanisms is presented in *Principles of Neuroscience, 5th edition* (Kandel et al., 2013), while Amthor (2012), Cozolino (2010a), Dispenza (2007), Ratey (2002),

LeDoux (2002), Lane and Nadel (2000), and other writers provide excellent summaries. More specifically, Niehoff (1998) describes many aspects of the biology of violence in her volume (also see Volavka, 2002), Sapolsky (2005) presents thoughtful commentary on the neuroscience of aggression in his work, while LeDoux (1996) and Cozolino (2010a) describe the effects of trauma on the brain particularly clearly and Damasio (2003) details the three previously mentioned subsets of emotions: background, primary, and social emotions.

Emotions are particularly difficult to study because they are "the result of multiple brain and body functions that are distributed over the whole person," rather than being localized within one part of the brain or body (Ratey, 2002, p. 223). Additionally, there is no single brain center for aggression (Volavka, 2002), so that malfunctions in any part of the brain, including the limbic area and the neocortex, may result in poor emotional regulation. Nevertheless, certain locations in the brain have been identified that are regularly associated with emotional functioning. More specifically, several discrete areas of the brain have been linked in a circuit that produces affective aggression and probably the related feeling of anger. Panksepp (1998, 2009; Panksepp and Biven, 2012) links the amygdala, hypothalamus, and periaqueductal gray (PAG) areas of the brain to what he labels the RAGE response. According to Panksepp, these three areas are hierarchical in that the amygdala's ability to respond to anger-provoking stimuli depends upon the well-functioning of the hypothalamus which in turn depends upon the well-functioning of the PAG. Thus, a lesion in the PAG would affect the entire system, whereas a lesion in the amygdala would have a lesser effect. As such, the PAG is central to the anger experience and possibly the most important area for the actual integration of the overall anger response (Panksepp and Biven, 2012). Panksepp notes that affective aggression is one of three basic kinds of animal aggression; the other two are predatory and inter-male aggression. Only affective aggression, however, is linked with what would normally be considered an angry state of being. Panksepp states one cause for this kind of aggression: "anything that restricts our freedom will be viewed as an irritant deserving our anger, contempt and revolutionary intent" (Panksepp, 1998, p. 189). He notes that restricting access to desired resources is another trigger for affective aggression.

The description above refers to normal mammalian displays of anger and aggression. As such anger and aggression are not necessarily problematic, even in the increasingly complex societies human beings create. They serve the function of activating the system against threat and toward sought-after but blocked resources. Furthermore, the relatively primitive circuitry described above is highly mediated in humans through higher cognitive processes centered within the prefrontal cortex of the brain. However, many kinds of damage, including that caused by stress and trauma, can strongly affect the functioning of the brain in these areas.

The *limbic system* is a useful term for a collection of areas in the brain that collectively have developed circuitry that creates, stores, and manages emotions. Some of these areas are subcortical, meaning they are older areas that developed relatively early in our species. These include the amygdala, thalamus, hypothalamus, and PAG nuclei. The amygdala is particularly crucial for emotions. It is both an early warning system telling us something may be dangerous and the place where emotional memories are stored. These memories are usually vague and always non-conscious. They create a sense of danger but cannot provide details or context.

Newer, cortical parts of the limbic system include the hippocampus, dorsolateral prefrontal cortex, and the orbitofrontal cortex. Here is where emotions become consciously experienced and labeled. These relatively newer parts of the brain are particularly critical in consciously turning off the anger response.

Here is a brief (and incomplete) list of brain nuclei associated with anger circuitry:

Amygdala: the brain's early warning center, highly responsive to threat, stores "emotional memories."

Thalamus: gathers sensory information and sends it on to the amygdala and to the frontal cortex.

Hypothalamus: initiates a flow of "fight or flight" hormones, including cortisol.

Midbrain PAG: the last step in the anger circuit before information goes to the muscles to act.

Hippocampus: stores declarative/episodic memories that consciously relate an emotional sense of danger to specific events and situations.

Dorsolateral Prefrontal Cortex: ability to prioritize behavior and awareness of emotional states of self and others.

Orbitofrontal Cortex: impulse control, understanding and utilizing cultural rules, ability to appreciate the consequences of one's actions.

As noted previously, anger is often a response to perceived danger. In animals and probably in humans as well, the quickest response to that danger involving anger or aggression follows this circuit: Sensory information (such as a loud noise) goes to the thalamus, where it is filtered and sent on to the amygdala. If the amygdala responds, it sends information to the medial hypothalamus to begin hormonal release and then on to the PAG to activate musculature (Siegel, 2005). Conscious validation or invalidation of the anger response goes through the dorsolateral prefrontal cortex, the orbitofrontal cortex, and the hippocampus. If the decision is made to stop the angry reaction, these nuclei send messages to the thalamus and hypothalamus to cease activating the system. All this can take place in less than a second.

Neuroplasticity

Therapy would be a useless profession if change were not possible. Significant change in anger patterns always involves changing specific neural networks in the brain. Neuroplasticity is the term that refers to the brain's continuing ability to make these changes by altering its internal structure. Neurons, as described below, can and do grow when used and shrink or even die when neglected. Thus, neurons have plastic properties – hence the word neuroplasticity.

The key players in the brain with regard to an angry brain are called *neurons*. The purpose of neurons is to convey information to each other and eventually to our muscles, glands, bodily organs, etc. They do so using both electrical and chemical processes. The human brain contains approximately 100 billion neurons, each of which is capable of connecting with up to 10,000 other neurons (Norden, 2007). Thus the number of possible interactions between neurons is virtually unimaginable. However, all neurons don't interact with each other. Instead neurons develop *neural networks* (sometimes called "nets") composed of thousands or hundreds of thousands of members that closely coordinate their firing patterns. These neural networks operate with several key principles. Two of the most famous principles are: *neurons that fire together wire together* and *use it or lose it* (Doidge, 2007). (See Figures 1.1 and 1.2 for illustrations of these principles.)

The first statement indicates that when neurons all fire simultaneously, the power of the electrical signal they transmit becomes synchronized and therefore more likely to affect one's behavior; the second statement indicates neural networks that are not used with regularity become weaker over time, while those used more frequently become stronger. Obviously both statements apply to the development and continuation of an angry brain. Every time someone thinks an angry thought or says an angry word, that individual is building a stronger anger network that fires faster and faster ("I have hair trigger anger – I get angry before I even have a chance to think") and by using that network habitually is guaranteeing its perpetuation. By contrast, that same person is neglecting opportunities to think positive thoughts, fails to recognize opportunities to experience positive emotions, and does not speak or act in more socially acceptable ways. That means his or her more positive brain networks fail to fully develop or are lost over time ("I used to be a happier person but now all I am is angry").

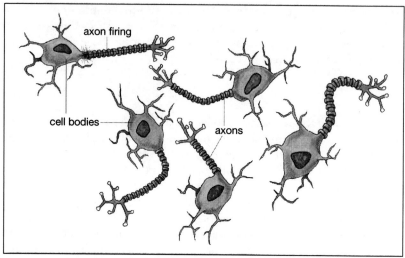

Neurons not in a strong network fire relatively randomly.

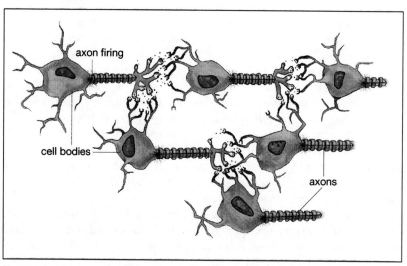

Neurons in a strong network fire almost simultaneously to increase the power of the signal.

Figure 1.1 Neurons that fire together wire together.

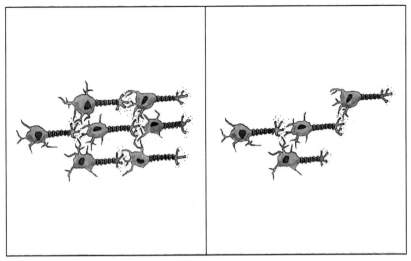

Number of neurons diminishes if network becomes relatively unused and neurons may be recruited into other networks.

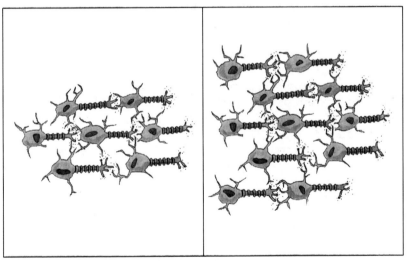

New neurons can be recruited into an actively utilized neural network.

Figure 1.2 Use it or lose it.

Here are some details of brain change that are important to understand (although perhaps too detailed to share with every client). As you may know, every neuron is separated from all others by a small space called the *synaptic gap* (or *synaptic cleft*). This prevents information from being transmitted simply by electrical means since electricity cannot jump this gap. Instead, the transmitting neuron (called the presynaptic neuron) must release chemicals called neurotransmitters such as serotonin and norepinephrine that float across the synaptic gap and relay the message to the receiving (postsynaptic) neuron. The message, by the way, is essentially to fire (send out an electrical spark) or not fire (Cozolino, 2009).

Three core processes underlie brain change. First, neuroplastic change begins when the axons of a neuron become covered with a fatty layer called myelin (Schwartz, Barres, and Goldman, 2013; Figure 1.3). Axons are the part of a neuron that sends electrical messages to other neurons. Myelination allows the electrical "spark" that begins at the start of the axon (near the cell body) to reach the tip of the axon at the same strength it began, as against losing power through leakage. Myelination greatly increases the speed and strength of axon electrical transmission. This more potent spark increases the likelihood that the receiving neuron will itself become activated and transmit signals to other neurons in the network to fire.

Note that myelination can actually decrease over time with disuse or disease. Multiple sclerosis is a common disorder caused by the loss of myelination on nerves and muscle fibers. This slows the speed and lessens the strength of movement directions from the brain so that the movements of individuals with multiple sclerosis become slower and more disordered.

Secondly, changes occur at the synapse (the space between two neurons) in a process called *long-term potentiation* (LTP; Figure 1.4). With regular use, the axon of the presynaptic neuron can over time release more neurotransmitter into the gap, while the dendrites of the postsynaptic neuron create more receptors that accept the neurotransmitter (Sapolsky, 2005). These alterations again greatly increase the probability that the neural network will stay activated and become stronger.

Thirdly, the receiving portion of a neuron, its *dendrites*, also change as the network develops. These dendrites become denser and filled with more receptors. The name for this process is *arborization* (Sapolsky, 2005) and there is a direct analogy with trees in that dendrites grow like the branches on a tree. Imagine a tree gradually taking shape as its first branches develop secondary branches and then the secondary branches grow even more branches. Eventually that single tree has thousands of branches. Neurons develop this shape over time and an arborized neuron has space for many more receptors than an undeveloped neuron.

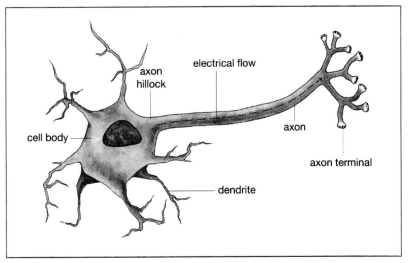

Relatively slow and weak electrical conduction from axon hillock to axon terminals.

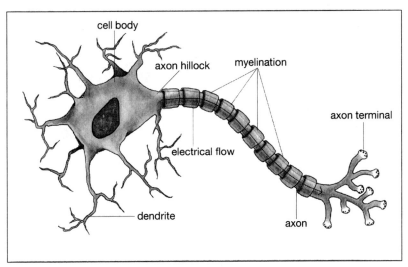

Relatively fast electrical conduction from axon hillock to axon terminals due to presence of insulation punctuated by gaps (Nodes of Ranvier) that allow electrical spark to reach terminals at full strength.

Figure 1.3 Myelination.

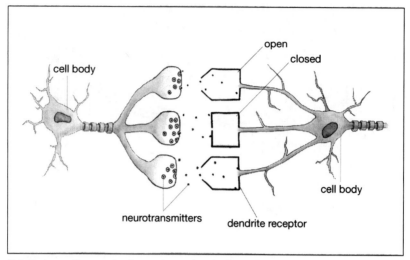

Relatively small amounts of neurotransmitters released.

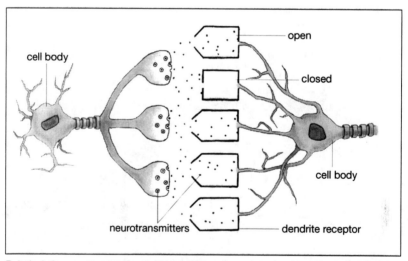

Relatively large amounts of neurotransmitters released as dendrites bring up more receptors which stay open longer and trigger axons to release neurotransmitters more quickly.

Figure 1.4 Long-term potentiation.

Arborization allows neurons to connect with thousands of other neurons. The result is a dense, tightly packed, and very potent neural network (Figure 1.5).

Taken together, these three brain processes of myelination, long-term potentiation, and arborization provide human beings with the ability to change over time to meet whatever challenges arise. The word that would best represent this state, if it were to become accepted, would be *neuro-flexibility*. This capacity for neuroflexibility is critical as we address the mind of the typical chronically angry person: overly rigid, too easily triggered for anger, biased toward anger and hostility, seemingly (but incorrectly) incapable of change.

People can change their brains. Angry people can train themselves to be less angry and in doing so will literally alter the composition of their brains. This information is invaluable for our clients. It means they have the ability, if they so choose, to alter the very substance of their brains. In my anger management and domestic violence groups, I present the material on neuroplasticity as a reason for hope. The brain constantly changes over time. The goal is for clients to take charge over how they want their brains to develop. However, neuroplastic changes seldom occur quickly. That means clients who willingly undertake a mission of reorganizing their brain must be highly committed to stay with that process over a period of weeks or months.

Ten Things to Know About the Angry Brain

What follows are ten comments about the brain that I share with my angry and domestically violent clients. I try to emphasize the practical implications of each point and how they can use this material in their lives.

1. Think of the angry brain as a survival machine – and anger as a survival-enhancing emotion

Our capacity for anger is one of six hard-wired emotions (the others are sadness, fear, joy, surprise, and disgust) that become available by birth. Each of these emotions has survival value in its own way. For example, a disgust reaction immediately tells you to avoid something that could make you sick.

The importance of this statement is that the client and therapist should not endorse a goal of never getting angry. Anger has great value and must be accepted as part of the human condition. Anger tells us that something is seriously wrong in a situation. It also gives people the energy to take action against the offending person, object, or condition. Recent studies (Cozolino, 2010a; Rodgers, 2014) indicate that anger seems to be

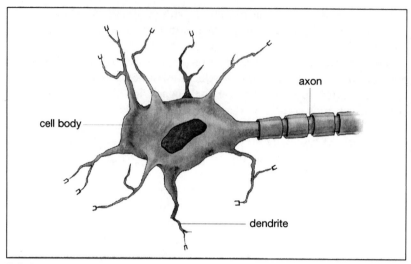

Relatively limited number and density of dendritic abor.

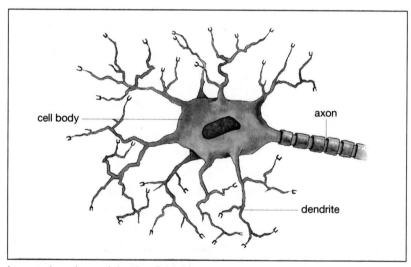

Increased number and density of dendrites.

Figure 1.5 Arborization.

primarily a left hemisphere phenomenon in the brain. This is significant in that the left hemisphere is associated with *approach*, while the right hemisphere is associated with *avoidance*. Angry people tend to move toward life's impediments in order to get rid of them. Approach is most sensible when the target is weaker than oneself so that victory is likely.

These victories may produce feelings of pleasure. Indeed, when I brought up this issue with my male domestic violence offender group recently, half of the participants (not surprisingly those with the worst histories of violent and antisocial behaviors) smiled while admitting feeling powerful and exhilarated while attacking their partners. However, others in the group reported just the opposite experience, an unpleasant sense of being out of control when violent. Panksepp and Biven (2012) note that although some people do display an appetite for activating the RAGE system (in particular when it leads to victorious encounters), still "for the most part RAGE feels bad ... [and] no person or animal enjoys the experience of persistent RAGE" (Panksepp and Biven, 2012, pp. 163–164). Presumably it will be harder for those clients who do derive pleasure from their aggression to give it up.

2. Much anger is defensive and protective – derived from and maintained by perceived threats

Death is the ultimate threat, probably the one for which all emotions are derived. Indeed, one's anger can transform into blind rage if we find ourselves cornered and unable to flee a dangerous situation. But, being social animals, humans have developed many other possible threats: the danger of being shamed, the threat of loss of a loved one to a rival, a sense that one's personal power and control over one's fate is being eroded, etc.

The problem here, with chronically angry individuals, is their tendency to perceive threats where others see none. These "false emergencies" seem obviously real to our angry clients, though, and the therapist must take care not to "pooh pooh" them and by doing so lose credibility. Nevertheless, one goal of anger management counseling is to help clients improve their discriminatory skills. Only then can they step away from a world populated by total enemies, suspicious characters, and so-called friends.

3. A core sense of safety is ultimately the best anger inhibitor

This point is especially crucial when working with domestic violence offenders (and domestic violence victims) as well as with very angry clients. Many offenders live in scary worlds. I am referring both to their real external environment that exists in the present and to their interior universe, much of which was created in their past. I believe that many clients would become significantly less angry and dangerous if they could transform these worlds. Counselors must be responsive to their clients' real concerns and understand how the day-to-day pressures of living in an unsafe environment promote angry and aggressive behavior as well as "paranoid" ideation.

How should we deal with these two senses of un-safety? First comes helping clients create a safer external environment. This may entail getting out of evidently unfixable antagonistic relationships ("My wife keeps threatening to call the cops and get me in trouble if I don't do what she wants"). Getting a lasting job certainly helps people feel safer. So does getting off probation for some of my clients who have been under a probation officer's authority for many years.

Now let's go into interior space. What would it feel like to live in a safer world? In my groups we discuss concepts like waking up unafraid, developing a capacity for self-soothing, creating a sense of personal competence, feeling loved and lovable, learning to take in comfort when legitimately offered, connecting with one's sense of humor, etc. The result of these changes would usually include developing a positive bias toward optimistic appraisal of ambiguous situations and a positive bias toward trusting others. Needless to add, these are long-term goals for many clients. Still, they are achievable goals. Later in this book (see chapter 8), I will describe how we help clients move gradually toward these goals during our 50-session domestic violence treatment program.

4. Anger is usually turned on unconsciously, but has to be turned off consciously

The non-conscious protective emotional centers of our brain are activated before we have cognitive awareness of a sense of threat. That means we react almost instantaneously to loud sounds, "funny" looks, noxious odors, bad tastes, and sudden touches. The brain's limbic system, its primary emotional reactor, goes through the brain's amygdala, a small sub-cortical nucleus (subcortical is a term referring to older parts of the brain that lay below the most recently developed outer covering, the cortex; nucleus refers to a cluster of neurons that are organized together and have similar cellular structures). The amygdala's main job is to quickly react to any possible sign of danger and to send out a warning that prepares the person for immediate action. The amygdala is also the place where people retain (as against consciously recall) the emotional feeling of past events (LeDoux and Damasio, 2013), such as the scary sensation that occurred to a man who was suddenly accosted by three masked men with guns.

The amygdala does not operate at the level of consciousness. Why? Perhaps because in times of imminent danger it would take too long to think of the best solution. Imagine a car bearing down on you as you cross a street. This is no time to consider the probability that it might miss you. It's far better to jump first and think about it later. Although thinking humans don't want to acknowledge it, the reality is that conscious awareness is a mixed blessing with regard to survival.

Conscious awareness, and the ability to begin inhibiting anger, appears soon after, but by then my angry client has already sworn out loud, while my violent offender may be midway through a punch. The fact that action precedes awareness creates a major dilemma in the field of anger management: we are always asking our clients to "think, think, think" when thinking may come too late to keep them out of trouble.

How can counselors avoid this trap? First, by asking our clients to "anticipate, anticipate, anticipate" and in so doing avoid potentially harmful situations. Second, by helping clients learn relaxation, stress-reduction, and mindfulness techniques that gradually lessen the amygdala's danger-triggered activation.

5. Changing the angry brain involves people changing their lives, not just their anger

One difficulty in modern human service delivery is the tendency to over-specialize. We create anger management groups and teach that topic as if someone were a broken car that we mental mechanics can fix by adjusting a few verbal or psychic gears. But everything connects with everything in people. I believe many clients sense this reality and may even be scared away from changing their anger patterns because of it. To paraphrase one of my clients: "Ron, my wife is just as angry as I am. If I quit yelling, what's going to happen to our marriage?"

Therapists can help here by asking at intake this question: "If you really quit getting angry so often, how do you think your life will change?" This simple question prepares the client for system-wide change. If you maintain an optimistic perspective, you can also help your client gain hope that his or her life will really improve through anger management.

6. People with angry brains distort the past, present, and future

One common myth is that we are capable of perceiving and remembering things exactly as they happened. But that's not how the brain works. Instead, it is keyed to retain the most salient information about an event and to discard most of the content as irrelevant (Schacter and Wagner, 2013). For example, a woman who has just been robbed at gunpoint may vividly remember the barrel of the gun pointing at her (perhaps too vividly, in which case it might look the size of a cannon), but not remember at all what the assailant was wearing.

One problem is that the brain over time can become increasingly biased. The brain filters information, with a tendency to attend to the novel and unexpected (Schacter and Wagner, 2013). Meanwhile, it tends to disregard more routine information because there is little potential threat in such data. But it is exactly this routine, non-threatening information that is critical for someone to begin feeling safer in a world perceived as dangerous. The result, all too often, is that an angry client disregards the very information that would tell him or her that it was safe to put down their weapons. We could say that an angry individual filters out the good and filters in the bad.

Because of this brain trait, angry people are especially inaccurate perceivers and recallers. They have a bias, both cognitive and pre-cognitive, toward misinterpretation. They consistently pull out negative aspects of interactions and later remember the situations as being far worse than they really were, or at least far worse than others would have interpreted them. In addition, they often are quite pessimistic in their predictions of the future. Their existential philosophy becomes "Of course I expect people to screw me over. It's been that way all my life." This negative mind set is all too self-fulfilling. The chronically angry person lives in a nasty world that he or she has done much to create.

Cognitive therapy is useful in challenging this way of perceiving the world. However, these negative patterns are deeply ingrained in the brains of angry individuals. They will need to make a strong and enduring commitment to alter them. Usually, though, clients can at least learn to recognize their most common negative interpretations of life in an "Oh-oh, I'm doing it again, I guess" manner.

7. Clients can change their brains

I've already discussed some of the main principles that underlie brain change earlier in this chapter. The main point here is that counselors need to convey this message to their clients.

This seems a good time to mention client oppositionality. Many angry clients enter treatment with the same "You can't teach me anything I don't already know" attitude they've utilized with who knows how many social workers, teachers, probation officers, psychologists, and other authority figures. To them you are just another authority figure and they are set to defy you as much as possible.

22

Fortunately, it is possible to sidestep anti-authority oppositionality. One way is to make an internal commitment to treat each angry client with respect, to honor their individuality, and to preserve their dignity. That is a general theme. More specifically, we can encourage each client to take control of their own change process by emphasizing that they and only they can create lasting brain change. They are the architects of their minds. For most clients this concept represents a new language, something they haven't experienced before and therefore are not biased against it. I emphasize this approach in the brain change-oriented domestic offender treatment program I facilitate (see chapter 8).

8. People with angry brains are continually training themselves to become more angry

One of my clients recently went on a harangue about how much he despised his ex-girl friend. He swore. He muttered violent curses. He called her a particularly cruel name. That's when I made him stop. All you are doing, I pointed out to him, is training your brain to hate. Every time this client indulges in these kinds of thoughts (which apparently he did many times a day), he is reinforcing his angry neural network. Keep doing that and that network will continue to become faster, stronger, and more controlling of his actions.

One domestic violence offender recently asked his group what they thought about him gaining revenge on his cheating wife by writing a nasty article on his Facebook page about her. To a man the group members sought to dissuade him. They discussed how their own acts of vengeance had usually backfired and left them feeling worse rather than better. True, they were probably better at telling him what not to do than listening to their own advice. Nevertheless, they clearly sensed that brains are not static entities. Rather, they are always changing, in this case either toward or away from chronic anger.

9. Positive interactive circuits must be developed to replace negative ones

It's not enough just to set a goal of becoming less angry. Clients need to consider with what they want to replace their anger. The idea is both to reduce the strength of one's anger circuitry and to increase the strength of other, chosen circuits. "Use it or lose it" is the key concept here (actually "Don't use it to lose it" and "Use it to grow it" would apply respectively to the network targeted for disuse and for increased use).

The counselor's opportunity at this stage is to help clients consider a wealth of positive possibilities. In other words, clients should be told they are free to choose what direction to travel. The main thing is to have a direction. Some obvious possibilities are to choose optimism over pessimism, to give praise rather than criticism to one's family, to develop a religious or spiritual program, to learn how to relax and enjoy life, etc. I believe it is important to have this conversation with every client, even those enrolled exclusively in group therapy.

10. Increased empathy is a major component of change for most angry clients

Empathy, pragmatically defined as "the ability to comprehend another person's thoughts, feelings and intentions," is a skill that can be learned, although it is likely that some people are gifted with more of this strain of emotional intelligence than others. Interestingly, the brain utilizes both very primitive and highly evolved parts of the brain in the pursuit of empathy. At the primitive level, a person's "mirror neurons" register the intentional motions of another person and fire as if he or she were making that same motion (say, for instance, reaching for a drink) (Iacoboni, 2009). These mirror neurons provide the substrate for empathy, although their firing does not alone constitute an empathic response. But at the same time much higher cortical areas are also involved so that we can consciously attempt to understand and get a feeling of the other. Although it is probably true that no individual can completely feel what another person is feeling or know what another person knows, still we can gradually gain a better understanding of the other through the empathy process. In one sense, then, empathy is an information-gathering series of hypotheses ("I wonder if she's feeling sad right now?") that become more and more accurate over time (Cozolino, 2010a).

Unfortunately, most chronically angry individuals are poor at empathy. That's at least partly true because taking a real interest in another human being makes it difficult to maintain one's animosity toward that person. One way that the world view of angry people often changes through treatment is that they become more interested and involved with others. Perhaps for the first time in their lives they come out of their defensive posture to realize that the world is full of fascinating people.

Healing the Angry Brain

Lou Cozolino (2002, 2010a) indicates that one major goal is to help clients integrate all their neural networks and in particular to integrate the affect and cognition systems. Since many clients have had to sacrifice their long-term well-being for the purpose of immediate survival in the face of stress and trauma, therapy should be used to reconnect circuits that have been disconnected. By doing so, clients will eventually gain far greater cognitive control over their behaviors as they lessen their tendencies to dissociate action and experience from conscious awareness. Cozolino describes several approaches that help clients develop these integrated neural networks, such as by simultaneously alternating the activation of the emotional and cognitive neural networks, creating "safe emergencies" that allow clients to master moderate amounts of stress, and co-creating new narratives that redefine the client's past and present experiences. These therapeutic endeavors eventually might raise the client's ability to tolerate and regulate affect, especially anger and fear. Cozolino cites the therapeutic approach labeled Eye Movement Desensitization and Reprocessing (EMDR) (Shapiro, 1995) as one specific technique that appears to help integrate neural circuitry in the manner described above. EMDR is rather mysterious in that nobody is sure how it works, but apparently the rapid alternating activation of stimulation of alternate sides of the face and body, and hence alternate brain hemispheres, creates opportunities for traumatized individuals to cease automatic dissociative reactions to memories or associations with the trauma. Panksepp (Panksepp and Biven, 2012) suggests that EMDR may work because the bilateral stimulation reaches into deep areas of the brain including the PAG, which he considers to be the most critical region for elaborating all primary-process emotions. He speculates that the eye movements may stimulate the flow of GABA, an inhibiting neurochemical, into these areas and so calm its hyperactivated state.

However, special techniques may not always be necessary when seeking to integrate neural circuitry with habitually angry clients. Taking a time out, for instance, helps clients do exactly that by cutting off the intensity of their emotional response before it short circuits a client's cognitive abilities. This simple technique, when practiced appropriately, helps clients learn how to proceed from "think or feel" to "think and feel," especially when followed by the question "Now what are you planning to do with your anger [in other words, how are you planning to use your anger to help you take action that is socially productive]?" It is obviously important, then, for anger management counselors to keep in mind the goal of helping their clients learn how to think and feel simultaneously rather than solely to promote the mindless ventilation of feelings or the creation of thought processes that are ungrounded in feeling.

Summary

The single most important concept to take from this initial chapter is that people have an amazing capacity to train their brains to think, feel, and direct behavior in specific directions. This capacity underlies the rationale for anger management and domestic violence offender treatment, that we can help people transform themselves. One direction we can promote is to help clients change from being chronically angry, because that emotion has been overdeveloped in the brain, to becoming emotionally balanced. Another direction is to help our clients not only change violent and disrespectful behavior into non-violent and respectful behavior, but to allow them to feel that they are in control of this process. The content of the rest of this book is designed to help clients achieve these results.

2

ANGER, THREAT, FEELING UNSAFE, AND DOMESTIC VIOLENCE

As noted in chapter 1, I believe that a core sense of safety is ultimately the best anger inhibitor. It may also be the most important inhibitor of acts of domestic aggression. The corollary to these propositions is that individuals who feel relatively unsafe, regardless of the apparent reality of this sense of unsafety, are more likely to develop significant problems with anger and aggression, including domestic violence.

Four aspects of this felt lack of safety will be explored in this chapter: a) research and theory about the stressed brain originally developed by Joseph LeDoux; b) the work of Donald Dutton and others that describes the increased risk for domestic violence associated with insecure attachment styles; c) romantic jealousy as an aspect of anger problems and an increased threat of domestic violence; d) Stephen Porges' polyvagal theory that indicates how people develop or fail to develop physiological mechanisms that inhibit our "fight or flight" reactions and so make normal social interaction possible.

The Stressed and Traumatized Brain: Fear and Anger

There are many possible links between physical aggression and brain dysfunctions. For example, violent offenders often show diminished prefrontal cortex brain activity (Ratey, 2002; Niehoff, 1998), implying that they may not understand moral concepts and are less able to inhibit subcortical areas associated with aggression. There is also a definite link between diminished serotonin levels and aggression (Niehoff, 1998); individuals with low serotonin levels are more likely to experience "knee-jerk" overreactions, becoming edgy and bad tempered. In addition, clients with attention deficit disorder and others who display signs of brainwave under-activity may become impulsively aggressive because of their need for brain stimulation (Volavka, 2002).

I have noted that I emphasize the need for felt physical and emotional safety as a condition for alleviating excessive anger. Unfortunately, decreased safety may increase an individual's proclivity toward angry outbursts. One especially interesting line of brain research focuses upon how the brain can be reconfigured by stress and trauma to become an organ that is selectively attuned to survival instead of thriving. Many clients who have been diagnosed with depression, impulsive anger, post-traumatic stress disorder and other anxiety disorders, or antisocial personalities share signs of suffering from impaired stress-response mechanisms.

The amygdala and hippocampus have been particularly well studied with regard to the long-term effects of trauma upon their interactions. Figure 2.1 illustrates how over time the natural balance between these two components of the brain can be disrupted, causing permanent alterations to how an individual perceives the world.

The stressed and traumatized brain has been studied extensively, in particular by Joseph LeDoux (LeDoux, 1996; LeDoux and Damasio, 2013). LeDoux suggests that post traumatic stress disorder and related phobic problems are best understood by a "sensitization" model in which continuing stress produces quicker and more intense reactions over time. LeDoux's main hypothesis is that long-term stress can cause permanent changes in brain structure as the brain becomes wired for survival rather than thriving. One set of changes that occur in the face of continuing or traumatizing threat is in the balance between activating and calming signals within the brain itself. The brain normally develops and maintains a balance between *excitatory/activating processes* (triggered by the chemical glutamate) and *inhibitory/sedating processes* (triggered by the chemical GABA). However, this delicate balance can be permanently altered by extreme or ongoing stress. That is because stress triggers the release of the hormone *cortisol* from the adrenal gland. Cortisol increases the intensity of fear reactions. Excessive amounts of cortisol particularly damage one area of the brain – the *hippocampus* – that is responsible for much of conscious (declarative) memory function, the labeling of emotionally threatening events, and for signaling to the adrenal gland to quit releasing cortisol. Therefore, the more stress damages the hippocampus, the more a vicious spiral ensues: the messages to quit making cortisol are reduced because of the damage, more cortisol is produced, which causes more damage to the hippocampus, which then sends even fewer messages to the adrenal gland to quit making cortisol, etc. In essence, this sustained level of excessive cortisol continuously prepares, but eventually breaks down, the body as it readies itself for immediate threats that may never appear (Cozolino, 2006).

Meanwhile, another nearby part of the brain, the *amygdala*, is an activator that tells the adrenal gland to keep releasing cortisol. The amygdala is concerned with creating the emotional content of memories. Over time stress causes the amygdala to become hypersensitive to threatening situations. The result is that the brain goes into a state of

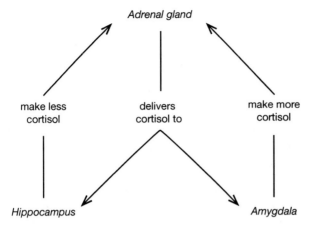

The normal brain achieves a balance between these two messages

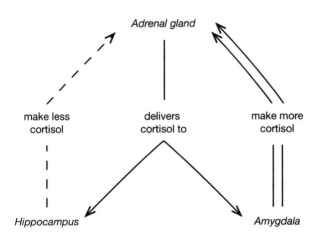

The stressed "survival" brain is out of balance

Figure 2.1 How the stressed brain becomes survival-oriented over time.

hyper-vigilance, as if serious threats were imminent. The body responds with continual flight or fight reactions, frequently to what others would consider minimally threatening or non-threatening cues.

The combination of a damaged hippocampus (as much as 16% smaller than average for traumatized people) (Teicher, 2002) and over-reactive amygdala in effect doubly prepares the stressed individual to live in a dangerous world. The brain has essentially been reconfigured for *survival* in a constantly threatening world. However, the individual with this kind of brain will function inefficiently in a safer world.

Cozolino (2006) writes that prolonged stress reduces the production of proteins important to the body's immune system, making chronically stressed individuals prone to illness and infection.

Stress also appears to damage the *corpus callosum* (Teicher, 2002), the part of the brain that connects the two hemispheres, making it difficult for traumatized or highly stressed individuals to integrate logical with emotional information that would help them respond appropriately to possibly threatening cues.

The amygdala is the main destination of what Joseph LeDoux labels the "low road" brain communication system. Here danger cues go directly from the thalamus to the amygdala, producing an instantaneous "freeze" reaction and then very rapid flight or fight behavior. The quality of information, however, is poor (Look out! There's a snake shape!!!!).

There is also a "high road" that runs from the thalamus through the visual cortex and then to the hippocampus. This takes longer, but provides more detailed information (Relax! It's a stick, not a snake) and integrates more information from past experience. Stress, abuse, and trauma tend over time to do more damage to the high road process than the low road. The result is that individuals are more likely to be flooded with vaguely understood, confusing, but very threatening sensations.

It is very difficult to eradicate emotional memories. One reason for this problem is that there are far more neuronal pathways from the amygdala to the cortex than from the cortex to the amygdala (Johnson, 2003). As a result, traumatic emotional memories are persistent, easily triggered, and can actually build in intensity over time. Also, the brain gives priority to the amygdala during threatening situations. Furthermore, situations are increasingly defined as threatening during cumulative experiences of trauma. The more often situations are perceived as threatening, then, the more control the amygdala will assume over day-to-day life.

The Anger and Aggression Connection with the Stressed Brain

Handling anger well presents difficult challenges to individuals even when their brains are functioning at maximum efficiency. But many clients who need help with anger management have far less than optimal brain function. Some have obvious damage due to falls or fights; others may have sweeping limitations caused by low general intelligence; and, since many angry people grew up in violent homes in which they witnessed and /or were subject to physical, verbal, and emotional abuse, they may have developed the same survival-oriented brain structures described above with excessively fearful clients.

The pathways regulating fear and anger (or the FEAR and RAGE systems identified by Panksepp and Biven, 2012) are very similar: "Research has uncovered surprising congruencies between the neurobiological mechanisms underlying stress disorders and those underlying aggression" (Niehoff, 1998, p. 50). Fear and anger have similar pathways in the brain, as one would expect from the long recognized "flight or fight" reactions people have in the face of danger. Anger, especially when experienced by the individual as defensive in nature, is, like fear, a core reaction to threat (LeDoux, 1996). Defensive aggression thus becomes one strategy to handle fear-invoking situations. Fear and anger then may become interlocked: "When [interpersonal] interchange has become hostile . . . the struggle to balance response and demand strains the physical boundaries of the nervous system and the dynamic interplay . . . degenerates into a vicious cycle, spiraling toward violence and rotating compulsively back toward fear" (Niehoff, 1998, p. 52). Some interpersonal violence can be described from this model as a developmental process between individual and environment that has created lasting, perhaps irreversible, neurobiological effects upon the violent person's brain.

Trauma resets the brain to favor defensive behavior. Specifically, stress may produce a condition labeled "limbic irritability" (Teicher, 2002), which in turn produces symptoms of aggression, exasperation, and anxiety. In addition, smaller amygdala size is associated with depression, irritability, and hostility (Teicher, 2002).

Many anger management clients were raised and may continue to live in physically and emotionally threatening environments. They may well need to have available a quick response mode to these threats that takes the form of defensive verbal or even physical aggression. This aggression is adaptive, but only if the individual's ability to assess threat is accurate. However, as noted above, the survival-oriented brain tends to misinterpret situations in the direction of perceived threat, becoming less and less accurate at assessing both whether or not a particular situation is threatening and the degree of threat involved. These people develop maladaptive patterns of anger and aggression: they become angry with the wrong people, for the wrong reasons, at too elevated levels of intensity, at the wrong times, and in the wrong places. Their frequently misguided sense of threat produces misguided incidents of aggression as they respond automatically but inaccurately to unsubstantiated and misinterpreted dangers.

This slide away from good reality perception can be progressive (Niehoff, 1998). Each angry reaction leads to false alarms to the stress system (increased norepinephrine, epinephrine, and cortisol, increased blood pressure, etc.) that further erode the ability of the brain to accurately assess risk. Eventually many survival-oriented individuals feel persistent tension, relentless suspicion, and a need for ceaseless vigilance. Their brains and bodies have been placed in a permanent defensive mode that can only be relaxed with great difficulty.

Attachment Theory

Over 50 years have passed since John Bowlby (1969, 1973, 1980) began developing his model of maternal attachment. Excellent reviews of the attachment model he and Mary Ainsworth developed and tested are provided by Badenoch (2008), Levine and Heller (2010), Johnson (2009), Berman and Sperling (1994), Karen (1994), Levy and Orlans (2000), and Wilson (2001), and, from a more neurobiological framework, Panksepp and Biven (2012). Although I cannot review this entire process in this volume, the key concepts Bowlby developed can be summarized:

Here is a definition of attachment: an enduring emotional bond that involves a tendency to seek and maintain proximity to a specific person, particularly when under stress. It is a mutual regulatory system that provides safety, protection, and a sense of security for the infant. Attachment is "an intense and enduring bond biologically rooted in the function of protection from danger" (Wilson, 2001, p. 38).

The key characteristics of the attachment process are as follows:

- The attachment system represents an independent behavioral system (it is not a drive but it is equally powerful).
- It is a homeostatic process that regulates infant proximity- and contact-maintaining behavior, allowing distancing and independence but ensuring the closeness of the caregiver as needed.
- Attachment is organized around specific attachment figures. Each relationship is unique, so that a parent's bonding connection with one child may be very different from his or her experience with another child.
- The physical goal of the attachment process is to ensure that the infant will survive its period of complete dependency. The concurrent psychological goal is for the infant to develop an internal sense of safety and trust.
- If attachment needs are well met, the infant will normally develop a sense of having a *safe haven*. He or she will feel a deep sense of belonging, that there is and will always be a place for him or her.
- If attachment needs are well met, the infant also develops the sense of having a *secure base* from which he or she can explore the environment. Thus, feelings of safety encourage risk-taking and exploration of the world.

- The attachment system is not always active: it is turned on when the attachment figure moves away from the infant or when the child feels threatened, disturbed, or needy.
- When threatened, disturbed, or needy, the infant then behaves in ways designed to restore adult proximity (crying, calling, crawling after, etc.).
- There is a standard sequence of infant reactions to attachment figure separation: *protest, despair, detachment*. Anger is often part of the protest phase. Detachment may be thought of as a reintegration phase in which the infant reestablishes an inner sense of quiet (with or without complete resolution of the attachment crisis).
- Children gradually develop by age 9–18 months (Diamond and Blatt, 1994) *internal working models* of their attachment world. These internal working models are mostly unconscious sets of expectations about whether and how well their security needs will be met by significant others. They are formulated in the right hemisphere since that hemisphere is dominant in the first three years of life (Schore, 1994, 2009). Internal working models include a conception of the self as worthy or unworthy, and positive or negative predictions about the consequences of attachment. They also provide a context for later social relationships (Cozolino, 2006; Dutton, 1998). The early dominance of the right hemisphere has significant implications regarding attachment experiences. Perhaps most important to understand is that the core sense of attachment security or insecurity can never be completely expressed verbally. Attachment is a "gut feeling," not a cognitive artifact. Attachment revolves around sensations of touch (Panksepp and Biven, 2012). That is why one hug is worth more than any number of words, no matter how calming and comforting they may be. Therapists would be wise to consider this reality even in our current "Don't touch your clients or you risk a lawsuit" atmosphere.
- Four basic attachment styles have been identified based upon the child's and mother's reactions to experiments in which children were temporarily separated from the mother:

  - Secure: the child feels distressed, seeks out mother, feels relief, returns to play.
  - Anxious/Avoidant: the child feels distressed but ignores mother when she returns, acting as if he or she were indifferent to the mother.
  - Anxious/Ambivalent: the child exhibits high levels of distress, and a mixed approach/rejection reaction when mother returns (e.g., hugs but arches away).

– Disorganized/Disoriented: the child displays no consistent pattern and/or unusual behaviors upon mother's return (e.g., fall to floor, turn in circles). This is speculated to be the result of the mother's unpredictability so that paradoxically the mother is both the source of insecurity and its solution.

These attachment styles are stable over time (trait-like) and consistent with the mother's parenting characteristics and attachment style. Parental behaviors predict children's attachment style: sensitive and consistently responsive parents tend to have secure children; parents who are unresponsive and rejecting of proximity tend to have avoidant children; inconsistent parents who alternate between unavailability and intrusiveness tend to have anxious/ambivalent children; excessively disturbed parents with very unpredictable behavior tend to produce disorganized/disoriented children.

- There are many positive results for children whose attachment needs are well met. These include: a) felt sense of safety and protection; b) basic trust and reciprocity; c) ability to explore the world; d) self-regulation of affect; e) identity formation as competent and worthy; f) the ability to balance the desires for autonomy and dependency; g) the establishment of empathy and consequently a pro-social sense of morality; h) a positive view of others and the world; i) resiliency in the face of adversity, stress, and trauma (Levy and Orlans, 2000).

Adult attachment can be defined as "the stable tendency of an individual to make substantial efforts to seek out and maintain proximity with one or a few specific individuals who provide the subjective potential for physical and/or psychological safety and security" (Berman and Sperling, 1994, p. 8). Although similar in form and function, adult attachment differs from parental/infant bonding in one important way. Adult attachment is more reciprocal in that both people can play the roles of caregiver and care receiver. In other words, they serve as complementary attachment figures, serving the dual purpose of comforting each other and preserving the dyadic unit.

Bartholomew, Henderson, and Dutton (2001) have developed an insightful model of adult attachment styles. They describe four main styles based on the interactions of two dichotomies: high or low personal self-worth and high or low perceived worthiness of others. The styles are labeled and described as follows:

- *Secure*: These adults have basic trust in themselves and others; they tend to be resilient, flexible, and adaptive; they are able to seek and receive support when stressed; they are also able to give support to others; they have a positive view of self, but can admit weaknesses and needs; they are generally interdependent in relationships; they can be comfortable with both intimacy and autonomy. Key terms: confident, good-natured, dependable, understanding (here and in the following descriptions key terms are taken from Klohnen and John, 1998).

- *Dismissive*: These adults possess high personal self-worth, but perceive others as of low worth; they appear to have little anxiety about interpersonal relationships; they tend to avoid relationship commitments; they defend against attachment anxiety by lessening need for attachment so that they appear to be quite self-sufficient; however, dismissive individuals may become very anxious when their attachments are lost or threatened if their defenses against feeling fail; they often pull away when partner seeks intimacy, especially withdrawing when others are stressed and needy; they treasure autonomy and self-reliance; they may be overly critical and controlling when helping partners; they are often perceived as cold and hostile by others; they don't use their partners as safe havens or secure bases (Fraley, Davis, and Shaver, 1998); they deny the value of close relationships; they may have limited and over-idealized memories of childhood. Key terms: independent, competent, rational, sarcastic.

- *Preoccupied*: These adults have low self-worth and perceive others as of higher worth than themselves; they display high anxiety but low avoidance; they seek acceptance, safety, and validation from others; they frequently become enmeshed in earlier unresolved attachments; their need for autonomy may be compromised because of a more compelling need for security; they demand emotional contact but may never be satisfied because of their unrealistically high demands ("I scare people away. I want to be so close, all the time, and they get nervous" – Bartholomew et al., 2001). Key terms: expressive, dependent, needs approval, self-revealing.

- *Fearful*: These adults perceive both themselves and others as having low worth; they are high on both anxiety and avoidance; they desire acceptance but avoid intimacy because they fear and anticipate rejection ("I'm afraid I'll say something that ruins the relationship" – Bartholomew et al., 2001); they need others to validate self-worth; conscious fear of anticipated rejection. Key terms: vulnerable, doubting, timid, distrusting.

Attachment theory was developed long before brain imaging of humans and animal studies made possible an understanding of the underlying brain mechanisms. Panksepp and Biven (2012) have recently described attachment as an epigenetic phenomenon. This means that certain genes that help children feel safe and secure are switched on or strengthened by consistently positive nurturing. These genes help regulate the flow of neurochemicals including endogenous opioids and oxytocin. The result is these children gravitate toward the optimistic, energetic, and adventurous cognitions consistent with the secure attachment style. Unfortunately, inconsistent, neglectful, or abusive parenting tends to activate and oversensitize the stress hormones described previously in this chapter. Worse, girls subjected to these unrelenting stress levels may then pass this sensitivity on to their offspring (Panksepp and Biven, 2012), partly because they haven't received proper parenting skills, but even more so because their genetic structure has been permanently changed.

Anger, Domestic Violence, and Attachment Styles

From an attachment perspective, "anger is triggered when there is a threat of separation and has the function . . . of ensuring that the attachment bond remains intact" (Holmes, 2001, p. xvii). Thus, anger has a positive function, serving to signal and underscore the protest stage of a separation crisis. Even episodes of domestic aggression may represent this kind of protest: "An assaulter's abusive episodes can be seen as an adult's version of protest when attachment needs are not satisfied" (Bartholomew et al., 2001, p. 60).

Unfortunately, adults who possess the three relatively insecure attachment styles (especially preoccupied and fearful) may well have distorted, exaggerated, excessive, and misdirected attachment needs. These people place unreachable demands upon their partners, wanting and needing far more than can reasonably be expected from another human being. They then become irate when those needs are not met. In essence, because they need their partners to make up for a lifetime of unsuccessful attachments, they create situations in which their intense separation rage is not resolved by reunion (Berman, Marcus, and Berman, 1994). Constantly fearing abandonment, these individuals ruminate over negative interactions, become hyper-vigilant and jealous, display high but inflexible self-disclosure, and see even their partner's normal withdrawals as evidence of abandonment (Dutton, 1998; Roberts and Noller, 1998), perhaps using violence to prevent their partner's withdrawal.

Relationship violence has been tied to specific attachment patterns. For example, both avoidance/dismissing and anxious/ambivalent attachment styles are associated with anger, shame, fear of negative evaluation, and pathological narcissism (Mikulincer and Florian, 1998). In addition, anxious/ambivalent partners often become excessively hostile and angry during conflict resolution discussions, perceive their partners more negatively, and become most angry and hostile when discussing a major problem (Rholes, Simpson, and Stevens, 1998), while fearful and preoccupied partners often have trouble leaving abusive relationships because of low self-worth that makes them think that violence against them is justified (Bartholomew et al., 2001).

Bartholomew et al. (2001) have linked the perpetration of abuse with adult attachment styles for both genders as follows:

- Dismissers: Individuals high on dismissiveness tend to be distant and callous ("Get away from me"). When they become angry in relationships they are likely to leave rather than argue due to the deactivation of their attachment system.
- Preoccupied and Fearful: The chronic anxiety about rejection and abandonment endured by these people leads to high levels of negative affect and anger.
- In general, the attachment dynamics of abusers are similar for males and females, hetero- and homosexuals. *Preoccupied* individuals, whose excessive needs for support and reassurance are inevitably frustrated, leading to increasingly demanding behavior, are especially likely to be both *perpetrators* and *recipients* of abuse for both men and women. However, while men who are *fearful* are also more likely to be *perpetrators* and *recipients* of abuse, women who are *fearful* are likely only to be *recipients* of abuse.
- The majority of the most severely abusive men studied by Bartholomew et al. (2001) were preoccupied or fearful. Furthermore, the more strongly preoccupied or fearful they were, the more severe the reported abusiveness.
- Regarding women who lived in abusive relationships, 53% were described as preoccupied and 35% as fearful. In addition, pre-occupied women stayed in relationships longer and had more contact after leaving, presumably because of their combination of strong attachment anxiety and an approach orientation toward conflict.
- The attachment style interactions between partners are important to understand in abusive relationships:
  - Two preoccupied individuals often become locked in highly volatile conflict.
  - The combination of a fearful woman and a preoccupied man best predicted male unidirectional violence. This pairing best fit the stereotypical model of a battering male and victimized female.
  - However, the pairing of a preoccupied woman with a fearful man was also common in abusive relationships and predicted both the most severe abuse and the presence of a mutually abusive relationship.

Cowan and Cowan (2001) note that insecure men with secure women partners produced the most negative and volatile relationship pattern in their research. It could be speculated that the men in these relationships felt a need to overpower, shame, belittle, and humiliate their partners in an effort to gain power and control over a person they correctly perceived as having greater confidence and possibly competence than they.

Finally, Roberts and Noller (1998) note that the pairing of two insecure individuals may prove to be a highly volatile combination, especially if one partner is scared of abandonment and the other fears intimacy. This statement describes the "chase and run" pattern often seen in couples therapy in which one partner, seeking intimacy, attempts to increase closeness, only to have the other partner, seeking autonomy, simultaneously attempt to increase the physical and psychological distance between them.

Romantic Jealousy, Fragile Self-Esteem, and Attachment

DiGiuseppe and Tafrate (2007) conducted an extensive review of the hypothesis that low self-esteem predicts anger and aggression. They found no empirical evidence that supported this belief. Indeed, they note that anger management counseling seems to have no measurable effect upon self-esteem, not even when the counseling is successful. They also suggest that anger and aggressive behavior is most likely when the angry person feels relatively powerful and superior to the offender. However, they have found that anger does follow perceived threats to high but unstable self-esteem (Baumeister, Smart, and Boden, 1996) and should be addressed in treatment. This high but unstable sense of self-worth is consistent with at least two insecure attachment styles, dismissive and preoccupied.

Romantic jealousy may be defined as: "A felt need to guard and protect one's relationship partner against the threat of a real or imagined rival." Jealousy always involves a comparison between the self and another, the rival, with regard to how attractive both may be to an actual or potential partner. Jealousy should be distinguished from "envy," which represents a state in which one person wants to take away something that belongs to another person (wealth, status, competence, an attractive mate, etc.) and if that is not possible at least then wants the rival to lose that asset. However, both these terms represent a state of anger that a person has toward a target having something the person wants, or towards a target wanting to take away what the person has (DiGiuseppe and Tafrate, 2007).

Jealousy exists on a continuum from "normal" (moderate in intensity, triggered by specific cues, may be an accurate sign of relationship distancing, seeks reassurance) to "excessive" (frequent, intense, minimal or no cues, needs repeated reassurance, causes relationship distancing) to "irrational" (delusional, no claim on the other person, paranoid projection). As Pittman (1989) notes, it is normal for someone to want to guard and protect his or her most valued objects and relationships. Pittman even describes a condition he labels "relationship drift," in which jealousy is triggered not by the partner's actual involvement in an affair, but because of a gradual distancing between the partners. Thus, a moderate amount of jealousy, from an attachment perspective, reflects an acceptable response to a real signal that the partnership is or could be endangered. However, many individuals come to counseling because they receive too many danger signals, many of which are inaccurate, and then they react too strongly to them. These chronically jealous people often become violent as they attempt desperately to keep their perceived rivals away from their all too vulnerable (in their eyes) partners.

The attachment model is particularly useful in describing and understanding some of the dynamics of jealous interactions. In particular, jealousy and attachment are similar in that both: a) function to maintain close relationships; b) are triggered by the threat of separation from the attachment figure; c) involve a range of emotions including fear, anger, and sadness; d) reflect both the actual current relationship concerns and the individual's internal working models of relationship stability (Sharpsteen and Kirkpatrick, 1997). Note that jealousy episodes most closely parallel the protest stage of attachment separation in that anger is more present than sadness for most people. Anger represents a protest against the perceived injustice of the situation (DiGiuseppe and Tafrate, 2007; Sharpsteen and Kirkpatrick, 1997).

Jealousy is particularly likely when an individual fears the loss of "formative attention," which is defined as "attention that sustains part of one's self-concept" (Parrot, 2001). This threat may induce the jealous individual to treat people as if they were property ("You belong to me") or an extension of one's ego ("You are me") or believe that a relationship represents a total merger of personalities (an "us" without two "I's"). All these beliefs turn the partner's normal distancing into a potentially devastating threat. The implicit message of the jealous person trying to protect these needs is "I am nothing without you. I can't live without you."

Relatively jealous people may have good general self-esteem but possess "weak spots" in their psychological profile, vulnerabilities that make them susceptible to anger and aggression. In particular, they may believe they suffer specific inadequacies in a major relationship area, such as being a good provider or sexual partner. Because of these deficits, they don't feel like a "keeper" and so anticipate rejection. Jealousy correlates with anxious-ambivalent attachment style (White and Mullen, 1989), with fearful attachment (Dutton, van Winkel and Landolt, 1997), to sensitivity to rejection (Leary, Koch, and Hechenbleikner, 2001), and to domestic abusiveness (Dutton et al., 1997). *Secure* individuals score lowest on jealousy measures (Knobloch, Solomon, and Cruz, 2001), but are most likely to directly express their anger toward their partners. Meanwhile, avoiders are more likely to turn their anger toward the rival, while anxious individuals are more likely to suppress their anger rather than confront their partner (Sharpsteen and Kirkpatrick, 1997).

Jealous individuals may sense, perhaps correctly, that their partners are far less committed to the relationship than they are. Of course, they may even correctly speculate that their partner is having an affair with a rival. Additionally, excessively jealous people frequently can detail a history of past betrayals (by past or present partners, as a witness to parental infidelity, and including their memories of their own lapses), which have increased felt insecurity, preoccupation, and fearfulness.

CASE STUDY

Excerpts from an Interview with a Jealous Man

Saul S, age 32, is an electrician with whom I tape-recorded four hours of directed conversation centering on his history of violent jealous outbursts. These episodes occurred in a string of dating and marital relationships that began with his first major relationship at age 16. These bouts of jealousy have continued, though in diminished form, through his recovery from chemical dependency and despite years of therapy. Saul's jealousy clearly is strongly affected by attachment considerations. As with many excessively jealous individuals, he demonstrates in his statements that his attachment style is a mixture of preoccupation and fearfulness. His core insecurity about relationships developed as he grew up in a chaotic household that included spouse battering, infidelity, alcoholism, and marital separations. It was then enhanced by his experiences with dating partners, the first two of whom were "unfaithful" to him. Here are some attachment-related excerpts from that conversation:

Becoming jealous: "I feel threatened by other people talking or being with somebody I care about and that affects my self-worth." "I guess it's fear, just being afraid that they [his partners] may choose to have interest in someone else . . ."
The feelings that accompany jealous episodes: "I would become tense, nervous, fearful. I always get angry."

Fearfulness: "That I won't measure up to their expectations, whatever they may be. I don't know if I fit in with what they want." The worst thing that your partner could do to you is [*finish this sentence*] . . . "not pay attention to me."

The initiation of a jealous episode: "I start out angry and demand answers. How do you feel about me? Do you care about me? Why do you do what you do? Would you do that if you cared about me?"

The purpose of a jealous outburst: "It's like I'm forcing the other person to tell me they care about me. They do love me."

A typical angry episode: "Yelling and screaming, at one time I threw a coffee table through the window. Pay attention to me or I'm throwing this through the window."

The costs of Saul's anger: "A lot of the time I end up pushing people away because I get angry with them. And then that seems to cause it to get worse because then I feel I don't fit in with their plans . . ."

The damage to the relationship because of Saul's jealousy and insecurity: "She would tell me she loves me but I couldn't grasp it because I felt something was missing. But after a while she didn't even want to say she loved me . . . I was pushing her away."

How Saul's relationships have ended: "The first one I went to jail, the second one I went to jail, the third one I went to jail. I would rather have them take me out of there than to have to leave on my own. It doesn't matter that you called the police because I'm not going to leave because of that, therefore you're not going to win."

Insecurity and defensive anger: "I feel I have a poor sense of self-esteem. It's just there. But I hate hearing them tell me I'm insecure. I would actually become angry with them and say how can you say I'm too insecure? How dare you?"

Preoccupied attachment style: "I feel I need acceptance from the other person. That I need to feel OK with myself. I need them to tell me I'm OK, that things will be fine, some reassurance. It's like you owe this to me."

Fearful attachment style: "I choose not to have many friends because the less I expose myself to other people, the less I feel they would really know who I am or a chance of being rejected by others." "I'm always suspicious. I expect my partner to try to hurt me and I guard against it."

Developing distrust after his first girlfriend cheated on Saul: "I became very distrustful, wanting to know where she was going, who she was going to see, if she was going to a girl friend's house or what. I just always wanted to know what was going on."

The cost of getting all the attention Saul allegedly seeks: "I have had that happen and actually I didn't care for it much. It was nice for a while but then it got old" [Saul actually has a need for autonomy, even though that need is usually subordinated to his need for attention].

Finding a sense of safety in Saul's most recent relationship: "I just felt good to be around her. I would be happy, content. Felt like I belonged and I still felt OK when she was gone but she wasn't."

Getting past the core insecurity: The best thing your partner could do for you is [*finish this sentence*] "pay attention to me, but I don't know if that's really the right way to say it. Maybe interact, communicate with each other, be supportive of each other."

Notice, in these last two excerpts, that Saul has indeed made significant progress in his quest to become less jealous and insecure. First, he has developed an improved ability to feel that he belongs with another person while retaining a sense of personal autonomy, a combination that better fits the concept of secure attachment than either preoccupied or fearful. Second, Saul still wants his partner to pay a great deal of attention to him, but at the same time he talks about being mutually supportive, another sign of increasing security.

Attachment Theory Related Treatment Strategies for Romantic Jealousy Concerns

White and Mullen (1989) mention several coping strategies individuals utilize to address their jealousy. These tactics include denying the problem, seeking to improve the relationship, trying to interfere with or punish the partner's actions, developing alternatives (meeting new people), derogation of the partner ("She's no good anyhow"), introspection ("What have I done?"), and demanding commitment by the partner. Certain of these strategies, especially seeking to improve the relationship and introspection, might move the jealous person toward security and away from preoccupation and fearfulness. Others, including derogation of the partner and demanding commitment, might only increase their perceived insecurity.

Therapists can employ several approaches that help clients address their insecure attachment difficulties. First, they can help their clients articulate a goal, namely to learn to feel like a "keeper" rather than someone their partner is likely to quickly discard. The analogy I utilize here is to ask the client to imagine that he or she is a seashell lying on the beach with hundreds of other shells. That person's partner or potential partner is walking down that beach, intent upon selecting one and only one shell to take home and keep forever. That person reaches down and picks up the shell that represents the client, carefully examining it, seriously considering taking it home. The question is this: "Do you believe you are a keeper?" Some clients believe that they are keepers, meaning that they do indeed think a potential partner would find them attractive and want to select them. Others, especially fearful clients, doubt that they could be attractive enough to gain another person's attention, much less be a keeper. Highly jealous individuals, though, especially preoccupied ones, tend to believe that their potential partners might very well select them, but that they will keep strolling down the beach, still looking for an even better shell, instead of heading home with their prize. Thus, they stay insecure no matter how long their partner is faithful. Setting the goal of learning to feel like a keeper, then, involves discussing with the client how that might happen, with emphasis upon developing an internal sense of worthiness as against attempting to keep one's partner off the beach of life.

It is also important to teach jealous individuals to value their partner as a separate person, not as part of oneself. Highly jealous people tend to engulf their partners because they carry a flawed life formula: $0 + 1 = 2$. They are the zero; their partner is the one; somehow partnership with that person is supposed to create a "2," filling in the client's tremendous sense of emptiness. That strategy might work for a while. Almost inevitably, though, it will fail because the client is all too aware of the reverse formula: $2 - 1 = 0$. They believe they can't live without their partner, that separation would once again reduce them to total emptiness. They need to recognize that the only relationship formula that really works is this: $1 + 1 = 2$.

Many jealous clients have a long history of relationship betrayals that include infidelity, abandonment, and physical and sexual abuse. Therapists need to help clients process their personal history of betrayals and infidelities, focusing upon the consequent loss of trust. This leads to the question of how realistically trustworthy is one's current partner. Sometimes that person is actually faithful, in which case the client must learn to distinguish that individual from everyone else. It is also important to challenge the jealous person to admit to his or her own infidelities; many jealous clients basically project their own sexual indiscretions onto their partners. They may also have concluded that, since they cheated on their partners, certainly all their partners will at least want to cheat on them.

Another useful approach is to help clients identify their main attachment style, their partner's style, and how the two styles might interact in ways that foster jealousy and insecurity. This is particularly useful when the client has the ability to abstract beyond specific individual experiences to recognize patterns in their life. It also helps clients realize that their engulfing behavior may be promoting increased dismissiveness from their partners; certainly not a desired effect.

Finally, the therapist may want to consider couples counseling if the relationship is stable and safe enough to do so. Mutual goals would include identifying attachment patterns, addressing any real problems with distancing in the relationship, what Pittman (1989) calls "relationship drift," discussing and deciding mutually acceptable third-party contact guidelines for the relationship, and developing mutually acceptable patterns of reassurance when either partner becomes insecure or jealous.

The partners of excessively jealous individuals may be seen independently as well. If so, they should be informed that: a) excessive jealousy is not a sign of love so much as a sign of insecurity and possessiveness; b) they should not allow the excessively jealous partner to control their lives by limiting their activities and relationships; c) they should quit trying to "prove" their innocence in situations where they are unjustly accused as against simply declaring that they refuse to be continually interrogated.

Polyvagal Theory

A sense of safety or unsafety comes from deep within people. Stephen Porges (2009, 2011), the developer of polyvagal theory, utilizes the term "neuroception" to describe how neural circuits distinguish whether situations or people are safe, dangerous, or life threatening. He states that "neuroception takes place in primitive parts of the brain, without our conscious awareness . . . Even though we may not be aware of danger at a cognitive level, our body has already started a sequence of neural processes that would facilitate adaptive defensive behaviors such as fight, flight or freeze" (Porges, 2011, p. 11). Porges' tremendous contribution to science comes from his decades-long effort to describe exactly what happens in the brain and body that allows people to feel safe in social situations.

Porges describes three different physiological systems that operate within humans. The most primitive is the "freeze" system, associated with unmyelinated nerve fibers emanating from the vagus nerve, which is the tenth cranial nerve (located on the brainstem). The freeze system would normally be activated only under dire circumstances, when someone is in grave danger. It produces immobilization, death-feigning, and loss of consciousness (Porges, 2011, p. 283).

The second system is labeled the sympathetic-adrenal system and allows for mobilization, including the fight or flight response. That has been described above in this chapter.

The third system can be labeled the "social engagement system" (Porges, 2011, p. 293). It involves two-way communications between a myelinated part of the vagus nerve emanating from an area called the nucleus ambiguous in the right brain hemisphere (Porges, 2011), the heart, the lungs, the throat, the digestive system, and facial and mouth muscles involved in communication (Cozolino, 2010a). Within this system the neurochemical oxytocin and other substances serve to allow social engagement and caregiving. The sympathetic nervous system becomes dampened, allowing the individual to listen better and to have greater emotional expression. This system protects the heart, enhances oxygenation in the brain, calms the individual, and permits social interactions (Porges, 2011, p. 283). In effect the myelinated vagus nerve system acts as a brake on the sympathetic nervous system to produce an internal sense of safety.

Porges uses the term "vagal tone" to describe a person's ability to regulate their bodily sensations, heartbeat, etc. He states that people with relatively higher vagal tone process their environment efficiently, while individuals with lower vagal tone and/or poor vagal regulation would be expected to exhibit difficulties in regulating their emotional state, attending appropriately to social cues and gestures, and in expressing appropriate emotions (Porges, 2011). Whereas higher vagal tone is associated with the ability to self-soothe and self-regulate, enhanced ability to attend to others and take in information, positive social engagement, and consistent caretaking, lower vagal tone correlates with irritability, emotional dysregulation, early childhood behavioral problems, hyper-reactivity to the environment, impulsive acting out, distractibility, withdrawal, and insecure attachment (Cozolino, 2010a).

These three systems are somewhat interactive so that individuals can rapidly adjust their heart rate and physiology to the rapidly shifting demands of the real world. Most importantly, Cozolino notes that "vagal regulation allows us to become upset, anxious, or angry with a loved one without withdrawing or becoming physically aggressive" (Cozolino, 2010a, p. 234). However, the efficacy of this task can be affected by one's genetic background and personal history. Secure attachment relationships in childhood will have a positive effect, while insecure relationships will tend to bias the system toward assessing ambiguous situations as more dangerous than they really are. Cozolino suggests that "We can hypothesize that many who engage in domestic violence, child abuse and other forms of aggressive behavior may not have had kinds of early attachment relationships required to build an adequate vagal system" (2010a, p. 234).

Helping Clients Develop a Relatively
Safe Sense of Themselves and the World

Is it possible within the somewhat limited context of anger management and domestic abuse offender treatment to help clients move toward a greater felt sense of safety? Don't these clients, some of whom could well be diagnosed with serious mental conditions such as borderline personality disorder, really need long-term individual therapy? While a referral for long-term treatment may be in order for some clients, it should be remembered that not every person's attachment vulnerability is strong enough to merit separate treatment. Another reality is that many clients will not possess the resources to obtain long-term therapy. The question becomes, then, how we can help clients deal with their attachment vulnerabilities within the context of anger management and/or domestic violence offender treatment.

First, it is essential to create a safe emotional climate within the individual or group therapy context. Clients need to feel that they can let their guard down in group without being shamed, disrespected, or punished. External safety gradually may lead toward internal safety.

Right hemisphere interventions such as relaxation training can also help clients develop a felt sense of inner control and contentment, a sense that they can call up their parasympathetic nervous system on demand. This internal ability to self-regulate frees clients from total dependence on their environment (and often their partners) for security. Mindfulness meditation training would be useful for that purpose as well.

Medication management may also need to be considered and can be implemented during treatment with deeply insecure clients. Certain medications help clients become less impulsively aggressive by increasing the "reflective delay" (Niehoff, 1998) between stimulus and response. These include antidepressants, anticonvulsants, anti-manic drugs, and opiate blockers that prevent craving. The basic goal of both therapy and medications is to help free the brain of defensively aggressive people from survival mode so that they can live better in (and help create) a safer world.

The concept of attachment is fundamentally interpersonal. Adult attachment insecurities ultimately must be healed within the context of intimate relationships. The clear implication is that couples counseling may be advised for many clients. This is particularly sensible for individual clients going through treatment with the intention of maintaining and hopefully improving their current intimate relationship. Emotionally focused therapy (Johnson, 2009) is a specific treatment model designed around attachment concepts that could be recommended for these clients to be pursued either during or after anger management or domestic violence offender treatment.

Let me acknowledge, however, that couples counseling is not the norm in domestic violence counseling. Indeed it is often prohibited on feminist therapy grounds (couples counseling implies that the woman partner carries some responsibility for the violence), because of the dangers involved, and because of the existence of no contact orders from legal authorities. Nevertheless, couples counseling may be appropriate if physical safety can be assured for all parties.

It is possible to make specific suggestions about how clients can move toward internal and external safety from an attachment perspective. These ideas have been organized around the four attachment styles as if any one individual possessed only one such style. Please bear in mind, though, that few people only identify with one style.

Secure attachment style and anger

In theory, anger will usually be associated with realistic threats to connection for clients who are basically secure. Furthermore, their anger will be proportional to the actual level of threat, serving as a signal of protest against actual or potential loss ("I don't like it when you stay out so late every night. We don't have any time with each other anymore"). Presumably their anger will soon cease after the concern has been relieved and the relationship rupture has been repaired. Consequently, the treatment focus will be to encourage individual exploration and couple discussion of realistic threats. Anger should be considered a bid for renewed contact and closeness by a client who senses that his or her partner has become so distant that the relationship itself is endangered.

Dismissive attachment style and anger

The anger of dismissive individuals frequently arises whenever a relationship partner attempts to lessen the physical, emotional, or psychological distance between them. The felt threat is to the person's autonomy and the immediate reaction is to push people away with anger, especially when the ability to distance or escape appears blocked (as when the partner walks in front of the television set and demands attention). Anger often takes the form of criticism and sarcasm as befits the dismissive person's stance of superiority and the reality that constant criticism is a very effective way to drive people away. Indeed, the first reaction of a dismissive individual to a partner's actual departure may be relief as the pressure to become more intimate lessens. However, dismissive individuals may occasionally become angry and jealous when their partners actually do leave as an unanticipated abandonment crisis develops. This abandonment crisis is usually described with words like "I didn't know she meant so much to me until I left. I know I neglected her before, but I swear I'll pay attention to her from now on if she'll only come back to me," but also as "How dare she leave me after all I've done for her. She's going to regret this."

The treatment focus with angry dismissive people centers on explaining their anger as a defensive reaction not so much to the partner's desire for closeness but to the client's own fear of vulnerability, dependency, and intimacy. These clients should be invited to explore closeness with their partners. However, care must be taken to ensure that they can maintain a sense of personal control during this exploration, lest they feel totally overwhelmed and withdraw.

Preoccupied attachment style and anger

Preoccupation may arise even in normally secure adults in the face of significant distancing that a partner denies ("I don't know why you think I'm having an affair. You're just imagining things") or sometimes as a result of a partner's gradual distancing (the "relationship drift" described by Frank Pittman; Pittman, 1989) that is either unacknowledged or uncorrected. However, certain individuals are chronically preoccupied, consumed by an internal working model that tells them they are not good enough to keep the person they love. Anger may easily arise with these individuals when the preoccupied partner senses the desire of his or her partner to achieve distance, even for short periods of time. This anger serves as a protest against abandonment, but often becomes confused with abandonments or rejections from the family of origin, previous adult relationships and past interactions with that partner. Anger may also arise when the preoccupied person fails to convince a partner to keep getting closer, since staying at the same emotional distance can be as unsatisfying and threatening as if the partner were actually leaving. Of course, actual rejections and abandonments may be the cause for tremendously angry attacks as the preoccupied person deals with tremendous feelings of rejection while reliving past rejections within the new one. Finally, and paradoxically, a partner's actual attempts at closeness may be angrily rejected as not being good enough since no one act of intimacy can make up for a lifetime of felt rejection.

The treatment focus with preoccupied clients revolves around explaining their strong anger as an often-exaggerated form of protest against separation. Such clients will need help learning how to take in whatever caring, love, and attention is available in the environment, while grieving and letting go of past attachment disappointments.

Fearful attachment style and anger

Fearful clients are often angry around the theme of distrust: "I know he/ she will betray me. They always do." This distrust may be expressed very actively, perhaps in the form of jealous accusations, but it may also appear in the form of passive aggression, as perfectly expressed by a client of mine who described how he fled abruptly a potentially significant relationship: "We started to get close, so one day I just left town without telling her I was going and never talked to her again." Additionally, anger may easily be turned against the self because of the fearful person's conviction that protest against relationship injustices are futile. Finally, Dutton notes that some fearful men also experience seething rage about past failures to meet their dependency needs: "Fearful men experience extreme chronic anger as an inevitable byproduct of attachment" (Dutton, 1998, p. 138).

Dutton (2007) writes that fearfully attached men experience high degrees of both chronic anxiety and anger, which is strongly correlated with borderline personality organization. He labels this pattern "intimacy-anger," describing a pattern in which such individuals desire social contact and intimacy, but experience pervasive distrust and fear of rejection.

The treatment focus with fearful clients relates their anger to their essential position of distrust. They must learn to challenge their mistaken belief that every potential relationship partner will take advantage of their neediness and vulnerability. Since they also feel relatively helpless about changing their fate in life (to be loveless), it is equally important to emphasize and teach assertiveness skills.

Summary

What can be done to help excessively angry clients, in particular those who function with the survival-oriented brain patterns described above? Niehoff writes that "The key to tempering violent behavior is adjusting the calculation of threat so that the intensity of the response matches the true demands of the situation" (1998, p. 264).

Therapeutically, angry and aggressive behavior may best be altered through programs that provide safety, promote attachment to others, and utilize right hemisphere targeted interventions as well as cognitive strategies that help the client address their initial protective and defensive reactions to perceived threat.

3

RAGE

Predictor of Out of Control Anger, Aggression, and Domestic Violence

What is Rage?

I define rage as "an experience of tremendous fury, far more intense than strong anger, which may be triggered by an immediate danger to one's existence or identity, or by a longer-term sense of unbearable injury or injustice."

> "I don't know what happened. I can't even remember what I did."
> "It felt like my brain was exploding."
> "That wasn't me. It's like Satan took over my body."
> "I felt completely out of control. I couldn't stop myself from screaming and kicking down the door."
> "At that moment I would have killed her if I had caught her."

These are the types of statements I often hear from clients talking about their strongest episodes of aggression. They are saying that something extraordinary happened, something they don't comprehend. Somehow their anger took a quantum leap and became qualitatively changed. This altered state of being is called rage.

Rage is an experience of excessive anger (and often other emotions) characterized by partial or complete loss of: a) conscious awareness (blackouts not due to alcohol or other drug reactions); b) a normal sense of self; c) behavioral control. It is a transformative experience, one in which people sense a "Dr. Jekyll and Mr. Hyde" alteration into a violent and unpredictable being (Potter-Efron, 2007).

Anger and rage feel quite different to the person experiencing them. Here is how one of my clients, a 30-year-old woman, described anger: "When I'm angry I yell and cuss. It's conscious, a power struggle, I'm in control." Here's her description of rage: "I see red. They tell me I said this and that, but I have no memory of it. Basically it's not me. It's me but shit's flashing in my head. They can go on for 2–3 hours. Afterward I feel mentally and physically exhausted, like I haven't slept for 72 hours."

Unfortunately, many anger management and domestic violence counselors are unfamiliar with the distinction between anger and rage. They mistakenly assume that standard anger management, communication training, or relationship skill-building will work to prevent or contain all of their clients' anger episodes. This can be a fatal error.

Nor do many researchers or authors differentiate rage from anger. However, Panksepp (2009; Panksepp and Biven, 2012) does describe a basic emotional system he labels RAGE (one of seven emotional systems he identifies. The others are SEEKING, FEAR, LUST, CARE, GRIEF/PANIC and PLAYFULNESS). His insights about the primitive origins of emotions are quite relevant to this chapter.

Panksepp argues that these seven systems developed so early that the basic mechanisms and pathways are shared by all mammals, some birds and perhaps even some lizards. These "raw emotional feelings" are part of a sub-neocortical circuitry that also generates emotional action readiness (Panksepp and Biven, 2012, p. 65). As noted in chapter 1, the anger pathway reaches its final pre-action destination at the periaqueductal gray region in the midbrain (the PAG). The sensations people feel when these ancient systems are activated cannot really be described accurately. Names such as anger, irritability, and hostility can only represent considerably higher "top down" (Siegel, 2011) interpretations of the experience. That is why my rageful clients struggle to explain their experiences. Two individuals were only able to respond to my inquiry about what they felt with one word: "intense."

Panksepp notes one critical research finding: strong electrical stimulation applied to these "lower" subcortical anger structures results in weaker neuronal activity in "higher" neocortical areas. This process is linear, in that the stronger the stimulation is to subcortical areas, the weaker the level of activity that is measured in neocortical areas. It seems likely to me that rage occurs when one's anger circuitry is so powerfully activated that the more primitive regions take over, as if they were saying to the neocortex "You can go to sleep for awhile. We'll handle this situation."

The mechanics of raging are poorly understood. It is possible that rages are somewhat similar to seizures, at least in their ability to induce an amnestic state. Certainly the person's executive control centers become disabled during a rage, so that even when raging individuals maintain consciousness they report an inability to control their behavior. Although treatment personnel may be tempted to dismiss this claim as responsibility shirking, it should be taken seriously. If indeed the client is being truthful, then discrediting his or her claim will seriously diminish the client/counselor relationship.

It is reasonable to postulate that several areas of the brain may be implicated during a rage. These would include:

- Prefrontal lobe under activity: impulsivity, poor judgment, difficulty learning other ways to handle anger.
- Anterior cingulate gyrus over-activity: obsessiveness, compulsivity, inability to forgive.
- Temporal lobe abnormalities: seizure-like dissociations, extreme violence.
- Limbic system dysregulation (including amygdala and hippocampus): excessive emotionality, inability to think, distorted cognitions.
- Hypothalamic and PAG overstimulation: dampening of the neocortex and "top down" reasoning ability.

Because of these possibilities it is important always to ask clients reporting rage symptoms if they are aware of having any accidents or other events that may have caused brain damage.

What could cause this massive degrading of the usually finely attuned balance between older and newer parts of the brain? One possibility is trauma or traumatic memories. Another is brain damage, as noted above. But I would suggest that it is the appearance of an apparently overwhelming threat that can trigger a rage episode in anyone, even someone with no history of trauma or brain damage (although certainly some individuals are more prone than others). One such situation involves being physically attacked. Indeed, it might help you survive if you could go into a rage state when under attack. But later in this chapter I will describe four other situations that also are threatening enough that they could trigger rages.

Varieties of Rage

Not all rage episodes are identical. Indeed, they vary in several dimensions. First, they can seem to come out of nowhere or to build up over time. These two patterns are labeled as sudden or seething rages. A *sudden rage* can be described as "an unplanned fit of tremendous fury during which a person loses partial or complete control over his or her feelings, thoughts, actions, and (sometimes) loses conscious awareness of his or her behavior", whereas a *seething rage* is described as "a long-term build-up of fury towards a specific individual, cluster of individuals, or group that includes a sense of having been victimized, obsessive thoughts about the situation, moral outrage and hatred toward the offenders, vengeful fantasies and (sometimes) deliberately planned assaults upon targeted offenders."

Second, not all rages are complete, totally out of control, potentially lethal phenomena. I distinguish them from two incomplete patterns, namely *near rages* in which a person gets very close to having an uncontrollable sudden rage but is able to stop and *partial rages* during which a person begins to rage but still maintains some control over what is occurring.

Third, I believe that at least five types of rages can be distinguished by the kind of threat that causes them. These are:

- *"survival rage,"* caused by real or imagined threats to one's physical safety or survival;
- *"abandonment rage,"* triggered by real or imagined threats of abandonment, betrayal, or neglect by important family members, partners, or close friends;
- *"impotent rage,"* initiated by feelings of helplessness and an inability to control important situations;
- *"shame-based rage,"* caused by real or imagined current or past experiences of shame and humiliation and the consequent threat to one's claimed social identity;
- *"moral rage,"* (outrage) resulting from an attack on one's most cherished values and the subsequent threat to one's moral identity.

The following questionnaire both describes the key elements in each type of rage and helps direct treatment for clients:

RAGE QUESTIONNAIRE

Today's date: _____

Your name: _____

Your gender: Male/Female

Your age: _____

<u>Instructions</u>

Please score each question by giving it the number that best describes how often you do the activities described below. Use the following key:

0 = No, I never do this or feel this way.
1 = Yes, I do this once a month or less often.
2 = Yes, I do this 2–4 times a month.
3 = Yes, I do this 2–3 times a week.
4 = Yes, I do this 4 times a week or more.

Sudden Rage Indicators:

_____ 1. My anger comes on both very quickly and very intensely.
_____ 2. I get so angry I lose control over what I say or do.
_____ 3. People say I act strange, scary, or crazy when I get really mad.

_____ 4. I have "blacked out" (not from alcohol or drugs) when I became very angry, so I did not remember things I said or did.

_____ 5. I get so angry that I worry I might seriously harm or kill someone.

_____ 6. I feel like I become a different person when I get angry – as if I am not really myself.

_____ 7. I become instantly furious when I feel that somebody has insulted or threatened me.

Score on items 1–7: ___

Seething Rage Indicators:

_____ 8. I am unable to quit thinking about past insults or injuries.

_____ 9. My anger about some past insult sometimes seems to grow greater over time instead of leveling off or diminishing.

_____ 10. I sometimes have intense fantasies of revenge against people who have harmed me.

_____ 11. I hate people for what they have done to me.

_____ 12. People would be amazed if they knew how angry I get even though I don't show it.

_____ 13. I think a lot about how unfair life is.

_____ 14. I have difficulty forgiving people.

_____ 15. I "seethe" in anger, but don't say anything to others.

_____ 16. I deliberately hurt people (physically or verbally) in order to pay them back for something they did to me.

Score on items 8–16: ___

Survival Rage Indicators:

_____ 17. I have gotten into a physical fight where it took several people to pull me away from the other person.

_____ 18. I threaten to severely hurt or even to kill people when I become very angry.

_____ 19. I startle easily in situations such as when somebody touches me on the shoulder from behind.

_____ 20. I feel like I am fighting for my life when I become angry.

_____ 21. I go into a "blind rage" when defending myself against real or imagined danger.

_____ 22. People say I am paranoid or that I falsely believe people are trying to harm me.

_____ 23. I have a "fight and flight" reaction during which I feel both really angry and really scared.

Score on items 17–23: ___

Impotent Rage Indicators:

_____ 24. I feel like exploding when people don't listen to me or understand me.

_____ 25. I blow up after thinking thoughts such as "I just can't take it anymore."

_____ 26. I feel both helpless and furious about situations I cannot control.

_____ 27. I pound the ground, break things, scream out loud, etc. when things don't go the way I want them to.

_____ 28. I get so angry I have to do something – anything – even if it makes the problem worse.

_____ 29. I harbor thoughts of violence or revenge towards people who have (or once had) power or control over me.

Score on items 24–29: ___

Shame-Based Rage Indicators:

_____ 30. I become furious when people seem to disrespect me.

_____ 31. My reputation – my good name – is something I strongly defend.

_____ 32. I frequently worry that people think I am stupid, ugly, or incompetent.

_____ 33. I get really mad after a moment of embarrassment, for instance if someone points out something I did wrong.

_____ 34. People say that I am way too sensitive to criticism.

_____ 35. I dwell upon put downs that I believe people have made about me.

_____ 36. I become irate when people seem to be ignoring me.

Score on items 30–36: ___

Abandonment Rage Indicators:

_____ 37. I become furious when I think about times when I have been abandoned or betrayed.

_____ 38. I struggle with intense feelings of jealousy.

_____ 39. I look for proof that people who say they care about me cannot be trusted.

_____ 40. Feeling neglected or ignored by the people I love seems almost intolerable to me.

_____ 41. I become preoccupied with wanting to get back at my parents or partners because they left me, neglected me, or betrayed me.

_____ 42. I feel cheated by my partner, children, or friends because I give them way more love, care, and attention than I get back.

_____ 43. I have been told that once I become really mad, I can't take in any reassurances or statements of caring from the people I am angry with.

Score on items 37–43: ___

Moral Rage Indicators:

_____ 44. I feel disgusted with people who break the rules.

_____ 45. I have become furious with people whose views differ from mine.

_____ 46. I feel personally attacked when people do things against my values.

_____ 47. I feel outraged by what some people try to get away with.

_____ 48. I am ready to fight to defend my values and beliefs.

_____ 49. I get so mad at people who have different values or beliefs I can feel myself losing control.

Score on items: 44–49: ___
Total score for all items: ___

Now that you have completed the questionnaire, please use the rest of the space on this page to answer these two questions: Do you think you have a problem with rage? Why?

This test has not been normed, so the following guidelines for interpretation are only suggestions.

If someone scores 2 or more points on any single item, it should be reviewed with the client.

If someone has three such sentences in any section of the quiz, the whole section should be reviewed and possibly targeted for therapy.

If someone averages 2 points or higher on the entire quiz (98 points total), then rage should be targeted as a major treatment priority.

It is helpful to have clients describe specifically how they experienced a rage episode. Here are some useful questions:

- About how long ago did this event take place?
- What was going on in your life about then that added stress to your life or might help explain what happened?
- Had you been drinking or drugging right before or during the rage (or withdrawing from a heavy period of intoxication)? If so, how do you think that affected you?
- Who was involved in the rage episode?
- What triggered the rage (maybe something someone said or did)?
- How much of what happened during the rage did you remember the next day (all, some, none. If some, what do you remember)?
- During the rage, what did you say? What did you think? What did you feel? What did you do?
- How did the rage end?
- How hard did you try to stay in control before or during the rage? What did you do to keep control? Did it work?
- Would you say that during the rage you were completely out of control, partly out of control, mostly in control, completely in control? Why do you say that?
- What happened to you after the rage? (Such as slept for hours, got arrested, wife left me, etc.)
- How often do you experience rages? Then and now?
- Are you taking any medications to help control your anger, emotions, or rages? If so, what are they? Do they help?
- What else do you do to try not to rage, or to control them once they begin?
- What advice would you give someone with a rage problem?

Clients who identify with rage issues have reason to be fearful and concerned about their lack of ability to contain their anger. They need their counselor to understand this fear and also their accompanying sense of helplessness. They also need guidance toward gaining better control over their raging. I suggest the following eight-step movement towards safety (Potter-Efron, 2007):

1. Be hopeful. Believe that you can learn how to stop raging.
2. Make a commitment to work hard and long to contain your rage.
3. Take the time to identify your rage patterns.
4. Look at your past near-rage episodes to learn more about how you personally prevent yourself from raging.
5. Look at your past partial rage episodes to learn more about how you stay at least somewhat in control even during a rage.
6. Make a safety plan to lessen your risk for sudden raging. A safety management plan might include gathering a support system, anger management training, and proper medication management if necessary.

7. Examine your current thoughts and behaviors to determine if you are right now developing or hanging on to any long-term resentments that could produce a seething rage. If so, then challenge those thoughts and change your behaviors.
8. Work on your long-term issues to make permanent changes in your sense of self and the world. The goals here are to feel secure, good about yourself, sane, and healthy.

Five Types of Rage

Survival rage

Many of my clients, especially those in domestic violence offender programs, grew up in and/or still live in dangerous surroundings. Consequently, they have become hyper-alert toward potential danger signs. This leads to the creation and maintenance of a *false-alarm system*, which in turn causes them to frequently and unnecessarily enter into survival rage mode. The goal, then, is to help clients turn down their alarm system so they get fewer false alarms. Before engaging in this type of therapy, though, it is critical to determine how physically safe the client is now. After all, it would be foolhardy to convince yourself that the world is a pretty safe place when one is in constant danger.

Treatment begins with creating a safe place in which to heal. This can be done through individual, couples, family, or group counseling. Once the counseling setting has been established as a place of safety, this will help clients create more safety in their lives. They can then better separate their relatively unsafe former life from a more secure present, making them less vulnerable to false alarms.

I have found it helpful for clients with survival rage to memorize a few brief safety reminder statements such as "I'm safe now," "Nobody is out to hurt me," or "I can trust . . . [name of partner or other person]." Trauma work may also be helpful, especially therapies that help clients better integrate the left and right hemispheres of the brain.

Impotent rage

This kind of rage is perhaps closest to the Power and Control model of domestic violence that will be described later. Its origins are as primitive as the baby fighting against being held too tightly and the adolescent running upstairs while screaming to be left alone. People need to feel in control of their own lives to feel safe. It's all too easy to lose control of your behavior when you feel you have no control over your life. Words associated with this feeling include: overpowered, weak, powerless, misunderstood, ganged up on, scapegoated, and helpless fury. No wonder, then, that my angry and domestically violent parents kept from seeing their children by court decree or hostile ex-partners sometimes feel enraged and ready to take action into their own hands, even while their group colleagues remind them that doing so will only make things worse. This situation is only exacerbated when the clients report that "I've tried everything but nothing has helped." They can feel overwhelmed with a sense of utter defeat and despair that can lead to a serious altercation.

Treatment for impotent rage has two dimensions. First, take effective action if possible. That means clients should take time to analyze their situation, determine what actions they have been taking simply are not working, and substitute new, more effective approaches. This is not an easy task as most individuals are generally wedded to habitual but ineffective behaviors, even more so when they are feeling very emotional about the situation. Clients must be gently dissuaded from these useless and perhaps dangerous activities.

The second dimension focuses upon helping clients better accept reality. For instance, I might ask clients what they want from the other person that they will never get (love, an apology, attention, etc.). They must recognize the limits of control. One of my domestic violence offender clients, for example, named his brain change plan (see chapter 8) "People can change, but I can't make them change." Now he needs to specify exactly what he cannot control about his girlfriend (in this case her hoarding behavior) and let go of the fears that underlay his previous "co-dependent" behavior. He also needs encouragement to develop some new behaviors that he can fill the vacuum created when he stops his old activities.

Shame-based rage

Humans have a genetically determined need to fit in, to belong within the safety of families and communities. Shame is an emotion designed to help people live within the norms and rules of their communities by making them feel bad about themselves when they break those norms. As such a moderate amount of shame can be quite valuable. Unfortunately, some people feel shame too often and too strongly. This creates the potential for shame-based rage.

Reviews of shame and its differentiation from guilt can be found in Potter-Efron and Potter-Efron (1989), Potter-Efron (2002), Tracy et al. (2007), Tangney and Dearing (2002), Dearing and Tangney (2011), and Schneider (1977).

Shame-based rage is quite dangerous and can lead to lethal violence. It is critical that treatment personnel be alert to this phenomenon. It occurs when people regularly experience potentially devastating feelings of worthlessness, incompetence, inadequacy, and unattractiveness. The threat here is to the person's felt acceptance in the human community (not just immediate family). Feelings of shame become intermingled with the fear of ostracism – being cast out or not allowed into an important group. This fear/shame combination ultimately reflects the dread of being unable to survive physically and emotionally apart from others.

This feeling of unworthiness can become unbearable. Typically clients report that they felt suddenly attacked by someone making a cutting remark about their appearance or personality, often in public: "She called me an idiot right in front of my friends!" Frequently the offender is an intimate associate because the opinion of that person is crucial to one's self-concept. Although the most common reaction to shame is to withdraw (Potter-Efron and Potter-Efron, 1989), some people aggressively attack the perceived shamer. Feeling deeply shamed, the client becomes enraged, counter-attacking by belittling, shaming, humiliating, assaulting, and even annihilating the other person. In essence, they project their shame outwardly. Note that the perceived shamer may not have said anything most people would interpret as shaming and certainly did not intend to shame the rager. What is critical is the perception of being shamed.

The key to treatment is to help clients break the link between shame and rage. But first the connection must be made in the client's mind. Questions such as "What were you feeling and thinking right before you lost it?" "How were you feeling about yourself when he/she said that to you?" and "In addition to anger what else were you feeling?" can help. Since clients seldom have a name for this experience, I do tell them about shame-rage and have them read about it (Potter-Efron, 2007; Potter-Efron and Potter-Efron, 1989, 2006). It is important for clients to identify the triggers (from others and self-talk) that prompt the start of a shame-rage event. Clients tend to have very specific vulnerabilities that often can be traced back to childhood ("Don't ever call me lazy, like my father did all the time"). When they identify the source of these vulnerabilities, they may gain better control of their reaction to them in the present.

It is important for clients to deal directly with their shame rather than converting it instantaneously into anger and aggression. This takes courage since shame is a very unpleasant feeling. They must deal with five core shame messages (You are no good; You are not good enough; You are unlovable; You don't belong; You should not exist). They must learn how raging temporarily relieves their shame, but ultimately makes them feel even worse about themselves. Let me add that it also takes a certain amount of courage on the part of the therapist to help their clients stick with a feeling that is certainly unpleasant to witness.

Clients with shame-rage tendencies need to learn to attend to what I call the Five A's: *attention* ("I'm listening to you"); *approval* ("I like you"); *acceptance* ("You are good enough"); *admiration* ("I can learn from you");

and *affirmation* ("I celebrate your existence"). These qualities are critical for the client to give to and to receive from their significant others.

Abandonment rage

I described previously (in chapter 2) how insecure attachment patterns can lead to excessive anger and domestic violence. The result of these attachment difficulties can generate true rages based on the fear of being abandoned or rejected. It's as if these individuals lived by a formula that looks like this: 0 (me) + 1 (you) = 2 (us). That means these people depend upon their partner to sustain them. Rages will occur when someone senses their partner might abandon them. The formula becomes 2 – 1 = 0, as in "I am nothing without you" and "I'll kill you if you try to leave me because I can't live without you." Note that it is the perceived threat of abandonment that might trigger an abandonment rage as against one's partner's actual behavior or intent. Also note that anything that symbolically reflects abandonment, betrayal, or rejection can trigger rages ("Julie said she'd just be gone an hour, but she didn't get home on time. I started worrying. I thought she'd run out on me just like my ex did"). Individuals who have abandonment rages often feel stunned by their own vehemence, but still see their reactions as justified by their partner's words or actions.

Treatment for clients who experience abandonment rage centers on the goal of helping them develop an internal sense of self-sufficiency. They need to learn self-soothing techniques and to realize they can survive and even thrive on their own. This is a lengthy therapeutic process involving fully grieving past losses, abandonments, betrayals, and rejections by significant others. In the meantime, they must commit to quit raging no matter how empty, lonely, hurt, or unsafe they feel. They also need to learn to take in sincere reassurances of love given by their partners and friends. They need to learn how to trust themselves and the world.

Moral rage

Values are visceral. By this I mean that one's most deeply held values, sometimes called sacred values (Berns and Atrin, 2012), are far more than intellectual beliefs. Sacred values have usually been learned during childhood, long before children can make discriminating choices. It is while parents still maintain God-like status that someone's most internalized values are incorporated into oneself. As such, these values may well invoke limbic system defenses when challenged. An attack on these values becomes in effect an attack upon that person's core identity. When this occurs, individuals may say that they feel sick inside, indicating that not only are they very angry but also disgusted by the people they perceive as violating their values.

This combination of anger and disgust may trigger a feeling of outrage. Those who challenge one's sacred values may be labeled disgusting, sub-human, pariahs, evil, sinful, lunatics, or monsters. This can then justify a full scale assault on the offending parties.

Outrage may well fuel domestic violence incidents. One example is a man who comes home to discover his partner in bed with another man. One of my clients put these words to his feelings: "What she did was disgusting. I spat on her. I threw her out of the house and then I burned all her clothes. She tried to apologize, but I told her to get away from me and never come back."

Outrage is difficult to treat if only because people cling to it as justification for the otherwise unacceptable things they did. Thus, they can claim to be otherwise non-violent people who did what they had to do under dire circumstances. The client's feelings of anger and disgust must be carefully acknowledged while not being endorsed beyond an "I can certainly understand how angry and disgusted you must have felt." Therapeutic work will be similar to helping people work through issues of hate while moving toward forgiveness. Empathy training might help clients remember that the person who offended them is a human being and not a monster. Ultimately, if a broken relationship is to be rekindled, the outraged party must be urged to turn toward the other (as against turning away in disgust).

More generally, clients with strong moral anger tendencies need to learn to pick their battles carefully. I tell them to imagine carrying a "moral handgun" in their pocket but that gun only has one bullet in it. They must learn not to go shooting their gun (mouth) off at every incident they perceive as going against their personal values. They certainly have the right to feel strongly about their values, but they do need to realize that they cannot demand that the entire world agree with them.

Summary

Rage is a qualitatively different experience than anger. As such, it is criti-cal for therapists in the fields of anger management and domestic vio-lence offender treatment to be able to recognize the signs of rage, including a partial or complete loss of awareness, the sense that one's mind and body are not one's own, a felt loss of behavioral control, etc. We can then help our clients identify which of five likely rage patterns best identifies their behavior: survival rage, shame-based rage, impotent rage, abandon-ment rage, or moral rage. Hopefully, then, we can help them make a commitment to do all they can to prevent and contain their rages.

Part II

ASSESSMENT

4

ASSESSMENT FOR ANGER
AND AGGRESSION

I have divided this chapter into two main sections: general concerns associated with diagnosing anger problems and specific instruments to use with clients to help determine the extent of their anger issues.

General Concerns about Anger Assessment

Assessment for anger problems is a particularly difficult task because of the great variety of issues that can be subsumed under that term, sometimes including propensity toward violence. Thus, the Buss-Durkee Hostility Inventory (Buss and Durkee, 1957) measures one particular aspect of anger, cognitive hostility, which in turn can be subdivided into expressive scales (verbal hostility, irritability, indirect hostility, and assault) as well as emotional or neurotic hostility (resentment and suspicion) (Felsten and Leitten, 1993), while the Minnesota Multiphasic Personality Inventory (Green, 1998) taps such features as sociopathic tendencies, resentment and "overcontrolled hostility." The Novaco Anger Inventory (Novaco, 1975), another well-known instrument, measures anger arousal.

One very interesting aspect of assessing anger problems is the relative lack of relevant diagnoses in the *Diagnostic and Statistical Manual of the American Psychiatric Association* (APA, 2014). Deffenbacher (2003) did address this deficiency and proposed several anger diagnoses ranging from a non-violent situational anger disorder through quite violent anger categories. However, these diagnoses and the implicit range of anger problems they invoke was not included in the DSM-5. Essentially the only diagnosis in which anger is a defining trait is *Intermittent Explosive Disorder* (312.34), which has the following description: a) recurrent behavioral outbursts involving verbal aggression such as temper tantrums and tirades *and* at least three physical acts involving physical aggression against people, animals, or property; b) these acts are far more intense than seems merited by the provocation; c) these actions are not premeditated or intended to achieve a specific goal; d) these outbursts cause the participant marked psychological discomfort or financial or legal problems; e) the person must be at least 16 years old; f) there is no better reason (such as a mental disorder) to explain the behavior. *Oppositional defiant disorder*, previously limited to children and adolescents, does now appear to apply to adults as well. That diagnosis addresses clients with angry/irritable moods, argumentative and defiant behavior, and vindictiveness. Additionally, the DSM-5 lists *conduct disorder* including behaviors such as aggression toward people and animals, property destruction, deceitfulness or theft, and serious violations of rules related to anger but focuses on aggression.

However, many psychological conditions, such as major depressive disorder, post traumatic stress disorder, and obsessive-compulsive disorder, that are described in the DSM-5 do involve the possible presence of anger or aggression. This anger may not always be present, though. Rather, this anger or aggression may be absent with some clients, occasionally present with others with the same diagnosis, and regularly present for still others with that diagnosis. Still, there are some fairly predictable associations between specific psychological diagnoses and certain ways that clients exhibit their anger. These correlations are described below.

Table 4.1 is intended as a guide to help practitioners recognize typical anger and aggression patterns associated with particular adult psychological diagnoses. It is meant only as a rough guideline but should help counselors notice links between certain displays of anger and aggression and possible psychological conditions or diagnoses.

Client Assessment

Two standardized assessments are particularly useful. They are the State-Trait Anger Expression Inventory—II and the Anger Disorders Scale. I discuss these two instruments first but then provide two other questionnaires I have developed, an Anger Intake Form and the Anger Styles Quiz.

The State-Trait Anger Expression Inventory

Charles Spielberger's State-Trait Anger Expression Inventory—II (STAXI-2; Spielberger, 1999) is a standardized, quick, easy to use, and easily understood questionnaire that taps several important areas of anger. Consisting of 57 items, the resultant product is an individualized assessment of an individual's tendency to become angry both immediately (State anger) and as a personality component (Trait anger). I have found the STAXI-2 to be quite useful, both for gathering information and for developing treatment plans.

Table 4.1 Adult Psychological Conditions and Associated Behaviors/Cognitions

Condition	Associated Behaviors/Cognitions
Adult attention deficit disorder	Frustration with routine tasks and obligations can increase tendency toward "oppositionality."
Alcoholism/ substance abuse	Disinhibits normal controls over anger and aggression; may be used to inhibit/suppress anger.
Antisocial personality disorder	Intimidation tactics are used to control others.
Anxiety disorders	Anger in the face of possible loss of control over external environment.
Attachment difficulties	Fears of abandonment trigger excessive vigilance, jealousy, demands for attention.
Bipolar disorder (manic phase)	Impulsive bouts of anger when immediate goals are blocked.
Borderline personality disorder	Strong tendency toward "splitting" increases development of hateful feelings and inability to forgive.
Dissociative identity disorder	Angry/rageful affect may be localized within one personality state ("alter").
Dysthymic disorder	Easily annoyed; cynical, and sarcastic.
Intermittent explosive disorder	Sudden inexplicable bouts of extreme aggression often accompanied by inability to recall incident.
Major depressive disorder	Increased irritability, angry rejection of others, impotent rage, suicidal ideation.
Paranoia/paranoid schizophrenia	Extreme suspiciousness; projection of own aggressive impulses onto others.
Post-traumatic stress disorder	Over-activated terror reaction triggers defensive, dissociative episodes.
Premenstrual dysphoric syndrome	Excessive irritability, over-sensitivity to criticism, over-reaction to perceived attack.

More specifically, the STAXI-2 measures these aspects of the anger experience: *State Anger* measures the intensity of a subject's angry feelings and the extent to which a person feels like expressing anger at a particular time. State anger is divided into the following components:

- Feeling angry.
- Feel like expressing anger verbally.
- Feel like expressing anger physically.

Trait Anger measures how angry feelings are experienced over time, so that individuals high in trait anger are more likely than the general population to become angry and/or to stay angry on a regular basis.

Trait anger is subdivided into:

- Angry Temperament, which reflects an individual's disposition to experience anger without specific provocation, and
- Angry Reaction, which measures the frequency that angry feelings are experienced in situations that involve frustration and/or negative evaluations.

The STAXI-2 also has scales that report *Anger-In*, which represents the desire and ability of the respondent to suppress their anger, and *Anger-Out*, which describes the person's tendency to directly express angry feelings to others. Note that these scales are independent of each other, which means that certain individuals may be high on *both* Anger-In and Anger-Out. Other scales measure *Anger Control-In*, a person's attempt to calm down and cool off, and *Anger Control-Out*, the respondent's control over the outward expression of angry feelings. Standardized tables are available for the general adult population and several subgroups such as younger adult males, adult females, etc., making interpretation of the STAXI-2 relatively easy and meaningful for specific populations.

Anger Disorders Scale

DiGiuseppe and Tafrate (2007) have developed both a take home test (in short and longer versions) entitled the Anger Disorders Scale and a structured interview format called the Structured Interview for Anger Disorders. Both are fashioned after a five-domain model developed by Power and Dalgleish (1997). The five domains are provocations, cognitions, motives, arousal, and behaviors. Symptoms assessed include such varied items as the breadth of things that might provoke someone, hurts and feelings of rejection, length of episodes, intensity of anger, physiological arousal, condemnation of the target, desire for revenge, anger held in, verbal expression, negative consequences from anger, and physical aggression toward objects and toward people. Note that higher scores on this scale do correlate with a greater propensity toward physical aggression, indicative of the overlap between anger, aggression, and domestic abuse.

The Anger/Aggression Intake Questionnaire

This set of questions is best administered in person but may also be given to clients to fill out independently. It takes roughly an hour to complete in session, depending of course on the verbosity of the client and the amount of detail desired by the therapist. As with most questionnaires, its reliability depends upon the truthfulness and completeness of the respondent's answers. Therefore every effort should be made to gather collateral information from the respondent's family, counselors, employers, and criminal justice personnel.

Although the specified purpose of this intake questionnaire is to gain assessment information, it also serves as a bridge to and motivator for treatment, since answering these questions often helps clients recognize the extent of their anger difficulties.

One important note: there are many opportunities while using this questionnaire to initiate discussions about the goals of anger management and the processes involved. I will highlight these opportunities as I discuss the questions after displaying the questionnaire below.

The Anger/Aggression Intake Questionnaire

1. Please tell me about any concerns you or others have about your anger.

2. Describe your <u>most recent</u> event involving your anger or aggression.
   a. When did this occur?
   b. With whom?
   c. How did it get started?
   d. While this was going on, what did you:
      - Think?
      - Feel?
      - Say?
      - Do?
   e. How did it end?
   f. Was there any use of alcohol or drugs by anyone involved?
   g. Was there any use of physical violence, force, threats, etc.?
   h. What effects (immediate or long-term) did this event have on you?
   i. What effects (immediate or long-term) did this event have on others?

3. Now please tell me about the <u>worst</u> incident you've ever had involving your getting angry or aggressive.
   a. When did this occur?
   b. With whom?
   c. How did it get started?
   d. While this was going on, what did you:

- Think?
- Feel?
- Say?
- Do?

e. How did it end?

f. Was there any use of alcohol or drugs by anyone involved?

g. Was there any use of physical violence, force, threats, etc.?

h. What effects (immediate or long-term) did this event have on you?

i. What effects (immediate or long-term) did this event have on others?

4. Frequency of problems. How often have you had trouble with your anger:

a. *This month?* __ None at all __ Once or twice __ Weekly __ Several times a week __ Daily __ More than once a day.

b. *Over the last six months?* __ None at all __ Once or twice __ Weekly __ Several times a week __ Daily __ More than once a day.

c. *Previously as an adult?*

d. *When you were a teenager?*

e. *When you were a child?*

f. *Would you say lately you are getting angry* __ more often than a year ago, __ less often than a year ago, __ about the same as a year ago?

g. *Would you say lately when you get angry that you have* __ more control than you used to over what you say and do, __ less control, __ about the same amount of control as before?

h. *Would you say lately when you get angry that you* __ do more damage than before, __ do less damage, __ do about the same amount of damage, __ don't believe your anger/ aggression is damaging?

i. *When you get upset are you more likely to get angry at* __ others, __ yourself, __ both yourself and others?

5. With whom do you get angry and how often do you get angry with them?
Code: D = DAILY; S = SEVERAL TIMES A WEEK; O = OCCASIONALLY

a. Partner/boyfriend/girlfriend	__D	__S	__O
b. Parents/stepparents	__D	__S	__O
c. Your children/stepchildren	__D	__S	__O
d. Other relatives	__D	__S	__O

 e. Employers/coworkers/employees   __D __S __O
 f. Teachers   __D __S __O
 g. Friends   __D __S __O
 h. Strangers   __D __S __O
 i. Others (whom?)   __D __S __O

6. Immediate stressors: What has been going on in your life now or in the last several months that has been causing you stress, concern, or anxiety?
 a. Financial troubles _____.
 b. Relationship problems _____.
 c. Health concerns _____.
 d. Job or school difficulties _____.
 e. Legal issues _____.
 f. Emotional problems _____.
 g. Concern about someone else _____.
 h. Religious or spiritual crisis _____.
 i. Other (what?) _____.
 j. How have these troubles affected your mood or behavior?
  _____.

7. Anger history.
 I <u>Family of origin.</u>
 a. Describe what the following people did or do with their anger, especially when you were growing up:
  i. Your father/stepfather:
  ii. Your mother/stepmother:
  iii. Your brothers and sisters:
  iv. Other relatives:
 b. Is there any family history of bad temper, assaults, homicides, or suicides?
 c. Were you spanked growing up? What do you think about that?
 d. Were you physically or sexually assaulted? If so, how do you think that has affected you, especially in the area of anger?
 e. In general, what did you learn about anger from your family?

 II <u>Friendship groups, culture, religious training, etc.</u>
 a. How do you think your attitudes toward anger and aggression have been affected by messages you received from members of:
  i. Your gender:
  ii. The opposite gender:

    iii.   Your nationality:

    iv.   Your race:

    v.   Your religion:

    vi.   Friendship groups or gangs you belonged in:

    vii.   Other people or groups:

8. Possible medical and/or psychological factors.

    a.   Do you have any current problems or past history of problems with:

   ___ Alcohol or drug abuse

   ___ Antisocial personality disorder

   ___ Anxiety disorders

   ___ Attention deficit disorder (with or without hyperactivity?)

   ___ Bipolar disorder

   ___ Borderline personality disorder

   ___ Brain injury, concussions, seizures

   ___ Chronic illness

   ___ Dementia

   ___ Depression

   ___ Diabetes or hypoglycemia

   ___ Disabling injury

   ___ Paranoia

   ___ Post traumatic stress disorder

   ___ Premenstrual dysphoric disorder

   ___ Schizophrenia

   ___ Other major illness or condition (What? _____)

9. Are you currently taking any medications? If yes, what are they? Have you noticed any change in the rate or severity of your anger episodes since beginning these medications?

10. Legal history relating to anger and aggression. Be specific.

    a.   Any current problems with the law?

    b.   Are you on probation or parole?

    c.   Are you coming here as part of a criminal diversion program?

    d.   Any past anger- or aggression-related legal difficulties?

    e.   Any brushes with the law because of your anger or aggression that did not result in any charges being filed?

11. Use of alcohol/drugs.

Substance	Current or recent use	Past use	Frequency
Alcohol			
Amphetamines			
Barbiturates			
Cocaine			

Inhalants
Marijuana or marijuana substitutes
Prescribed medications
Opiates (heroin etc.)
Other (designer drugs etc.). What?
Drug combinations. What?

12. What connections could there be between your use of these substances and your anger or aggression?
    a. When I use _____ I often become more angry than usual.
    b. When I use _____ I can become violent.
    c. When I use _____ I get argumentative.
    d. When I use _____ I become controlling or demanding.
    e. When I use _____ I have poor judgment.
    f. When I use _____ I get jealous or paranoid.
    g. I only get in trouble with my anger when I use _____.
    h. Others tell me I get angrier or more violent when I use _____.
    i. Mixing _____ and _____ makes me more aggressive.
    j. I often use _____ to try to cool down.
    k. Another connection between my using and my anger is: _____.
    l. I don't see any connection between my use of alcohol or drugs and my anger or aggression _____.

13. How have you attempted to control your anger?
    a. ___ I never have.
    b. ___ I talk to myself. What do you usually say that helps you cool down?
    c. ___ I leave the scene. Where do you go? What do you do?
    d. ___ I talk with people. With whom?
    e. ___ I go to a self-help group like AA.
    f. ___ I do something physical. What?
    g. ___ I do something else. What?

14. What do you think is the first thing you need to do to help you control your anger or aggression?

15. What else do you need to do?

16. How hopeful are you that you can become less angry or aggressive?

17. Is there anything else you can tell me that might help me understand your concerns about anger and aggression?

Discussion of the Anger/Aggression Intake Questionnaire

The first and last questions are open-ended, designed to help clients feel somewhat in charge of a mutual exploration process. Starting out less programmed also gives the counselor an opportunity to gauge the client's motivation. Imagine the difference in a respondent who responds to the first question with "Actually, I don't think I have an anger problem. My probation officer is hung up on it, though. She claims I'm angry but she says that about everybody" vs. one who states "My anger's getting worse and worse. I'm scared I could kill someone one of these days. I need help."

The second and third sets of questions ask informants about the details of two anger/aggression episodes, their most recent and worst incidents. If the last episode was also their worst, then the questioner can instead ask for a "typical" incident to augment the last one. These items prepare clients to think about anger in two ways: 1) that anger and aggression episodes frequently occur in discrete, describable units; 2) that each episode involves cognition, affect, and verbal and/or physical actions. A third aspect of these questions is an immediate probe for alcohol or drug use (to be extended later in the questionnaire). The inquiry about immediate and long-term effects of the anger episodes helps the questioner determine how much insight the respondent has about his or her behavior. Finally, item "i" is a first check for empathy: does the respondent show any remorse or even awareness of how his or her anger/aggression affects others such as the immediate recipient of that anger or witnesses to it such as children?

The fourth set of questions helps determine the extent of the client's anger. It's important to know how often the client gets angry. Just as critical, though, is gathering information about the client's movement over time with regard to this material. In other words, has the client been getting angrier over time, less angry, or staying about the same? If the client does report significant change here, moving toward more or less anger, the counselor should ask the respondent how and why that has happened. This fourth set of questions also sets the stage to introduce three *goals* for anger management: to get angry less often; to stay in better control even when angry; and to do less damage to oneself and others when angry. Finally, the last question in the fourth set is an initial inquiry into the direction of the client's anger: inward, outward, or both. I will discuss this issue in more detail later in this chapter.

Question 5 recognizes that people frequently are highly selective about the targets of their anger or aggression. While some informants state that they get angry with just about everyone over just about anything, most report that their anger is more limited. One person may only get mad at spouse and children, another primarily targets employees, still a third "authority figures." The implication here is that these individuals have all the tools they need to manage their anger, since they demonstrate they can do so over and over again in many settings. The interesting question, then, is how can they take those skills and apply them with their spouses, children, coworkers, authority figures, etc.?

The sixth question regards the client's immediate stressors. My belief is that people break down under the weight of stress and that the greater the number of significant stressors in someone's life the more likely they will break down. Some people become anxious, others depressed. But some people, perhaps including the immediate respondent, do become more angry and aggressive when stressed. If that is the case then counseling should begin by focusing upon how the client can lessen the amount of stress he or she is enduring. Also, individuals who indicate they are highly stressed become good candidates for relaxation and stress management training.

The seventh set of questions represents inquiries into the client's history, in particular family of origin. How was anger handled back then? Were there any models of how to deal effectively with conflict? Or were the client's parents unfortunate models of losing control, becoming abusive, being excessively critical, etc.? Please note the last family of origin question: "In general, what did you learn about anger from your family?" This question implies that what was once learned can now be challenged.

The seventh set also asks about broader early life influences that may have shaped the respondent's beliefs about anger and aggression. Note that the phrasing is intended to put the client in control. Nobody is insisting that he or she was affected by race, religion, or gender. But he or she may indeed ascribe some attitudes, beliefs and actions to these influences. If so, it will be important to discuss and perhaps challenge them.

Question 8 screens for possibly significant medical and psychological conditions often associated with anger and aggression. Note that these conditions may sometimes be the primary *cause* of a client's anger. One example would be someone who reports that he or she never had an anger problem until afflicted with depression. Another possibility is that medical or psychological conditions may *exacerbate* an already existent anger problem. For instance, someone may say "I've always been pretty angry, but since I hurt my back it's been a lot worse." Finally, one's anger may be functionally *independent* even of a serious condition such as alcoholism, as witness someone who says this: "Yes, I get angry when I've been drinking. But I get just as mad just as often when I'm sober." Thus, it is important to identify ongoing medical and psychological concerns and then to look carefully at their relationship to the client's anger issues.

The ninth question asks about medications the respondent consumes. This serves three purposes: 1) sometimes clients don't know the name of conditions for which they take medications; 2) the medications may hint at a client's anger-related conditions, as with someone who takes anti-psychotics; 3) it is important to screen out the possibility that a client's anger or aggression may be the result of mis-medication or over-medication.

The tenth set of questions is about legal problems related to aggressive outbursts. Note that some clients are reluctant to admit their past and present legal difficulties, in part because of their tendency to deny and minimize their problems.

Alcohol and drug use are the focus of question sets 11 and 12. While no substance is always associated with anger or aggression none are entirely free from possible implication either. That's why it's critical to ask clients who consume these commodities questions that pin down exactly what effect they have upon his or her anger or aggression. For instance, does the client smoke marijuana to try to cool down? Does the respondent regularly become violent when drinking whiskey? Is a par-ticular combination of substances, such as cocaine and alcohol, especially predictive of anger or aggression? It is certainly possible, given their answers to these questions, that some clients will need to be directed toward alcohol and drug treatment. These people must be helped to realize that all the anger management skills they develop will be useless unless they also address their alcohol and drug problems. Treatment for anger may have to be deferred in this situation, although simultaneous treatment for the two problems may also be feasible. Note that I discuss the relationship between alcoholism, drug abuse and addiction more thoroughly at the end of this chapter.

Question 13 allows the counselor an initial view of the client's already developed anger management resources. Does he or she know how to take a time out? Can the client relax? Does that person have a support system of people who will help cool him or her down? Asking these questions also gives the counselor an opportunity to mention several ways people can learn to handle their anger and so makes a transition to treatment.

Questions 14 and 15 remind clients that they are responsible for making changes and also imply that they are in control of the process ("What do you think . . .?"). This is especially useful because many angry individuals are quite oppositional and automatically resist being told what they must do.

Question 16 asks about the client's degree of hopefulness. This question helps counselors frame their task realistically: the goals are to help clients become angry or aggressive less often, to stay in better control when they do become angry, and to do less damage to themselves and others when angry.

The final question is open-ended, to allow the client to express anything else that they feel might explain their problems.

The Anger Styles Questionnaire

A primary unit of analysis in the behavioral assessment of anger is the discrete anger episode, a length of time that stretches from the moment something occurs that triggers a person's anger until the time when the issue is resolved or abandoned. Episodes like this can take place in seconds, especially for individuals who describe their anger as impulsive and quickly over, to years, for those who cannot let go of perceived injuries.

My name for the triggering event, whether it comes from an external source or is internally generated, is an "anger invitation." Most people receive many anger invitations every day. Clients who develop anger problems are usually those who accept a greater number of those invitations than others. But sheer quantity is only one interesting aspect related to the consideration of anger episodes. The more important issue is exactly how people respond to the anger invitations they receive. My co-author Patricia Potter-Efron and I have identified through clinical observation at least eleven consistent patterns of response. These patterns are labeled "anger styles." Anger styles are repeated, predictable ways in which people handle situations in which they could or do become angry. Each style may be utilized appropriately in certain situations. However, people get into trouble when they overuse or misuse one or more styles, for instance when someone develops a habit of excessive moral anger and becomes outraged over minor ethical transgressions.

The Anger Styles Questionnaire (adapted and modified from Potter-Efron and Potter-Efron, 2006) is designed to help counselors identify which anger styles a particular client utilizes frequently.

Anger Styles Questionnaire

Directions: Please answer the following 33 Yes/No questions by circling the most correct answer based on the ways you generally handle your anger. There are no correct answers. If you think that the best answer would be "Sometimes" then still try to select a best "yes" or "no" answer, but add the letter "S" to your response.

1. I try never to get angry.   Yes/No
2. I get really nervous when others get angry.   Yes/No
3. I feel I am doing something bad when I get angry.   Yes/No

4. I often tell people I'll do what they want but
   then frequently forget.   Yes/No
5. I frequently say things like "Yeah, but . . ." and
   "I'll do it later."   Yes/No

---

6. People tell me I must be angry but I'm not certain
why they say that.   Yes/No

7. I get mad at myself a lot.   Yes/No
8. I "stuff" my anger and then get headaches,
stomachaches, etc.   Yes/No
9. I frequently call myself ugly names like "dummy,"
"selfish," etc.   Yes/No

10. My anger comes on really fast.   Yes/No
11. I act before I think when I get angry.   Yes/No
12. My anger goes away quite quickly.   Yes/No

13. I get really angry when people criticize me.   Yes/No
14. People say I'm easily hurt and oversensitive.   Yes/No
15. I get angry easily when I feel bad about myself.   Yes/No

16. I get mad in order to get what I want.   Yes/No
17. I try to scare others with my anger.   Yes/No
18. I sometimes pretend to be very angry when
I really am not.   Yes/No

19. Sometimes I get angry just for the excitement
or action.   Yes/No
20. I like the strong feelings that come with my anger. Yes/No
21. Sometimes when I'm bored I start arguments
or pick fights.   Yes/No

22. I seem to get angry all the time.   Yes/No
23. My anger feels to me to be like a bad habit
I can't break.   Yes/No
24. I get mad without thinking – it just happens.   Yes/No

25. I get jealous a lot, even when there is no reason. Yes/No
26. I don't trust people very much.   Yes/No
27. Sometimes it feels like people are out to get me. Yes/No

28. I become very angry when I defend my beliefs
and opinions.   Yes/No
29. I often feel outraged about what other
people say and do.   Yes/No
30. I always know I'm right in an argument.   Yes/No

31. I hang onto my anger for a long time.	Yes/No
32. I have a hard time forgiving people.	Yes/No
33. I hate many people for what they've done to me.	Yes/No

Each set of three questions describes a separate anger style. Specifically,

Questions 1–3: Anger avoidance
Questions 4–6: Sneaky anger (passive aggression)
Questions 7–9: Anger turned inward
Questions 10–12: Sudden anger
Questions 13–15: Shame-based anger
Questions 16–18: Deliberate anger
Questions 19–21: Excitatory anger
Questions 22–24: Habitual hostility
Questions 25–27: Fear-based anger (paranoia)
Questions 28–30: Moral anger
Questions 31–33: Resentment/hate

I have found this questionnaire to be quite valuable in planning treatment priorities. (However, please note that the reliability and validity of this questionnaire have not been researched.) Basically, a client who answers "yes" to all three items in a set certainly utilizes and probably over-utilizes that anger style in daily living. Even one or two positive responses merit careful probing about when, where, and with whom the client utilizes that particular anger style.

The following paragraphs briefly describe each anger style.

Three anger styles, the *hidden* styles, share a common feature: people utilizing them are partly or mostly unaware of and/or unable to accept their anger. The first of these is called *"anger avoidance,"* an anger style practiced by people who believe anger is bad, scary, or useless. These individuals cannot use anger appropriately in their daily lives. Instead they tend to deny, ignore, and minimize their anger. Unable to listen to the messages in their anger, these people often become enmeshed in situations they dislike but cannot escape. The therapeutic focus for clients who are consistently anger-avoidant is to help them learn how to accept and utilize their anger.

The second hidden anger style is *passive aggression*, which is labeled "sneaky anger" in our book. Passive aggressive individuals often feel powerless and dominated by others. They tend to be unassertive and resentful, despising the people in their lives who they believe are trying to control them. However, passive aggressors have discovered one tactic that defeats these powerful opponents. They thoroughly frustrate others through inaction, making doing nothing a sort of art form that they have mastered. Unfortunately, passive aggression, when overused, traps the user in a perpetual inertial state. Masters at doing nothing, their lives stagnate and become purposeless. Therefore, treatment for passive aggressive individuals must emphasize helping them develop positive purposes and goals in life in addition to helping them become more assertive and expressive with their anger.

"*Anger turned inward*" is the third hidden style. Individuals with this pattern avoid conflict by redirecting their anger against others toward a safer target, themselves. They often develop patterns of self-neglect, self-sabotage, self-blame, self-attack, and even self-destructiveness. Therapy with these clients may involve helping them give themselves permission to recognize and utilize their anger. This subject is covered more extensively in the last chapter of this book.

Four anger styles can be grouped together as the "explosive styles." Individuals with these styles periodically demonstrate their anger through dramatic outbursts. "Sudden anger" is the most easily recognizable of these patterns, in which anger emerges as rapid, usually short-lived, intense bursts. Clients with strong tendencies toward sudden anger often respond well to classic anger management tactics such as taking time outs that are designed to delay the expression of anger long enough for the client to regain control.

"*Shame-based anger*" is another explosive style. Here individuals rapidly convert feelings of shame into anger and rage (see chapter 3). They then attack their attackers, the people they believe are shaming them or might be planning to do so. The presence of debilitating amounts of shame-based anger may be associated with domestic abuse (Dutton, 1998), since intimate associates most frequently trigger (both accidentally and sometimes intentionally) their partners' shame. Clients with this style of anger are often volatile and physically dangerous. They often need long-term therapy that addresses the shame underlying their anger and aggression.

"*Excitatory*" anger represents the third explosive anger style. Individuals with excitatory anger tendencies actually seek out their anger because becoming irate and getting into arguments triggers feelings of excitement and intensity. They will need help making and keeping a commitment to calmness and moderation as well as finding pro-social ways to vent their need for excitement.

The last explosive style can be named "*deliberate anger*." Deliberate anger is purposely displayed in order to intimidate others. People who regularly utilize deliberate anger have discovered a simple two-word reality: "anger works." Because they get what they want when they get angry, they keep doing so, sometimes appearing tremendously irate even though they are not really angry at all. Clients with this pattern will need to be confronted about faking their anger for instrumental gain. They also often need to learn other ways to ask for what they want and need from others since they tend to have poor social and communication skills.

The final four common anger styles are labeled the *chronic* styles. Individuals who utilize these styles frequently have developed long-term anger patterns that keep them angry, bitter, and resentful.

Habitual anger is my name for the initial chronic style. People high on habitual anger usually think and act in ways that continually perpetuate their anger. Anger becomes their default emotion of choice, automatically appearing in situations where others would feel other emotions or have no affective response at all. A client with habitual anger, for instance, might respond to being told he was loved with annoyance ("Why do you say that all the time? It bugs me") or respond to getting praise at work with defensiveness ("Oh sure, they say they like my work, but they're just trying to make me work harder"). Cognitive treatment for habitual anger is very appropriate with its emphasis upon automatic and irrational thinking processes.

"*Paranoia*," or more generally "*scared*" or "*distrust-based anger*" is the second chronic anger style. Here anger is projected onto others and then defended against with "defensive" anger and aggression. The result is that paranoid individuals become hyper-vigilant and live in a world in which few people, if any, can be trusted and in which the danger of attack is imminent. Treatment for clients with strong paranoid tendencies should be directed first toward helping them recognize the extent of their projections and secondly to helping them feel safer and more trusting.

Moral anger is another chronic style. People who become morally angry continually perceive their anger as justified, righteous, for a cause greater than their own self-interest. Like all of these styles, moral anger can be used well or poorly. Used at its best, the morally angry individual becomes an advocate for a socially significant purpose. Used poorly, people wrap the cloak of righteousness around them and refuse to take it off, treating even the smallest conflicts as moral battles and turning opponents into devils and monsters. Counselors working with clients in this area need to concentrate upon helping these people become more empathic and accepting of others' points of view.

The final anger style is named *resentment/hate*. Resenters tend to be people who store up incidents in which they feel maltreated instead of trying to handle each one in a timely fashion. Over time their anger becomes rigid and inflexible, building into a solidified sense of hatred. Those that have harmed them become despised and treated as loathsome and unforgivable. This anger can last from weeks to decades and is very resistant to intervention. Treatment for hatred usually centers on the concept of letting go of old wounds and getting on with life. The key term is "forgiveness," a topic that will be discussed in detail in a later chapter of this book.

Anger Assessment as a Bridge to Treatment

Effective assessments act as a bridge to treatment when they point out and prioritize specific topics that need work. The Treatment Planning Form will help counselors summarize their assessment information so that they can present clear treatment directions and priorities to their clients.

Treatment Planning Form

1. Prioritize these three anger goals with regard to the client's immediate need to develop skills in these areas:
   _____ Prevention _____ Containment _____ Problem Resolution
   Name one specific skill in top area to develop: _____.

2. Prioritize these four treatment areas with regard to the client's immediate need to develop skills in these areas:
   _____ Behavior _____ Thoughts _____ Feelings _____ Spirit
   Name one specific skill in top area to develop: _____.

3. Prioritize people/life spheres on which to concentrate attention:
   ____ Partner ____ Child/Children ____ Parents ____ Siblings
   ____ Work ____ Teachers ____ Friends ____ Driving ____ Legal
   Figures ____ Strangers ____ Others (Whom? ____)

4. Name any complicating factors that must also be addressed to help the client manage his or her anger:
   ___ Alcohol or drug use
   ___ Depression, anxiety, etc. (which?: _____)
   ___ Immediate stressors (which?: _____)
   ___ Anger/aggression of other family members
   ___ Legal concerns
   ___ Other (what?: _____)

5. From the STAXI-2, which of these problems need attention (at least 65% on test scale):
   ___ Immediate Anger (State Anger)
   ___ Trait Anger: Angry Temperament
   ___ Trait Anger: Angry Reaction
   ___ Anger-Expression Out
   ___ Anger-Expression In
   ___ Anger-Control Out
   ___ Anger-Control In
   ___ Total Anger (Anger-Expression Index)

---

6. Which of the following anger styles need to be addressed (indicated by the client checking at least 2 of 3 items in designated section of questionnaire)?

____ Avoidance ____ Anger-in ____ Sneaky ____ Paranoia
____ Sudden ____ Shame-Based ____ Deliberate ____ Addictive
____ Habitual ____ Moral ____ Resentment

7. What else needs to be addressed? _____.

Anger, Alcoholism, and Addiction

I briefly discussed the complex relationships between alcohol and drug abuse/addiction and anger/aggression in the intake questionnaire presented earlier in this chapter. Here is more detailed information.

There is a broad parallel between alcohol and drug abuse/addiction and anger/aggression. For example, deficits in the brain's production of serotonin and dopamine have been implicated in the development of both concerns (Volavka, 2002). In addition, anger serves many similar functions to addiction that differ from person to person. Anger can be as exhilarating as a stimulant drug such as cocaine. Alternatively, some people develop chronic, lower intensity anger problems remindful of individuals who are habitual maintenance drinkers. Also, certain people experience transformative experiences when angry, feeling more powerful and intelligent just as some individuals utilize mind-altering drugs such as LSD for the same purpose. Finally, anger can even have sedative effects, as noted by Jacobsen and Gottman (1998) in their description of anti-social "pit bull" batterers who actually become physiologically calmer even as they yell and scream at their partners.

One important question is how treatment of one of these concerns impacts the other. This is particularly vital because the two conditions are seldom treated simultaneously, even though they certainly could be. Instead, chemical dependency counselors tend to insist that clients go through addiction treatment before dealing with their anger, while anger and abuse specialists sometimes reverse the equation. Given the realities of the field, let us begin with the possible effects of alcohol and addiction treatment on the client who also has a significant anger/aggression problem. Here are four possible results of beginning with chemical dependency treatment: a) alcohol/drug treatment may take care of the problem completely; b) alcohol/drug treatment may help clients have fewer anger problems or to be less violent than before but not completely reduce their anger levels to normal; c) alcohol/drug treatment may release anger that had been inhibited through substance use; d) there may be no connection at all – they are independent variables.

The first result, that alcohol/drug treatment may take care of the problem completely, does happen occasionally. Here clients report that they almost never get excessively angry and absolutely do not become physically aggressive, except when they are under the immediate influence of alcohol or drugs. As long as these clients "keep the plug in the jug," presumably they will have no strong anger problems.

The second result, that alcohol/drug treatment may help clients have fewer anger problems or to be less violent than before but not completely reduce their anger levels to normal, is in my experience more common than the first. This reflects research that consistently indicates alcoholics have considerably more chronic anger than the average population (Potter-Efron, 1991; Walfish, 1990), even after treatment. Even a casual reading of the *Alcoholics Anonymous Big Book* (Alcoholics Anonymous, 1976) reveals a strong concern among the writers of that book about the necessity for dealing with long-term resentments in order to avoid relapse. It seems very reasonable, then, to suggest that many clients who undergo alcohol and addiction treatment be referred to anger specialists to continue their recovery work.

The third possibility, that alcohol/drug treatment may release anger that had been inhibited through substance use, cannot be overlooked. This situation is most likely to develop with individuals who have utilized addictive processes to "stuff" their anger. These people will often score positively for anger avoidance and passive aggression on the Anger Styles Questionnaire described earlier in this chapter. Newly sober, these people might get hit by a tidal wave of previously suppressed anger, which, if not predicted and for which they are unprepared, could easily trigger a relapse.

White (2004) provides an interesting summary of several ways in which substance use and anger/aggression might interact:

1. Independent. No relationship. A person's substance usage has no correlation with his/her anger.
2. Rationalizing effect. People use their state of intoxication to explain and diminish responsibility for their anger episodes.
3. Causal. Here the person only becomes angry or aggressive when under the direct influence of a chemical substance.
4. Additive. The individual already has an anger problem that is increased when using mood-altering substances.
5. Synergistic. The combination of certain chemical substances and anger becomes explosive and dangerous.
6. Neutralizing. Individuals use some chemical substance in an attempt to diminish or avoid their anger.

7. Contextual. Someone only becomes aggressive when they utilize mood-altering substances in specific situations (such as at a tavern or at family of origin reunions).

As White notes, it is important to remember that there may be no connection at all between a particular client's anger and substance-use pattern. The two are independent variables, so that the client might remark "Sure, I drink when I'm angry. But I drink when I'm sad, and happy, and when I'm not feeling anything at all." Clearly, all the alcohol and addiction treatment in the world will not touch this person's anger problems because the two entities are unrelated. He or she will need to be treated separately for this completely different concern.

Another important consideration is the relationship between the use of specific mood-altering substances and an individual's experience of anger. Although these experiences vary widely, there are some predictable correlations. Table 4.2 (adapted from work originally created by Michael Miller, MD, and presented in Potter-Efron, 1991) briefly describes the overall risk that use of a particular substance will exacerbate a person's anger or aggression problems and some of the reasons why the danger is increased.

Table 4.2 Anger/Aggression Relationship to Alcohol/Drug Use

Drug Group	Overall Risks	Why?
Alcohol	High	Societal permission/expectation; disinhibition; withdrawal; irritability; pervasiveness within society.
Sedatives and Barbiturates	High	Promotes irritability; assaultiveness; self-destructive attacks.
Cocaine and Stimulants	High	Highly associated with irritability and impulsive attacks; amphetamine use (long term) can produce psychotic-like personality changes.
PCP	High	Produces angry/assaultive tendencies.
Steroids	Medium–High	Seems to encourage anger and aggression, especially in already susceptible individuals.
Inhalants	Medium	Generally incapacitates users, but associated with aggressive lifestyles.
Opiates	Medium–Low	Generally diminishes all emotions during use. Aggression to procure drug money main problem.
Cannabis	Medium–Low	Mistakenly assumed to diminish anger/aggression. Can exacerbate underlying paranoia.
Hallucinogens	Low	May exacerbate underlying psychotic delusions.

What might occur if the client first receives treatment for anger/aggression while still displaying addictive behaviors? Possibilities include: a) the client's continuing addiction problems make it virtually impossible for him or her to learn anger management techniques; 2) the client can learn and even utilize these techniques well when sober but not when under the influence of alcohol or drugs; 3) the client can learn and utilize anger management skills on all occasions, even when intoxicated and despite continuing addiction patterns. I find the second alternative to be most common with my clients, although I certainly have experienced the other two frequently. This may partially be due to the belief in American society that getting drunk or high allows people to take a "time-out" from normal inhibitions. However, I do not believe that is the only or best interpretation. It seems that many anger management clients simply cannot bridge the learning gap between their sober and intoxicated states. In other words, what they learn sober does not generalize to what they say and do while intoxicated. The implication of this limitation, of course, is that angry clients with alcohol or addiction patterns must be challenged at least to curtail if not eliminate their use of mood-altering substances.

The following sets of questions are designed to help clients understand the linkages between their use of alcohol and drugs and their anger and aggression issues as well as to help them recognize that they must deal effectively with both concerns:

1. How does your use of alcohol or drugs affect:
    a) how often you get angry?
    b) how strongly you get angry?
    c) how likely you are to become violent?
        • against yourself?
        • against others?
        • against objects, pets, etc.?

2. How does getting angry affect your drinking or drug use?
    a) Does it give you an excuse to use?
    b) Does it affect your choice of drugs?
    c) Is your anger a regular part of the way you relapse?

3. Are there times you want both to get angry and to get high?
4. When does this happen (e.g., shame episodes, depression, etc.)?
5. How do you plan to stop or control your anger if you don't deal with your alcohol or drug use?
6. How do you plan to stop or control your drinking/drugs if you don't deal with your anger?

7. Is there any way you can think of to use the energy and strength of your anger to help you deal with your drinking or drug problems?

CASE STUDY

Assessment of a Chronically Angry Client with Multiple Problems

Rick, age 33, works as a job estimator for a siding and roofing company. He has been married three times and has one child from his first marriage, which only lasted a few months, and two children with his current wife Amanda. Here is a summary of selected information taken from the general intake questionnaire, the STAXI-2 and the Anger Styles Questionnaire. I also consider how Rick would be classified in terms of levels of anger and types of domestic abuse, possible relevant psychological diagnoses and the specific effects of alcohol on his behavior. Note that numbers set in brackets refer to the number of the question on the Anger and Aggression Intake described earlier in this chapter.

[1] Rick's assessment began with this statement: "Ron, I'm desperate. I get so angry I see red. I can't stop. I want to stop. Can you help me?" And Rick meant what he said; he became so angry several times a day that blood rushing through the capillaries of his eyes caused him literally to see red. [2] As for his most recent angry incident, Rick had just yesterday shoved a potential client after "we got into a pissing contest and he said I didn't know what I was talking about." Nor was that the first time Rick had lost his temper at work. In fact, he had been fired from his last job after repeatedly arguing with his boss.

When I asked about specific aspects of the recent episode, Rick remembered this thought: "I won't let that bastard show me up." The accompanying sensations included accelerated heart rate and rapid breathing, along with a feeling of rage. What he said right before he shoved the guy was "Get out of my G . . . D . . . face, you a . . . h . . . ." Finally, he shoved the man hard enough to make him fall down, told him to "go to hell," and stomped off. It took him several hours to calm down, after which he went to the office, expecting to get fired. But, amazingly, the customer never called to complain. Still, Rick realized he had lost control again and that he needed help.

[3] Rick has had far worse incidents than this. He admitted that he beat his first two wives (but not Amanda) and that was why those marriages fell apart. The worst event he remembered occurred

in his twenties when, after drinking copiously, he got into a drunken rage and destroyed his entire living room, causing over $4,000 worth of damage. The police arrived in time to stop him from killing himself with the gun that by then he was holding to his temple. He was arrested, taken to a mental health ward at the local hospital, and eventually charged, ironically enough, with malicious damage to his own property. For that crime he served a few months in jail, went through an alcohol education class that had no effect upon him, and endured a year's probationary period.

[4] Rick gets significantly angry at least twice a day. That's been true his entire adult life, although he does say he is winding down a bit. He tends to be less physically aggressive than in the past, but more "cutting" with his words. [5] The primary targets of his wrath are his wife and kids, but nobody is exempt as he regularly gets angry at friends, family, strangers, work associates, and drivers.

[6] Life has been particularly hard on Rick lately. His wife has been very depressed; both of his sons have been diagnosed with Attention Deficit Disorder; the bad economy has affected his work commission and so "I'm in debt up to my eyeballs." He's feeling overwhelmed, constantly irritable, ready to snap at anything.

[7] Rick grew up in a troubled and violent household in which he witnessed his alcoholic Dad beat his depressed Mom. That man never hit Rick. Instead, he constantly belittled him, telling Rick he was a "worthless piece of s . . ." and worse. The family dissolved when Rick was nine years old. After that he lived mostly with his grandparents, whom he described as "good people who were way too old to handle us." When I asked Rick what he had learned about anger as a child, his response was "Don't let nobody ever push you around and don't trust nobody."

[8] I then went through the list of behavioral and mental problems listed in Item 8 of the questionnaire. Several possible concerns emerged, including alcohol abuse (discussed later), antisocial personality disorder based on his long history of oppositionality and aggression, borderline personality disorder because of strong traits of jealousy, insecurity, and need for relationship reassurances, and dysthymia hinted at by statements such as "I never really feel good about anything. Every day's a gray day." He also is very distrusting of others, so much so that he implied in a paranoid fashion that people were plotting against him. [9] Rick had never been treated, nor was he taking any medications, however, for any of these conditions.

[10] Rick was not currently in any legal trouble. In addition to the incident described previously Rick also has a history of relatively minor scrapes with the law, including domestic abuse charges from his previous marriages.

[11, 12] Alcohol is Rick's mood-altering substance of choice, although he has certainly used other substances including marijuana, ecstasy, and amphetamines. He drinks three to four times a week up to a twelve-pack at a sitting. He says that sometimes drinking actually calms him down at first, but then it tends to make him more irritable, argumentative, and jealous. Later, when I asked him how he hoped to control his anger if he kept drinking, he admitted that he probably would not be able to do so and committed at first to "cutting down" and then to quitting drinking entirely, a goal that he has not been completely successful in accomplishing. He declined specific treatment for alcoholism, however, saying that he'd been through all that twice before and it didn't work. Still, he has been generally successful at reducing the effects of his drinking upon his anger and aggression in that he does not drink any more just to give him an excuse to get mad.

[13] Rick had seldom actually attempted to control his anger since he has thought of it as part of his personality more than a series of choices that he could make. His main effort has been just to walk away when he gets mad. However, that doesn't work very well because he spends the time away stewing over alleged insults rather than relaxing. [14] When I asked Rick what he needed to do first to help himself control his anger, he said that he needed to learn how to let go of his anger instead of obsessing like that. [15] He added that he also wanted to learn how to be more accepting of others and to be less demanding.

[16] Finally, Rick told me that he wasn't very hopeful he could change, but he was willing to try. [17] He repeated that he was desperate to change, because he realized now that he was living a miserable life.

Rick took the STAXI-2. He turned out to be very high on both Anger-In (90th percentile) and Anger-Out (95th percentile) and quite low on Anger Control-In (20th percentile) and Anger Control-Out (4th percentile). He placed in the upper 5% of adult males on the STAXI-2. All these scores describe an individual with a massively significant anger problem, one that is pervasive and characterlogical in nature.

Rick's Anger Styles Questionnaire was highly positive for five anger styles: sudden anger, shame-based anger, paranoia, habitual anger, and resentment/hate. Again, high scores in this many areas indicate a broad anger problem that will undoubtedly take much time and effort to repair.

With regard to Eckhardt and Deffenbacher's diagnostic categories for anger, Rick would almost certainly be diagnosed with a generalized anger disorder with aggression. As for the domestic aggression typology described earlier, Rick would fall primarily into the "antisocial" category, but with significant aspects of "needy" and "derivative" characteristics, illustrating the point that real human beings seldom can be definitively placed in one simple category.

Rick's assessment led to the following treatment plan: 1) Rick made a commitment to the goals of becoming angry less often, becoming less intensely angry, and doing less damage when angry; 2) He agreed to read two books on anger, the first with an emphasis on facing the reality of being chronically angry and the second a workbook on anger skills development; 3) In terms of anger styles, Rick chose to begin work in the area of dealing with his sudden anger, to be followed as soon as possible with the themes of shame-based anger and resentment; 4) Rick agreed to minimize his alcohol consumption and to consider making a commitment to abstinence if he could not contain his anger when drinking; 5) He agreed to a referral to a neurologist for consultation with regard to his taking anti-seizure or other medications to keep him from seeing red.

Summary

A thorough assessment is the first step toward successful anger management counseling. I have presented several guides toward this goal in this chapter. Specifically, I have discussed the use of a standard intake interview, the State-Trait Anger Expression Inventory, the Anger Disorders Scale, and an Anger Styles Quiz. In addition, I have described materials intended to help practitioners in this field be better able to distinguish different levels of anger and aggression and different types of domestic abusers. Finally, the dual relationship between anger/aggression and psychological problems and another dual relationship between anger/aggression and alcoholism and addiction were considered and an assessment case study was presented.

5

DOMESTIC VIOLENCE

Core Information and Assessment

The field of domestic violence offender treatment is in its infancy. Basic questions such as what is domestic violence, who commits acts of domestic violence, and how do people justify these acts are still being debated and discovered. I will discuss these core issues first in this chapter, then describe theoretical models of domestic violence and their treatment implications, and end with material on assessment of domestic violence offenders.

What is Domestic Violence?

Battering, spouse abuse (Neidig and Friedman, 1984; Harway and Hansen, 2004), *intimate partner violence* (Jordan et al., 2004), *intimate partner abuse* (Hamel, 2014), *Domestic violence*. All these terms have been used to describe physical and verbal behaviors that hurt, intimidate, or diminish a close family member (usually but not always a relationship partner). Some, but not all, of these actions are illegal. Some, but not all, of these actions are psychologically oriented. Domestic violence may refer to a single event or to a continuing pattern of behavior. It may refer to impulsive, unplanned behaviors, or to carefully constructed plans carried out over months or years. In other words, there is no exact understanding of domestic violence.

Clients often enter treatment very confused about why they got into trouble and what they need to do to stay out of future trouble. To help clarify the issue I begin with a summary of the state of Wisconsin's mandatory arrest policy, the law that usually applied to them if they were arrested.

Note that many men argue that item #4 above results in *de facto* discrimination against them, since they often are arrested simply because they are the stronger partner. This claim inevitably comes up in every group. Counselors are advised to acknowledge the element of truth in their argument while returning the discussion to their taking full responsibility for what they did.

Domestic Violence Law in Wisconsin

1. Wisconsin Mandatory Arrest Law.
   The police must arrest someone if called to a domestic abuse situation.

2. "Domestic Abuse" officially means:
   a) Intentional infliction of physical pain, injury, or illness.
   b) Intentional impairment of physical condition.
   c) First, second, or third degree sexual assault.
   d) A physical act that causes another person to fear imminent engagement in the three things mentioned above.

3. An arrest will be made if:
   a) The officer believes acts of domestic violence occurred.
   b) Either: i) The officer believes acts of domestic abuse are likely to occur again; or ii) There is evidence of physical injury to the victim.

4. If both people have been violent, the officer does not have to arrest both parties. Instead he can choose to arrest the person he/she thinks is the "primary physical aggressor." The decision is based upon the relative degree of fear or injury of each person and any history of domestic abuse between these people. It is *not* based on who initiated the violence.

5. Arrest is *not* based upon the consent of the victim. It is entirely up to the police officer. (The same is true for prosecution of the case by the district attorney.)

6. The officer's decision does not have to be based upon the presence or absence of visible signs of injury or impairment.

7. If arrested there is a 72-hour no contact order (which sometimes may be waived by the victim).

Not in the law, but important to remember: there are no excuses, justifications, or exceptions written into the law. That means no matter how justified someone feels about having committed an act of domestic abuse, he or she could be arrested.

Arrest criteria, though, hardly encompass the bulk of what is considered domestic violence. For instance, behaviors such as verbal abuse, economic control, isolating one's partner, and even passive aggressive non-actions may be included in a list of domestic violence activities. Indeed, the term "violence" is often used metaphorically rather than literally.

Is there a common core to all these behaviors? A feminist interpretation is that the common denominator is a man's desire to establish and maintain power and control over his partner. However, this interpretation is too limited in light of evidence that women frequently perpetrate acts of physical violence against their male (and female) partners. A reasonable expansion would be to say that an act of domestic violence refers to any attempt, by either gender, to establish and maintain control over one's intimate partner. This definition does not imply that the behaviors are always conscious or intentional. The key question is whether the behaviors did have the deleterious effect of diminishing the other's control over their life.

There are two problems, though, in this definition, the first being the possibility that almost any behavior could be interpreted by the alleged victim or the courts as an act of domestic violence. Here is an example: "My wife Anne called my probation officer. She told him I was abusing her because I wouldn't take the kids when she wanted me to babysit them. The p.o. told me I was being controlling. But Anne wanted me to take them when I was supposed to be at work just so she could go out drinking with her friends. What am I supposed to do?" Being falsely accused of using controlling behavior is a real problem for many of my clients, especially those who already have bad reputations with law enforcement officials. It is important to remember that the primary goal for domestic violence offender treatment is to increase the level of physical safety for all parties even while promoting further life style, attitude, and behavioral changes.

The second problem is almost the reverse of the one above. Domestic violence is limited to partner abuse in the above definition. But what about the son who beats up his father? What about the father who sexually abuses his daughter or the mother who beats her child? All of these appear to be acts of domestic violence. Although these behaviors may be covered by other laws as well, it is not uncommon for our program to receive referrals to our domestic violence programs for all these offenses.

Here is my best definition of domestic violence: any behavior, by either gender, which is intended to intimidate, injure (physically or emotionally), or control one's intimate partner, family member, or person with whom one is living.

How Common is Domestic Violence?

Most studies of domestic violence prevalence focus only upon physical interpersonal violence. A thorough review of these studies was carried out by Desmarais et al. (2012). They report that across all studies approximately one in four women (23.1%) and one in five men (19.3%) experienced physical violence within an intimate relationship. Furthermore, they found that almost one fifth (19.2%) of individuals reported intimate physical violence in the year prior to the study. However, they note that studies varied tremendously in reported rates of interpersonal violence and differed in their definitions of intimate violence.

Which Gender Commits Acts of Domestic Violence?

Medeiros and Straus (2007) extensively reviewed the research on gender domestic aggression rates. They state that the evidence in over 200 studies supports the conclusion that men and women assault their opposite gender partners at approximately the same rate. Desmarais et al. (2012a, 2012b) also reviewed the research literature on gender perpetration of domestic violence. These reviewers reported a wide range of rates (which emphasizes the relatively poor level of knowledge at this time), ranging from 1.0% to 61.6% for men and from 2.4% to 68.9% for women. Surprisingly, the overall rate of female-perpetrated violence was higher than male-perpetrated violence (28.3% to 21.6%). It is reasonable to conclude from these reviews that domestic violence offender models that dismiss female violence are misguided.

Is Domestic Violence Unidirectional or Bidirectional?

Historically domestic violence has been viewed as unidirectional and specifically as always directed by men at women. Research, though, does not support this model. Instead, a recent thorough review of the literature (Langhinrichsen-Rohling et al., 2012) indicates that 57.9% of domestic violence episodes are bidirectional, meaning that both parties participated. When violence was unidirectional, females were twice as likely as males to be the aggressor (28.3% to 13.8%). This certainly suggests that the role of women in violent relationships is as important to consider as that of men.

There is one important consideration here, though. Most men are larger and stronger than their female partners and so they do commit more acts of severe abuse.

Reasons People Use to Explain or Justify
Acts of Domestic Violence

A Partner Abuse State of Knowledge (PASK) review of offender motivations revealed that the most frequently endorsed motivations were: a) a *desire to retaliate* for having been hurt emotionally by the other person; b) *to express* anger, jealousy, or other feelings difficult to put into words; c) *stress*; d) an attempt to *get the other's attention* (Langhinrichsen-Rohling, McCullars, and Misra, 2012). Both men and women endorsed these reasons at approximately similar rates.

Hamel (2014) describes research findings based on an instrument he helped create, the Reasons for Violence Scale, and administered to men and women in domestic violence offender programs. *Power and control* is one motivator in which there was little support for the hypothesis that men were more motivated than women by this goal. *Self-defense* rates in non-clinical samples varied from 5% to 35% for men and from 0% to 21% for women, but were much higher from samples of men and women in batterer intervention treatment programs (67% of men and 61% of women). This great difference illustrates the significance of knowing what group is being sampled when domestic violence is researched. Other motives found regularly included *jealousy* (50% of female offenders and 32% of male offenders) and *retaliation* (71% of female offenders and 61% of male offenders). This sample group also claimed a much higher rate of self-defense (65% of women and 57% of men).

In sum, it appears that domestic violence offenders believe they have many reasons for their behavior. It would seem likely that any one individual could endorse several of these motives. Clinically, it is important to address all of these motives in individual or group counseling. It is also important to acknowledge our clients' reasons while maintaining a firm stance that there are no acceptable reasons for domestic violence.

Risk Factors

Jordan et al. (2004) conducted a literature review and cite the following factors that increase the likelihood that a woman will become injured or killed in an episode of domestic violence. These included: offender's access to guns; attempting to separate from partner; exposure to parental violence; violence begins before marriage; forced sex; abuse of victim during pregnancy; alcohol consumption by the woman; a history of prior abuse by the partner; a history of generalized aggression by the male; threats to kill the woman or of suicide; and control of the woman's activities.

More recently, Capaldi et al. (2012) overviewed studies that described risk factors for the occurrence of domestic violence within a relationship. The following conditions increased the likelihood for domestic violence: younger age; deprivation such as unemployment and low income; minority group membership; childhood exposure to abuse; conduct disorder in childhood and during adolescence as well as a diagnosis of antisocial personality disorder in adults; drug use in both genders and alcohol use primarily in women; anxiety and depression primarily in women; negative emotionality – consisting of emotional volatility, poor impulse control, defensiveness, and jealousy; hostile attitudes toward women by men; pro-violent beliefs by either gender; dating couples as against married partners; low relationship satisfaction; high couple conflict. Some support for insecure attachment was also found, in particular between domestic violence and preoccupied or avoidant, but these findings were mixed.

Some preventive factors against dating violence were also noted. These included positive and involved parenting; encouragement of nonviolent behaviors, and peer support.

Anger's Relationship with Domestic Violence

Several postulates apply to the relationship between anger and domestic violence:

It is important to separate the *emotion of anger* from the *behavior of domestic violence*. Domestic violence should be viewed as a form of aggression. Theoretically, then, individuals may be both angry and aggressive, either angry or aggressive, or neither. This leads to two corollaries: a) Do not assume that all participants in domestic violence offender treatment programs need anger management skills training; b) Do not assume, as the Power and Control model argues, that anger management is irrelevant to domestic violence offender treatment. One implication, then, is that it would be wise to have some form of anger screening during assessment of domestic violence offenders.

There is a definite correlation between clients with high anger and those who commit acts of aggression. For instance, Kassinove and Tafrate (2002) found that high trait anger individuals (as measured by the STAXI-2) reported negative verbal reactions in 74% of the situations they experienced anger, and physical aggression in 22% of these anger episodes. This indicates that many domestic violence clients will indeed need anger management skills training. It also suggests that clients attending anger management programs should be screened for domestic violence behaviors.

Anger is more closely connected with expressive than instrumental violence. Expressive violence, sometimes called hostile aggression (Kassinove and Tafrate, 2002) is associated with statements such as "I got so mad I didn't know what I was saying or doing." This occurs when someone's anger escalates beyond their ability to contain it. At this point the person's higher level cognitive abilities have been dampened in favor of threat-based limbic system reactivity. Instrumental violence, on the other hand, is more intentional in nature. Theoretically a domestically violent person may have no anger whatsoever as he or she thoughtfully commits acts of physical, verbal, or psychological nature in order to dominate one's partner. Indeed, Jacobsen and Gottman's (1998) "cobras" (discussed later in this chapter) seem to fit this concept in their highly sociopathic, non-empathic behaviors. Note, though, that there is no clear division between expressive and instrumental violence and that any person's act of domestic violence may incorporate both elements (Hamel, 2014).

Many research studies do indicate a strong correlation between high levels of anger and domestic violence behavior. These studies date back to the 1980s. For instance, spouse abusers have higher levels of anger, hostility, and depression than non-abusers (Maiuro et al., 1988; Margolin and Wampold, 1981).

More recently, Babcock et al. (2004) report that married violent men are generally more angry than married nonviolent men, as are younger dating men. Another study indicates that the instigators of intimate partner violence regularly reported higher levels of anger and hostility than nonviolent men (Norlander and Eckhardt, 2005). Dutton, focusing on attachment dynamics of domestic violence, states that: "insecure attachment patterns [that are correlated with domestic violence] are essentially maladaptive methods of regulating affect, particularly anger and other emotions stemming from loss (Dutton, 2007, p. 33). It seems reasonable to conclude, then, that an excess of anger and an inability to manage anger are specific concerns of a substantial percentage of clients referred for domestic violence offender treatment.

In general it is advisable to include anger management skills training as a significant component of most domestic violence offender treatment programs. This conclusion seems appropriate given the findings above. What is remarkable, then, is how little attention historically has been placed upon anger management in domestic violence treatment programs. The reason for this neglect can be traced directly to the theoretical and political dominance of the Power and Control model (see later in this chapter). Hopefully, though, this pattern of neglect is gradually being replaced with awareness that anger management must be an integral part of most domestic violence offender treatment programs.

Theoretical Models of Domestic Violence

Any discussion of the recent theory of domestic violence in American society must begin with the Power and Control model. I will discuss its strengths and weaknesses, then go on to the development of offender typologies. Finally I will discuss the need for the creation of gender-inclusive treatment models.

The Power and Control model

Approximately 50 years ago Thomas Kuhn published his famous treatise on the paradigmatic theory of scientific revolutions (Kuhn, 1996). In it he described how a particular breakthrough model will take over a field, guiding research by setting parameters about what is and isn't important. Einstein's theory of relativity would stand as an excellent example. Over time, though, theorists and researchers begin questioning the model as the limits of its effectiveness become clear (for instance, that relativity cannot be conceptually integrated with quantum theory). Some practitioners within the field hold on tightly to the older paradigm, while others speak out against it, at first tentatively and then with increasing insistence. Finally, the now "old" paradigm is discarded in favor of a new one, only to have the cycle repeated. The paradigmatic model is controversial and not applicable to all fields. However, it seems to fit almost perfectly into developments in the field of domestic violence offender treatment.

The paradigm in question is called the Power and Control model, or sometimes the Duluth model, since its creators are from that northern Minnesota city. Built upon feminist theory in the 1970s, advocates of the Power and Control model place female victims within a patriarchal family and societal structure. Physical aggression by men, then, is viewed as just one way that men maintain their dominant status (Graham-Kevan, 2007). The hallmark of the model is the famous Power and Control Wheel (Pence and Paymar, 1993) that considers eight different areas in which men utilize power and control to maintain dominance. These are the use of a) coercion and threats; b) intimidation; c) emotional abuse; d) isolation; e) economic abuse; f) using children; g) using male privilege; h) minimizing/denying/blaming. The singular contribution of this wheel is that it extends the discussion of relationship dominance beyond physical coercion and into many other spheres.

The Power and Control model essentially created the field of domestic violence treatment. More importantly, it raised the collective consciousness of Americans and changed the treatment of domestic violence from being a private affair between couples into a societal concern. As such there can be little question that many lives have been saved because of this model and its determined advocates.

One unfortunate result of the total dominance of the Power and Control model, though, has been its stifling effect upon scientific discourse. This is because paradigmatic models are just as important for what they leave out as for what they contain. This is especially true for the Power and Control model. Its advocates specifically preclude psychological interpretations of the causes of domestic violence, couples therapy, anger management, and anything else that might distract from holding men and only men responsible for all acts of domestic aggression. Mutual violence or female-initiated acts of relationship aggression are either ignored or considered to be defensive. Many advocates of this model have brooked no questioning of its primacy. Furthermore, several states have legally mandated that all domestic violence offender programs must adhere to the Power and Control model, thus effectively squelching dialogue.

These limits would be tolerable if indeed the Power and Control model was singularly effective. However, research into domestic violence offender treatment effectiveness has not borne this out. While the Power and Control model does appear to be somewhat effective, it is no more so than other approaches (Eckhardt et al., 2013) and perhaps less. A recent comprehensive meta-study in the state of Washington found that six Duluth-style programs had no effect at all upon five year recidivism rates while five other widely varied programs collectively reduced recidivism by one third (Whitaker et al., 2013). The reality is that domestic violence offender treatment is still in its infancy. What is most needed, therefore, is an open-minded approach that allows for a number of different models to be attempted as the field seeks a new and better paradigm. For instance, anger management centered programs need to be developed and tested against the general success rate.

The Power and Control paradigm gradually has come under question. Today, most facilitators of domestic violence offender treatment programs tell me that they do use the Power and Control concept, "but I also use . . ." In other words, what is most valuable about the model is being incorporated into a larger body of theory and practice. I believe this is a positive development. One problem, though, is that many shelters for battered women still fiercely advocate for the Power and Control model, creating a tension between some offender treatment facilitators and shelter personnel.

Domestic violence offender typologies

One major development in the field has been the creation of many typologies of offenders built around the idea that not all offenders are alike. Several such typologies are noted below.

Saunders (1992): *Family-Only Aggressors*: least angry, depressed, and jealous; suppressed feelings; least marital dissatisfaction; least psychologically abusive.

Generally Violent: most aggressive outside of home; severely abused as children; most severe violence; violence most highly associated with alcohol use.

Emotionally Volatile: highest levels of anger, depression, and anxiety; frequent alcohol use associated with violence; most psychologically abusive; least satisfied in marital relationship.

Groetsch (1996): *Type One*: least dangerous; normal male/abnormal circumstances; no premarital abuse; feels remorse; situational and isolated abuse; very treatable.

Type Two: moderately dangerous; several character defects; some premarital abuse; feels limited remorse; some use of weapons; abuse neither situational nor isolated; moderately treatable.

Type Three: very dangerous; personality disordered; ongoing and systematic pattern of abuse; frequent past and premarital abuse; frequent use of weapons; no remorse; not treatable; focus on consequences.

Jacobsen and Gottman (1998): *Pit Bulls*: insecure; highly unstable relationships; most violence with family members; emotionally dependent; great fear of abandonment.

Cobras: highly antisocial; non-remorseful; feel entitled; non-empathic; seek gratification; high alcohol and drug abuse; don't fear abandonment but will not be controlled.

Dutton (1998): *Overcontrolled*: flat affect or constantly cheerful persona; tries to avoid conflict; high social desirability; chronic resentment; overlap of violence and alcohol use; avoidant, dependent, and passive-aggressive traits.

Impulsive/Undercontrolled: cyclical phases; high levels of jealousy; relationship-only violence; high levels of dysphoria, depression, and anxiety-based rage; fearful/angry attachment style; borderline personality traits.

Instrumental/Undercontrolled: generally violent; antisocial history; violence acceptable; usually physically abused as child; low empathy; dismissive attachment style; macho attitude towards violence.

Based upon the literature and my own counseling, I suggest the following four-group typology for domestic abusers. Note that I include both genders in this typology

1. Low-level Aggression/Non-pathological
   This is a broad category that includes individuals of both genders who are occasionally physically aggressive within intimate relationships but who do not suffer from significant DSM Axis Two pathologies and whose aggression is relatively minor. This low-level aggression is nevertheless unacceptable and should not be considered standard or acceptable behavior. Subtypes of this type of domestic aggression could include: a) Occasional Couples Relationship Aggression characterized by temporary emotional overload, minor aggression, and remorse; b) Groetsch's Type One aggressors facing situational problems that produce occasional but more severe violence; c) men who have learned classic "male dominance" cultural roles and whose aggression serves to maintain those roles (but who have the capacity to modify their behavior once they realize it is no longer rewarded by society); d) perhaps Saunders' "family-only" and

Dutton's "overcontrolled" men whose poor communication style and excessive desire to appear worthy are part of their perceived male role and can be altered.

Treatment for these individuals should emphasize: education focused upon accepting the goal of non-violence within relationships; stress reduction; anger and conflict management training; individual and/or couples counseling as needed. The concept of creating a non-violent system may be as important here as that of becoming a non-violent individual, especially when excessive anger and aggression occur within two or more family members.

2. Needy

These are individuals whose aggression is maintained by severe ego deficits. They have strong borderline personality traits and many could be classified as having an Axis Two Borderline Personality Disorder. Their adult attachment styles are usually a combination of preoccupied and fearful. Their violence usually occurs as they experience (or anticipate the possibility of experiencing) emotional or physical abandonment. They tend to be extremely jealous and possessive. They feel empty inside and consequently cannot self-soothe. The theme of their violence is "I can't live without you so I can't let you go."

Treatment: education focused upon the rights of others to have a life of their own; relatively long-term individual therapy designed to help the individual fill the internal emptiness with a sense of self, a greater sense of safety, and self-soothing ability. Couples counseling may be appropriate but must involve helping the client gain awareness that he or she has expected and demanded way too much from their partner (namely, to make them feel whole) and make a serious commitment to curtail those demands. Meanwhile the partner could gain from an increased understanding of the aggressor's psychological situation as long as he or she is strongly encouraged to separate caring for their partner from taking care of their partner. The theme of couples work would be to help the couple become less enmeshed and more interdependent.

3. Antisocial Traits

These individuals have significant oppositional and defiant tendencies. Some merit the Axis Two label "Antisocial Personality Disorder." Their attachment style is usually "dismissive" but they have strong feelings of entitlement. This combination translates into "I have no interest in meeting your needs but I fully expect you to meet mine." Low empathy, high generalized violence, deliberate use of intimidation tactics, and frequent alcohol/drug abuse are concurrent characteristics. They jealously guard their partners not because they can't live without them, but because they possess them and won't let anyone else have them. These individuals are frequently referred by law enforcement personnel as part of their corrective experience (in other words, as half punishment and half hope they might actually get something from the program).

Treatment: many authors consider these individuals pretty much beyond hope in terms of education and therapy. Both individual therapy and couples therapy are normally excluded and partners are usually counseled to leave the relationship. Instead, the emphasis is upon providing and maintaining consequences against acts of violence. However, some people with antisocial tendencies may benefit from educational efforts that focus upon helping them develop pro-social values (guilt, empathy, respect, etc.). Some individuals may have conversion experiences when exposed to AA or religious organizations that help them value others. Group and individual counseling should not be ruled out entirely, especially for clients who don't have full-fledged antisocial personalities and who seem capable of developing beyond their entitlement concepts.

4. Derivative Aggression

These domestic aggressors have a major physical or psychological condition that explains much or all of the person's aggressive behavior. Such conditions could include alcoholism (if virtually all acts of aggression occur while the individual is intoxicated or going through withdrawal), paranoid schizophrenia, severe depressive episodes, post-traumatic stress syndrome, chronic pain, etc. Note that counselors must walk a narrow line with these clients, neither totally excusing their unacceptable behavior just because they have another problem (for instance, not telling the drinker that it is the alcohol and only the alcohol that is the cause of his or her behavior) nor dismissing these concerns as unimportant. Rather, an effort must be made to understand the exact connections between the violence and other disorders to gain an understanding as to how much of the client's domestic aggression may be secondary to another condition.

Treatment here would give major attention to the contributing physical and psychological conditions that help explain the client's aggression. These conditions might be addressed before or concurrently with treatment for anger and aggression.

Graham-Kevan has summarized typological formulations in this manner: "The typology research reviewed suggests that perpetrators of partner violence differ on the prevalence of personality disorders. In particular, the most violent subgroups are frequently found to contain individuals who exhibit more antisocial behavior, are generally more violent, and are generally more resistant to mental health intervention than others (2007, p. 158).

The main value of typological constructions should rest in developing individualized treatment plans for each client based on into which typology category that person best fits. However, this may prove difficult in practice, given that most treatment takes place in groups. Also, it should be noted that real human beings seldom fit neatly into typological divisions. Rather, as one of my clients noted, "Well, yes, I fit into that secure attachment, mostly, but sometimes I'm fearful and I think I was dismissive with my first wife." Facilitators of group programs should be aware of these typological distinctions and craft their programs for relevance to all types of offenders.

Gender-inclusive treatment model

Although the Power and Control model remains strong in the field, it is no longer dominant. Indeed, it appears that this model is gradually being superseded by a broad range of competitors. A fairly recent development in the field has been the presentation of domestic violence offender treatment programs that are applicable to both men and women. Hamel (2007) lists several propositions of this perspective. He supports these propositions with a broad literature review. Here I will just describe the model.

Hamel lists the following core postulates of a gender-inclusive model: a) interventions should be based upon a thorough, unbiased assessment; b) all treatment modalities should be considered, based on the facts of the individual case; c) both men and women can be victims and/or perpetrators, and everyone is responsible for his or her behavior; d) the causes of partner abuse are varied but similar across genders; e) victim/perpetrator distinctions are overstated, and much partner abuse is mutual; f) both genders are physically and emotionally impacted by abuse; g) "gender inclusive" does not mean "gender neutral" or "gender equal"; h) the gender-inclusive approach is a feminist approach; i) regardless of perpetrator gender, child witnesses to partner abuse are adversely affected and are at risk for perpetrating partner abuse and becoming victimized as adults; j) family violence is a complex phenomenon, with reciprocal interactions between the individual members.

It follows from Hamel's postulates that a good assessment would not make any gender-based presumptions about who initiated or continued the aggression or what motivated the individual to act. Differences in the extent and intensity of violence would lead toward better crafting of an appropriate treatment plan. Treatment modalities might include individual counseling, group therapy, couples counseling, family counseling, etc. There should not be a philosophical or political bias against any particular treatment modality.

Most critically, gender-based assumptions that men are always offenders and women victims are discarded in this model. Therefore designing men's groups around the desire for power and control and women's groups around victimization is inappropriate, especially in the light of knowledge that many people, perhaps the majority of offenders, both attack and are attacked. Neither partner should be labeled as the sole offender or recipient of violence in these situations. Labels such as the term "perpetrator" (all too often shortened to "perp") should be discarded because they vilify one party and condemn that person to a lifetime of evil.

Also, men as well as women can be the target of physical assault ("She's slapped me, threw a hot iron at my back, cut me with a knife . . ."). Both genders can suffer lasting emotional damage when they are the target of abuse, even if they are at the same time offenders themselves.

Hamel does note that women suffer far more serious physical injuries than men in violent interactions because of men's greater strength and size. He states that treatment should take into account differences between the genders in biology, personality, communication, and social roles.

Hamel's argument that a gender-based program is a feminist program means that a truly feminist perspective would "seek to protect all members of the family system and holds perpetrators of both genders accountable for their behavior" (2007, p. 14).

Hamel cites a wide range of research studies that indicate the children who witness incidents of violence between their parents often suffer symptoms including poor self-esteem, aggression, depression, and poor social skills. These deficits appear to occur regardless of the gender of the abusive parent or parents. And, because domestic abuse between adults, child abuse, and sibling abuse tend to overlap, family therapy may be advisable or even necessary to challenge family norms perpetuating familial aggression.

This gender-inclusive model obviously has been designed in direct opposition to the Power and Control model. I believe the weight of evidence supports a gender-inclusive model because the similarities between genders regarding domestic aggression outweigh the differences. However, as Hamel notes, due weight must be given to real differences between the genders.

Evidence-based intervention models

Collectively, the field is moving, along with mental health counseling in general, towards utilizing interventions that are "evidence-based," which in practical terms indicates interventions that can claim statistical support. These interventions tend to be cognitive/behavioral in orientation, if only because such interventions are most easily subject to testing (DiGiuseppe and Tafrate, 2007). Theoretically, "what works?" should be the only question informing the design of treatment programs utilizing this model. So what have researchers discovered so far about what interventions do seem most effective?

Curriculum-based *primary prevention* programs appear to be at least modestly effective in lessening future acts of domestic violence. These programs often take place in schools and are aimed at teenaged dating situations. They provide participants with knowledge about domestic violence, help shape anti-violence attitudes and beliefs, and encourage people to seek help if they find themselves involved in a violent relationship (Whitaker et al., 2013). Whitaker et al. note that because prevention is generally cost-effective, programming is badly needed to prevent interpersonal violence before it begins.

Cognitive behavioral therapy has been relatively well documented to diminish relationship violence and to improve overall emotional functioning (Eckhardt et al., 2013). This type of intervention helps clients process their emotional reactions without immediately acting upon them. In effect they tilt one's brain toward neocortical dominance over amygdala-centered impulsive behaviors.

Readiness to Change and other motivation-enhancing programs have received some tentative support (Eckhardt et al., 2013). Presumably these programs are effective by first acknowledging clients' doubts and then winning them over to wanting to change their behavior. One example of a program that incorporates motivational encouragement is this author's brain-change centered program described in chapter 8.

Eckhardt et al. (2013) report in their meta-survey of domestic violence treatment programs that a strong therapist–client relationship and group cohesion appear to improve program efficacy.

No single therapeutic modality has emerged as definitively superior to others, including the Power and Control model (Eckhardt et al., 2013). Therefore it is unwise for any government or other authority to insist that all domestic violence offender treatment programs be based on that model. On the other hand it is equally inaccurate to state that the Power and Control model is less effective than other programs.

Eckhardt et al. (2013) summarize their extensive review of treatment effectiveness research in this way: a) some intervention programs for intimate partner abuse perpetrators and victims are effective; b) however, the quality of research underlying these findings is not of consistently high quality; c) nevertheless, if one were to ask the question of whether there is evidence indicating whether programs are indeed effective at preventing new episodes of violence, the answer would be conditionally affirmative.

It is probably best to think of current domestic violence offender treatment as at an early developmental stage. It seems critical to continue to encourage experimentation with new approaches while refining the ones, in particular cognitive behavioral and motivation enhancement, that appear relatively effective. In the meantime, I recommend that counselors integrate a number of relatively accepted approaches including anger management, cognitive-behavioral therapy, power and control dynamics, etc., while they also emphasize their particular strengths and skills. The reason to emphasize one's particular strengths is that it is important that treatment providers believe in the effectiveness of their approach in order to increase the motivation of their clients. If we, the providers, are not especially enthusiastic about what we bring to the sessions, how could we expect our clients to hope this program will change their lives?

Assessment of Participants

Assessment of domestic violence offenders can be difficult and time consuming. It is wise to allocate two to three hours of individual appointment time if possible, each session separated by days so that clients can fill out various questionnaires between sessions. Some questions you need to consider include:

- Is this person truly an offender? (Mistakes happen.)
- What type of offender (as based on various typologies)?
- How dangerous has this individual been?
- How dangerous could this person be in the near future and later on?
- Is this person currently involved in a violent or potentially violent relationship?
- Does this client have a history of domestic violence behaviors in previous relationships or does this appear to be a particular relationship issue?
- Has domestic violence been unilateral or bilateral? If bilateral, what if anything is happening with the client's co-perpetrator?
- How willing and cooperative is the client, as against angry, defensive, or passive?
- Does the client have children and what is his/her involvement with them?
- How angry does this client appear to be?
- Is the client's violent behavior primarily expressive, instrumental, or both?
- What negative motivations (e.g., staying out of jail) or positive motivations (e.g., getting back with girlfriend) exist for this client to complete treatment?
- What is the client's legal status (e.g., on probation, restraining order or no contact order)?

Assessment tools

There are several published assessment tools that are useful in the assessment process. Perhaps the best known is the Conflict Tactics Scale and its revised version, the CTS2 (Straus, Hamby, and Warren, 2003), both designed to measure the severity of domestic violence behaviors. Another helpful instrument is the CAT-2, the Controlling and Abusive Tactics Questionnaire (Hamel et al., 2015). This 37-item instrument (39 items with males) measures behaviors labeled "derogation and control," "jealous hypervigilance," and "threats/control of space."

A more specific Danger Assessment has been developed by Campbell (1995) that queries behaviors such as possession of weapons, sexual aggression, and threatening verbalizations.

Patricia Potter-Efron and I have developed the following Relationship Behavior Questionnaire to assess the relative range of violent and controlling behaviors committed by an individual as well as violent behavior that he or she has received in an intimate relationship. This questionnaire can be used during both assessment and treatment as it generates much discussion and disclosure.

Relationship Behavior Questionnaire: Control, Intimidation, Manipulation

Please make a check beside the statements below that describe any controlling behaviors you have used in your primary relationships. These are mostly with intimate partners, but can also be with your children, relatives, and people you have lived with.

RAGE. Goal = to destroy. May include partial or total loss of awareness. May result in severe damage to self or partner.

Done by You:
___Murder or attempted murder
___Broken bones
___Bad bruises
___Choking to unconsciousness

___Violent rape
___Deep bite wounds
___Stabbing
___Stomping (repeated kicking)

___Other (What? _____)

Done to You:
___Attempted murder
___Broken bones
___Bad bruises
___Choking to unconsciousness

___Violent rape
___Deep bite wounds
___Stabbing
___Stomping (repeated kicking)

___Other (What?_____)

PARTLY CONTROLLED VIOLENCE. Goal = to get what I want or to retaliate against the other person for something they have done. May cause injuries but usually less severe than with rage.

Done by You:	Done to You:
___Hitting	___Hitting
___Choking/suffocating	___Choking/suffocating
___Hard shoving or pushing	___Hard shoving or pushing
___Pounding, punching	___Pounding, punching
___Throwing against wall	___Throwing against wall
___Kicking	___Kicking
___Biting	___Biting
___Twisting skin or limbs	___Twisting skin or limbs
___Slapping	___Slapping
___Burning	___Burning
___Forced sex	___Forced sex
___Taking/not returning children	___Taking/not returning children
___Other (What?_____)	___Other (What?_____)

RESTRAINING BEHAVIORS. Goal = to keep partner from leaving. This is a serious violation of another's rights.

Done by You:	Done to You:
___Holding on to other	___Holding on to other
___Blocking, locking the door	___Blocking, locking the door
___Taking, destroying phone	___Taking, destroying phone
___Refusing to allow privacy	___Refusing to allow privacy
___Following or tracking partner	___Following or tracking partner
___Keeping partner from friends/family	___Keeping partner from friends/family
___Keeping almost total control of money	___Keeping almost total control of money
___Other (What?_____)	___Other (What?_____)

INTIMIDATION TACTICS. Goal = to scare partner into obedience.

Done by You:	Done to You:
___Threats of violence	___Threats of violence
___Yelling or screaming	___Yelling or screaming
___Name-calling, swearing	___Name-calling, swearing
___Throwing objects	___Throwing objects
___Breaking things (own/other's/both)	___Breaking things (own/other's/both)

___Punishing kids to hurt partner

___Threatening to leave

___Threatening to take kids

___Threatening financial ruin

___Threatening to harm or kill self

___Other (What? _____)

___Punishing kids to hurt partner

___Threatening to leave

___Threatening to take kids

___Threatening financial ruin

___Threatening to harm or kill self

___Other (What?_____)

SHAMING TACTICS. Goal = to destroy other person's self-worth. Indicating in some way that the partner or person you are fighting is no good, not good enough, unlovable, doesn't belong, or should not even be.

Done by You:

___Belittling (You're stupid, ugly, worthless, sick . . .)

___Blaming (Anything that goes wrong is the other's fault)

___Public humiliation of the other person

___Negative comparisons ("You're not as good as . . .")

___Fault-finding (commenting on what the other does wrong)

___Refusal to give praise or appreciation to other

___Other (What?_____)

Done to You:

___Belittling

___Blaming

___Humiliating

___Comparing

___Fault-finding

___No praise

___Other (What?____)

PASSIVE AGGRESSIVE TACTICS. Goal = to control through negative interactions.

Done by You:

___Ignoring the other

___Refusing to discuss serious issues (finances etc.)

___"Forgetting" on purpose

___Showing up late or not at all

___Playing dumb ("I don't know how")

___Stalling or going slow

___Other (What? _____)

Done to You:

___Ignoring other

___Ignoring issues

___Forgetting

___Showing up late

___Acting dumb

___Stalling

___Other (What?_____)

Another instrument I utilize regularly with incoming clients is the Revised Safe at Home Questionnaire (Begun et al., 2008), a 36-item instrument that measures a client's readiness to change by placing them into the pre-contemplation, contemplation, or preparation/action stages of personal motivation.

There are several other questionnaires and instruments that could be used selectively with clients. An excellent description of these tools is available in Hamel's *Gender-Inclusive Treatment of Intimate Partner Abuse* (Hamel, 2014).

What about seeking collateral information? Should you attempt to contact the offender's alleged victim or current partner? Should you contact the client's children? Here laws are important in that while some states mandate at least informing the victim that the offender is in treatment (California), many other states prohibit any contact at all. If you work in a state with some flexibility, then consider these pros and cons about making collateral contact:

Pros: gain better information, especially if the client has been minimizing his behavior; discover the victim's sense of current safety or danger; encourage periodic feedback from the victim as to the progress or lack of progress of the client; encourage the victim's right to stay free from violence; sets the stage for later couples counseling where appropriate.

Cons: the victim could be re-traumatized by your bringing up the subject of intimate violence; the victim may not be truthful and may minimize or maximize the partner's violence as well as his or her own violence; the offender may be angered and feel distrustful when informed that you have made contact with the victim, thus lessening trust and self-disclosure; it is possible that merely contacting the victim will increase that person's risk of receiving more violence.

In general I advise caution regarding collateral contacts. When clients tell me they are eager to return to their relationship or to do couples counseling, I inform them that we can discuss those matters after the client has successfully completed at least half of our program, thus insuring that I will have time to better assess the client's situation.

Summary

The modern conceptualization of domestic violence is far from complete. Indeed, there are many questions concerning how it should be defined, what causes domestic violence, who perpetrates it, and how to treat it. Consequently I have described several models for understanding this phenomenon: power and control, typologies of offenders, gender-inclusive, and evidence-based approaches. I believe treatment specialists, researchers, and scholars need to be very open to new developments that will almost certainly arise as we come to better understand the causes and cures for domestic violence.

Although assessment and treatment are often treated as separate entities, the reality is that treatment begins with assessment and that assessment continues throughout treatment. Formal assessment tools and time periods should be viewed as initial opportunities to develop a therapeutic relationship with a client as against a purely statistical or mechanical enterprise. This effort is then carried into treatment.

Part III

TREATMENT

6

INTERVENTION APPROACHES IN ANGER MANAGEMENT

Intervention Philosophies and Approaches

When reviewing the literature on anger management it is easy to be struck by the wide range of proposed interventions. While certain methods, in particular cathartic ventilation techniques, have lost favor because research fails to support their utility (Tavris, 1989; Bushman, Baumeister, and Stack, 1999), many others have been shown to be effective at least with some clients in some situations. These include cognitive therapies such as those proposed by the rational-emotive techniques of Beck (1976, 1999) and Ellis (Ellis and Tafrate, 1997; see also Kassinove and Tafrate, 2002); assertiveness training (Alberti and Emmons, 2001); social skills training (Kassinove and Tafrate, 2002); relaxation training (Smith, 1999); meditation and mindfulness (Hanson, 2009; Eifert, McKay, and Forsythe, 2006), and systematic desensitization (Evans, Hearn, and Saklofske, 1973). Tafrate (1995) concluded that several techniques were effective, in particular strategies that targeted self-statements, physiological arousal, and behavioral skills. Multi-component programs, such as Novaco's (1975) stress inoculation program, were also found to be effective, although not necessarily more effective than single-component programs. The overall effectiveness of anger management programs is appraised later in this chapter.

These treatment modalities spring forth from underlying philosophical views about the nature of problematic anger. Historically, three main philosophies have dominated psychological approaches to anger problems over the last several decades: *ventilation*, *reduction*, and *management*. More recently they have been joined by a relative newcomer, namely *mindfulness*.

Ventilationists tend to view the core problem in anger as emanating from people's tendency, under societal pressure, to suppress and repress their emotions. The treatment goal, then, becomes giving permission to individuals to fully express their feelings, including anger. Hopefully, the cathartic experience produced in this manner will help clients relieve their stress, drain their anger, and get on with their lives. Classic gestalt therapy (Polster and Polster, 1973), with its emphasis upon completing unfinished business, exemplifies this approach.

Reductionists, on the other hand, focus upon people's tendencies to be too strongly emotional rather than too repressed in their emotions. Ellis' rational-emotive therapy (1962; Ellis and Harper, 1975) fits this model, with its emphasis upon recognizing irrational thought processes that subsequently produce excessively powerful emotional states. In general cognitive therapy techniques have held up well in research studies (DiGiuseppe and Tafrate, 2007), consistently indicating that their use does produce modest gains in the areas of anger management and domestic violence treatment. They do demand a fair amount of mental competence from clients, though, and therefore are not always successful with participants who are especially anxious, unable to concentrate, or who have somewhat limited intelligence.

The anger management approach differs from the cognitive approach in taking a more positive view of anger, seeing it as a valuable resource but one that must be used carefully. Assertiveness training is one example of a management approach (Alberti and Emmons, 2001), with its concept that appropriate anger expressiveness exists in a middle ground between excessive anger, labeled aggression, and deficient amounts of anger, labeled passivity.

Mindfulness, sometimes called mindful meditation, accepts anger as part of the human condition, but helps participants learn how to accept their anger without having to act (or act out) with it. A typical mindfulness statement would be to imagine anger as a cloud in the sky that will eventually pass without your having to do anything (Thich Nhat Hahn, 2001). ACT theory (Eifert et al., 2006) is a recent therapy technique that attempts to bridge the gap between Eastern and Western philosophies while utilizing mindfulness meditation to deal with anger. While mindfulness is a promising and creative approach to anger management, it is also quite foreign to most of my angry and domestically abusive clients and so does encounter initial resistance.

I believe that each of these four philosophies has value for the overall treatment of anger. Certainly I see many clients who do "stuff" their anger in exactly the manner described by the ventilationists. These people tend to turn their anger inward, suppressing it, converting it into physical symptoms, or even physically attacking themselves with their anger since they themselves are the only allowed target for their aggression. Meanwhile, other clients do indeed work themselves into totally useless frenzies of rage because of unnecessary anger-increasing thoughts; they desperately need help learning how to reduce their exaggerated bouts of anger. A third group of individuals mostly needs skills training so that they can express their anger in a pro-social manner that increases the probability for a successful conflict outcome. Still others benefit immensely from locating the still point at their center through mindfulness meditation that allows them to let go of their anger. Furthermore, many clients could benefit from many or all of these approaches.

The philosophies described above in turn reflect the ambivalence of American society toward the expression of anger. Stearns (1994), in his book *American Cool*, notes that over the last 200 years Americans have gradually given themselves more permission to express their emotions in general, but with the caveat that they should not lose control of those same feelings. In other words, it's good to state one's emotions at a moderate level, but not too strongly. Additionally, it is definitely not acceptable to lose control of your emotions. Doing so reduces one's status from full adult toward that of a child. Furthermore, I would add that expressing emotion for its own sake is suspect in American society. Being emotional simply to be emotional seems to be considered a rather narcissistic indulgence. Instead, the emotion of anger is supposed to be functional, specifically to communicate to others that something is wrong. It is meant to lead to effective problem resolution, not simply to being ventilated for its own sake. Certainly this movement in American society toward disallowing the excessive expression of anger has spread across many venues, most prominently in the home, where parents are admonished not to scream at their children and spouses not to verbally or physically aggress against each other (the development of feminist theory with its accompanying challenge to traditional male privilege, including the use of anger and aggression to maintain power and control, has also contributed strongly to this aspect of anger management) and in the workplace, where bosses and supervisors no longer can simply yell at their employees without fear of negative repercussions. Most anger management programs reflect this general philosophy of allowing the expression of anger in moderation, while discouraging excessive anger and acts of aggression.

Three goals for anger and aggression management emerge from the consideration of the philosophies and traditions stated above: 1) to help clients prevent the development or expression of unnecessary anger; 2) to promote the moderate expression of anger while containing excessive ventilation of angry thoughts or aggressive behaviors; 3) to help clients learn appropriate conflict resolution skills. The key words I use with my clients, then, are "prevention," "containment" (or "control"), and "resolution" (Potter-Efron, 2002). I explain to clients that the first goal for most of them (with the exception of those who excessively suppress their anger) is to help them become less angry. In particular, I want to help them become more effective at sorting through their "anger invitations," namely all the things they could become angry about, so that they can quit wasting their time and doing damage to others by becoming unnecessarily angry about things that are essentially trivial or that they cannot control. The second goal, containment, applies in situations where it is reasonable for them to become angry. Here the goal is for these people to learn how to express their anger without losing control. Their task is to tell others about their anger without losing their cool. Finally, these individuals must learn how to utilize their anger in the service of problem-solving. That means learning conflict resolution skills such as compromise, negotiation, and fair fighting.

The anger and aggression management programs I have developed are multi-component models. My reasoning is that since anger and aggression concerns are tremendously varied, ranging from "stuffing" one's anger through violent attacks, no single set of interventions will be universally effective. Rather, practitioners will fare best by utilizing a broad range of interventions and selecting from them those that best match the needs, strengths, and abilities of each particular client. This model is applicable for both individual and group therapy, although certainly there is a practical limit to flexibility, especially when designing and implementing anger education groups. Nevertheless, I believe that therapists should be able to use a wide range of therapeutic models and skills so that they can approach each client with personally designed intervention strategies.

Treatment Intervention Areas in Anger and Aggression Management

There are four main areas for therapeutic intervention in anger and aggression management counseling.

Behavior – Key word: change
Cognition – Key word: choice
Affect – Key word: regulation
Existential – Key word: meaning

This chapter is organized into four main segments, each representing a major intervention focus. These are: i) behavioral change; ii) cognitive reformulations; 3) affective modulation; iv) existential/spiritual growth. Naturally, these areas overlap in actual practice. For example, a client who learns at the behavioral level to take a time out when aroused will almost certainly be simultaneously challenging old automatic thoughts while perhaps also attempting to relax. Still, one client will need a more behavioral emphasis, while another would be better to focus upon cognitive interventions, body awareness, or existential concerns. While most clients will probably benefit from addressing all four of these intervention areas, many may only need help in one or two spheres.

"*Change*" is the key word when client and counselor are focused upon behavioral interventions. The goal of behavioral interventions is to help clients alter their anger- and aggression-provoking, maintaining, and exacerbating actions, which may be either physical or verbal. Taking a time out is an example of a behaviorally focused intervention.

"*Choice*" is the key word in the area of cognitive intervention. Here the goal is to help clients learn to recognize and alter specific thoughts and thinking patterns that provoke, maintain, and exacerbate their anger and aggression. Disputation techniques, in which clients identify certain "irrational" thoughts and replace them with more "rational" ones, exemplify the cognitive approach.

The key word in the third intervention area, affect modulation, is "*regulation.*" The goal in this sphere is to help clients learn how to modulate their emotions, in particular anger, so that they do not become physically and emotionally over-stimulated and then lose control over their actions. Relaxation training is a typical example of affective intervention.

Finally, "*meaning*" is the key word in the existential/spiritual realm. The goal is to help clients discover the greater meaning of their anger or aggression in their lives so that they can replace negativity, cynicism, and despair with optimism and hope. Forgiveness training represents one area of existential/spiritual interventions. I also place mindfulness meditation techniques here because of their profound effect upon the user's spirit, although mindfulness certainly influences all the above categories.

These four intervention areas complement each other. For instance, the likelihood for effective behavioral change is certainly increased as a client makes new cognitive choices. However, such changes may only be possible when the client learns how to control his or her bodily anger reactions, thus involving the affective sphere. But all of these skills may feel meaningless to the client, and therefore left undone, until that person gains a sense of hope for the future and lets go of paralyzing resentments. Still, it is important to be able to decide where to focus one's energies, especially when engaged in individualized anger management. The information presented below is meant as a guideline to help the practitioner decide where to place emphasis.

Behavioral Approach: Introducing Clients to an Objective Change Focus

The immediate goal when working at the behavioral level is actual behavioral change, as against a change of attitude, seeking information, or gaining insight. Of course, most motivated clients coming for anger or aggression management already have a goal: to quit getting angry and/or aggressive. But that goal is quite vague. Furthermore, just stopping

Choosing the Best Treatment Modality

Behavioral emphasis. Attend here when clients:
a) Need immediate skills training to lessen their risk for anger outbursts or violence.
b) Need quickly to change what they are doing that provokes their anger and/or the anger of others.
c) Have anger that comes in sudden bursts that is difficult to contain.
d) Possess little ability to utilize abstractions, metaphors, or analogies.
e) Have developed habitual and ingrained patterns of aggressive behavior.

Cognitive emphasis. Attend here when clients:
a) Need to change thinking patterns that exacerbate their anger.
b) Can work on anger prevention as well as anger containment.
c) Can move from single cognitive explanations to a more general level of abstraction.
d) Need help with specific cognitive distortions such as paranoid ideation or exaggeration.
e) Frequently take excessively morally righteous or critical stands to defend their beliefs.

Affective emphasis. Attend here when clients:
a) Need to alter their bodily stress reactions to contain strong fight or flight reactions.
b) Appear to be both angry and anxious.
c) Need improved awareness of their bodily anger symptoms and reactions.
d) Demonstrate the presence of a strong shame-rage reaction pattern.
e) Appear to have a powerful need for excitatory, stimulating activities including becoming intensely angry.

Existential/Spiritual emphasis. Attend here when clients:
a) Need help understanding the greater meaning of their anger in terms of frustration of their life goals, needs, and yearnings.
b) Complain of bitterness, long-term irritability, and despair.
c) Could benefit from an emphasis upon the resentment process and forgiving others.
d) Need help forgiving themselves.

getting mad is really only half a goal, since no preferred behaviors are proposed to replace those the clients want ended. For these reasons I normally try to help clients expand their goal statement in two ways. First, instead of just quitting getting angry, I suggest the following quantitative goals that are all targeted upon the reduction of negative behaviors: a) to become angry/aggressive less often; b) to stay angry/aggressive for shorter periods of time; c) to become less intensely angry/aggressive; d) to do less damage when angry through aggressive behaviors and words (either to others or to oneself). Since these are quantitative goals, it is necessary to discuss at least informally and sometimes to obtain objective information about the client's actual angry behavior. The second part of goal setting involves what I call the *substitution principle*, defined as naming what kinds of behaviors could replace the client's old angry and aggressive actions. Initially very few of my clients, especially the more angry ones, can describe these more positive behaviors, perhaps because their minds are so primed to notice and react to negative environmental stimuli. Many clients need help just to name such basic behaviors as speaking in a soft voice instead of yelling, giving praise to family members instead of criticizing, smiling instead of frowning, or working cooperatively with colleagues instead of walking away.

Some readers may be concerned about possible confusion here between anger and aggression, since anger *per se* is not a behavior but an emotion (although the distinction between affect and action has been breaking down in the light of brain research into the complex interrelationships between physical states, actions, and feelings) (Damasio, 2003; LeDoux, 1996). Although I agree with this differentiation in principle, it is important to recognize that most clients who need anger management do not make fine distinctions between their angry feelings and their aggressive behaviors. Therefore, it seems reasonable to describe under the term "behavioral interventions" those approaches that ask clients to focus upon the active elements of their combined anger and aggression. The result is an immediate emphasis not upon the "why" of their anger but upon questions like these:

- How do you get angry: What do you say and do?
- When and where do you get angry?
- With whom do you get angry?

Perhaps the single most important question from a behavioral perspective is "Exactly how do you get angry?" Most clients do so with a combination of anger-provoking thoughts and anger-increasing actions. Chronically angry clients become angry and then act in highly predictable patterns. Most people don't get angry in new and creative ways every time they are upset. Instead, they tend repeatedly to think the same thoughts and make the same actions. Thus, angry behavior is habituated behavior. But habitual behavior is highly resistant to change. As noted in chapter 1, long-standing habits are the result of perhaps millions of neurons that fire in synchrony. Chronically angry clients must accept the reality that they will need thorough behavioral retraining if they want to diminish, much less extinguish, these habits. One implication of this situation is that old behavior must not only be minimized but also not rewarded (by others or internally by the client), while new behavior must be strongly rewarded and encouraged whenever it occurs. "Use it or lose it" is the applicable neuroplastic principle, but it may take months for habitual anger-activating networks to diminish and to be partially replaced with anger-deactivating networks.

The following questions often help clients realize early in counseling that they can and must make a real commitment to change if they wish to lessen their anger and aggression problems. Each question or set of questions has a specific purpose that is described after the question.

1. *"With regards to controlling your anger/aggression, what are you doing now that is not working?"* *"What will happen if you keep on doing what you are now doing?"* These two questions help clients recognize that what they are doing is directly and primarily contributing to their anger and aggression problems and so they must change their actions if they want to improve their lives. At a motivational level these questions help move them away from blaming others and toward taking personal responsibility for their behavior.

2. *"What behaviors could you change right now?"* This question points clients toward immediate action. One reason for this is that in my experience most angry clients are not very patient. They want immediate results and need quick rewards to stay motivated. It is important to get angry clients focused upon the possibility of immediately changing some very specific behavior that will quickly demonstrate to them that they really can gain control over their anger and aggression.

3. *"What specific behaviors are you willing to change? To stop? To start?"* Here the emphasis changes from theory to practice. Hopefully, clients will not leave even their first session until they have made a clear and concrete commitment to altering one or two very specific anger-increasing behaviors. A good commitment will include their being able to state exactly what they will attempt to cease ("I won't demand that my step kids say they love me when I put them to bed") and a positive substitute behavior ("Instead I will just tell them I love them and leave it at that").

4. *"Will you commit to these changes regardless of what others do?"* This question is especially valuable in couples therapy. Asking it

helps avoid the bargaining trap in which both people basically say they will curtail a particular behavior if and only if their partners curtail one of theirs. In effect, agreeing to this bargain then gives the power of maintaining the behavioral changes to one's partner. If either person fails to keep his or her promise, then both can revert to anger-provoking actions. For that reason it is much better to have each partner commit to changing his or her behavior regardless of the other's actions. But even in individual or group counseling the question is important because it tweaks out the client's hidden bargains ("OK, I'll quit yelling but she better start treating me better or I'll go back to it").

5. *"How will you and others be able to see that these changes are occurring?"* Sometimes clients talk a lot about how they are changing their attitude. That's certainly important and should not be discouraged. However, from a behavioral perspective attitude change is only important if it results in actual behavioral change. The question here is exactly what new actions and words will people hear and see displayed by the client instead of criticism, shouting, threatening, hitting, etc.

6. *"If these changes work, what would come next?"* This question sets the stage for further success, but also lets clients know that behavioral change is a gradual process that usually occurs in steps. It is not enough just to alter one or two actions. Nor can everything be altered at once. Rather, clients will be assisted to make a series of changes over time that eventually will help them lead lives free from excessive anger and aggression.

7. *"What positive long-term results do you expect in your life because of these changes, for yourself? For others?"* Here clients are encouraged to visualize the final result of their considerable effort. But again the goal is not simply to have a pleasant vision of a better life. Rather, each statement that clients make about a more positive future ("I see me and my husband back together. We're not arguing. We're holding hands and really happy to be with each other") needs to be translated into operational procedures ("So what do you need to start doing right now to help make that vision real?").

Selected behavioral interventions

I will briefly discuss several behaviorally focused interventions in this section. (Readers wanting more detailed exercises on many of these interventions are referred to my client workbook (Potter-Efron, 2001).)

Personal commitment to change. This simple intervention asks clients to make an immediate commitment to curtailing their angry behavior.

But, in order to give this promise a positive focus, I ask clients to make this pledge:

I, _____,

promise to stay calm for 24 hours,

beginning at _____a.m./p.m.

on _____ day, _____.

This promise, which as you can see borrows from the Alcoholics Anonymous philosophy of living one day at a time, presents a workable goal for clients that goes beyond their agreeing only to "stuff" their anger for a while. It leads to discussion of how they can both stop angry and aggressive behaviors and how they can maintain a physiological state of calmness.

Time out. This is the single most important behavioral intervention clients can learn, especially if they have an active pattern of aggression. However, I emphasize that time outs should not be overused. They represent a fall back position when clients realize that they are feeling overwhelmed by their anger and are about to lose control. That is when they must take a time out as against saying or doing things that are hurtful to others and ultimately to themselves. Time outs should not be used just because someone is feeling a little anxious or annoyed with another person. Even more critically, they should never be utilized as a way to escape talking about important concerns or to punish one's partner.

A good time out has four components: "recognize, retreat, relax, return." First, clients must learn to *recognize* the signs that they are heading toward a blow out. Some of these signs are physiological, such as a quickening heart rate or a rising voice pitch. Others are actions like making fists. Cognitive signs, for instance thinking that someone is a jerk, also are critical to recognize, as are verbal cues such as when a client regularly says out loud "You have no right telling me what to do" just before losing control. Next, clients must *retreat*, meaning that once they realize they are close to losing control, they must quickly leave the situation. It certainly helps if they can tell their partners something like this: "I'm really starting to get angry. I better take a time out. I'll be back in a while." It also helps when the partners of angry clients allow and encourage these time outs rather than complaining about them or, far worse, trying to keep the person from leaving. Third, clients must then go somewhere to *relax*. The critical task is for clients to do something while away that actually calms them down, perhaps taking a walk, reading a book, or having a cup of decaffeinated coffee, as against walking away but continuing to stew over alleged insults and eventually returning just as angry as when they departed. Unfortunately, sometimes this step is difficult, as when a harassed mother of three wild children knows she needs to get away but has no one to take over watching the kids. But even then perhaps she can go to her room and briefly close the door. Finally, clients must *return* so that they can more calmly address the concerns about which they became so angry. This last step cannot be skipped. Clients must realize that time outs are designed to help them deal with reality, not to escape it. Normally, this whole process will take from about fifteen minutes to several hours, although some clients may need longer than that in exceptional circumstances. Clients should be encouraged to return as soon as they reasonably can. They should, however, check in with themselves so that they do not return before they are ready and only to get into another argument over the same issue.

Anger/Aggression logs. Quantitative data about the frequency of a client's angry and aggressive behavior can be useful to gather for three reasons. First, collecting information early in treatment provides a numerical baseline. If a client gets angry three times a day the first week of treatment, then reduces that number to once a day by the end of treatment, that constitutes a significant improvement. That changes counseling from an all or nothing proposition in which any incident of anger or aggression is perceived by client and counselor alike as a failure to a more realistic framework in which the goal is to effectively reduce the number of episodes of anger to manageable proportions. Second, gathering data is an active process that tends to motivate clients toward change. Several of my clients, for example, have returned from a week's charting to tell me they were astonished at how often they became angry the first few days but that they have already dramatically reduced the number of episodes. Third, collecting this information helps clients understand that anger usually occurs in discrete episodes and that the choices they make during those incidents are critical: whether or not to become angry, how to express their anger, etc. This recognition sets the stage for future cognitive interventions focusing upon the concept of choice.

I ask clients to collect the following information about each anger/ aggression episode: a) date; b) time; c) a brief description of what happened; d) what you felt; e) what you thought; f) what you said; g) what you did; h) what were your choices? Normally, I only collect this information one time, early in treatment. However, some anger management programs do collect this kind of data more regularly, especially residential or inpatient programs in which the client's behavior can be closely monitored.

Praise. While many behavioral interventions targeting the reduction of negative behavior are most useful early in treatment, those that target the development of positive actions begin to dominate later in the process. One example is helping clients learn to substitute giving praise instead of criticism. This is not easy for most clients because they have become habituated to looking for the bad rather than the good in others. They need both to retrain themselves to notice the good and then to comment on it out loud. To help them do these first tasks, I provide a list of things they can praise (Potter-Efron, 2001): accomplishment ("Good job"); effort ("Good try"); thinking ("You figured it out"); appearance ("Nice smile"); creativity ("That's interesting"); morals/values ("Thanks for being honest"); concern for others ("You're so generous"); common sense ("You're very practical"); taste ("You have great taste"). Note that clients should be instructed to follow the parenthetical statements noted above with specific information (for instance, "You did a good job changing that tire, Pat") rather than being left in a generalized form. In addition, angry clients are very likely to follow praise with criticism ("You did a good job changing the tire, Pat, *but* you put the hubcap on at the wrong angle"). They should be told not to do that since criticism that follows praise essentially negates the praise.

Fair fighting. I mentioned previously that one goal of anger management is to help clients improve their problem-resolution skills. In general, angry clients are often poor at problem resolution at least partly because they simply do not possess effective communication skills. Furthermore, chronically angry individuals become more concrete and rigid in their thinking and inflexible in their words and actions when they feel stressed. Just watching people repeat themselves, saying exactly the same thing again and again during an argument, is convincing evidence for the disruptive effects of anger upon communication.

Simple and specific do and don't lists can be helpful in these circumstances. I've compiled one such list to help angry clients argue better. The "don't" list includes avoiding hitting, pushing, shoving, holding, and threatening others; interrupting; name calling; saying "always" and "never"; making faces; standing up; yelling, etc. The "do" list advises clients to stick to one issue at a time, breathe calmly, listen, be clear and specific, be willing to compromise, etc. I then ask clients to extract a smaller list of two or three main ideas from the larger group that would be most helpful for them. The idea is for them to write these ideas down and carry them in their wallets or purses at all times, consulting their personalized shortlist before or even during conflicts.

Cognitive Aspects of Anger Management

The majority of anger management programs that I have encountered are primarily or at least significantly cognitively oriented in that they focus upon helping clients learn to recognize and alter specific thoughts and thinking patterns that provoke, maintain, and exacerbate their anger. Kassinove and Tafrate (2002) note that there are two somewhat distinct cognitively oriented approaches. The first, developed by Aaron Beck (1976, 1999), places its emphasis upon helping clients assess their automatic thought patterns in order for them to be better able to perceive and respond to situations more accurately and realistically. The second, developed by Albert Ellis (1962; Ellis and Tafrate, 1997) and labeled "rational emotive behavior therapy," places more emphasis upon helping clients develop a more flexible approach in response to daily problems.

Some key principles of cognitive therapy as related to anger are these:

1. Anger will be increased or decreased by how people interpret the situation they are in. A person's appraisals of a situation activate or deactivate anger.
2. Many situations can be seen as "invitations" to anger. People always have a choice to accept or decline these invitations.
3. However, angry individuals have developed "automatic" (habitual, inflexible, fleeting, and only partly conscious) patterns of thinking that lead them to accept more anger invitations than others, usually without realizing that they have other options.
4. Certain beliefs consistently increase a person's anger. These include:

   a) Beliefs that justify one's angry and aggressive thoughts and actions ("I had a right to get angry after what he said to me").
   b) Beliefs about one's personality ("I'm just an angry person and I always will be").
   c) Beliefs about being helpless ("My anger takes over. I can't do a thing to stop it").
   d) Beliefs that give responsibility away ("It's her fault. She deserves my anger").
   e) Beliefs about the world that support getting angry ("The world's a bad place. You can't trust anybody").
   f) Beliefs that anger/aggression are good solutions ("Getting mad makes you feel good").

5. Anger-producing thoughts can be replaced by anger-reducing thoughts. Negative thinking patterns can be altered with practice.

The appraisal process, the first item above, is a central concern in cognitive therapy with angry individuals. Lazarus (1991) discovered that people increase their anger when they conclude that another's actions not only hurt them but also were unjust, preventable, intentional, and/or blameworthy. An example would be a man whose best friend "steals" his girlfriend. That man might argue that his friend's behavior was unjust because it violated the principle of loyalty to your friends, that his friend could have prevented this from happening by just staying away, that he believes his friend intentionally set out to take his girlfriend away from him, and that the offense is so heinous that his friend deserves punishment.

With regard to the third point above, Hauck (1974) describes the process of becoming angry that takes place mostly at an automatic, half-conscious level. He details a six-step process: 1) I want something; 2) I didn't get it so now I'm frustrated; 3) That's awful and terrible; 4) I can't stand it. I must have my way; 5) You are bad for frustrating me; 6) Bad people ought to be punished. Notice the leap from the fourth to the fifth stage here in which the angry person makes a moral judgment against the other. This tendency to turn the opponent into a symbol of evil increases both the angry person's total anger and the desire to attack and destroy the adversary.

The point made earlier that clients can indeed change their thought patterns to replace anger-provoking and anger-increasing thoughts with anger-declining and anger-decreasing thoughts, represents the primary rationale for cognitive therapy. That is why "choice" is the main word I emphasize during anger management counseling. Many clients simply do not realize that they possess far more freedom to choose their pathways in life than they have thought. Once they understand their choices they often feel empowered because now their previously automatic angry reactions can no longer dictate their lives.

Selected cognitive interventions

Initial questions designed to increase cognitive awareness. The following questions help clients become more aware of the part that cognition plays in anger:

1. What thoughts do you have that seem to make you mad or add to your anger?
2. What happens to you when you think these thoughts?
3. Do you have any anger-increasing thoughts you just can't get out of your mind?
4. How accurate/realistic/true do you think those thoughts are that get you angry?
5. Do you ever try changing or challenging these thoughts?
6. Would you like to start changing some of these thoughts?
7. What other thoughts could/do you think?
8. How would you be different if you really could think these new thoughts regularly instead of the old ones?
9. Are you ready to start practicing these new thoughts?

These questions don't have to be asked in strict sequence or all at once. Rather, they can be intermingled with other materials at any time during intake or counseling. Note that the third question probes for a client's obsessive thoughts, such as "That's so unfair what she said to me." These thoughts are particularly tenacious and difficult to counter. Also, they seem so obvious to clients that they may not even mention them unless asked. Nor do clients question the validity of these obsessive cognitions. The eighth question represents a bridge between strictly cognitive considerations and the more broad existential aspects of anger (discussed later in this chapter). The ninth question lets clients know that altering their thought patterns takes time, energy, and effort.

Confronting denial. Many clients deny or minimize the extent of their anger problems. Some do so by refusing to admit that they frequently feel exceptionally angry. Others admit their anger but blame everyone else for it. The effect of challenging such denial head on by demanding clients accept their anger problems is often disastrous. All it does is trigger oppositionality. Fortunately, many clients can be helped to accept their anger and aggression problems by getting them to list and describe the consequences of their anger and aggression. I utilize a pie chart (Potter-Efron, 2004) listing the major spheres of life most frequently affected by a client's anger and aggression. These are: health, family, work, school, finances, friendships, the law, values, mood, and spirit.

Notice that getting clients focused upon this material creates a bridge between their behavior and their cognitions. This is especially true for clients whose behavior has damaged them in several areas of life. For instance, a single client might easily report having to get stitches after smashing his fist through a window, a divorce largely attributable to his anger, doing jail time for fighting, money problems related to having to replace broken objects, etc. Also, this material is entirely self-centered and so clients do not have to be empathic (many angry people have little empathy for others). All that matters is that their anger is ruining their lives.

Also, notice the parallel here with traditional addiction counseling, another area where denial is strong. The first step of the AA program is "We admitted we were powerless and our lives had become unmanageable" (Alcoholics Anonymous, 1976). I tell clients that admitting the full effects of their anger is the equivalent of the "unmanageability" section of the first step. I don't ask clients to accept being powerless over their anger, however, although some clients certainly feel that way. The point is that it is difficult to maintain denial when facing reality.

Challenging a single anger-provoking "hot thought." Many angry individuals possess poor abstraction abilities. Therefore they need help challenging their anger-provoking cognitions one thought at a time. The goal is to help them come up with one "cool thought" that can replace the hot thought. I explain to clients that hot thoughts are the ideas they think to themselves that instantly make them angry. These thoughts are usually short, vague, and over-generalized, such as "Nobody tells me what to do," "I can't take it anymore," and "How dare you say that to me." I also mention that hot thoughts have two other names. Sometimes they're called "trigger thoughts" because these thoughts act like the triggers of a gun. Another name is "automatic thoughts" because they occur so quickly in the client's mind. The goal is to help clients identify their hot thoughts. That can usually be accomplished best by helping them reconstruct their most recent angry and aggressive incidents.

The next step is helping clients develop their cool thoughts. Examples help, such as changing "Nobody can tell me what to do" to "It's OK. I'll decide what I want to do after I hear what they say." It's important, though, to remember that each person has his or her own unique cool thoughts. What works for one person may not work for another, so each hot thought/cool thought has to be individually hand crafted. The test of a cool thought is simple, though. It should help the client feel calm. So if "It's OK. I'll decide what I want to do after I hear what they say" doesn't calm the client down, then the question is what could he or she think that would?

The disputation process. Some clients can learn a more abstract approach to cognitive change so that they can more generally challenge their anger-provoking thought patterns. The model I utilize is my own version of materials developed by Albert Ellis (Ellis and Harper, 1975). The goal is to help clients learn the process with which they can substitute positive, non-anger provoking thoughts for negative, "irrational" thoughts. The five aspects of this process, as I present them to clients, are:

A: The Antecedent = an anger invitation = something you might get angry about.
B: The anger-provoking Belief(s) that convince you that you have a right to be angry.
C: The Consequences of your beliefs: anger, hostility, aggression.
D: Your Disputation – A thought that substitutes for "B" and is far less anger provoking.
E: Effects (positive). Your new, less angry or aggressive behavior.

Here is an example:
A: Your boyfriend calls to tell you he has to cancel his date with you tonight.
B: You think: "That's awful! What a betrayal! How dare he do that to me."
C: You start yelling at him, accusing him of betraying you.

D: New thought: "Wait a minute. He's a good guy. This is a disappointment, not a disaster. I can handle it OK."

E: You calm down quickly, quit yelling, accept his apology, and make plans for another date.

Clients still need to utilize this technique one negative thought at a time. However, once they realize that there is a consistent way they can work to change negative thoughts into more positive ones they become more adept at doing so on their own, without needing the immediate help of a counselor.

Affective Anger Management Approaches

Anger and aggression are usually full brain and body reactions to a threatening event (Niehoff, 1998), although the threat can be immediate or potential, real or imagined, weak or strong. As such, anger and fear responses are frequently intertwined so that any threatening situation may trigger fight, flight, or freeze reactions and sometimes the same trigger will produce different reactions at different times. However, chronically angry clients react far more often with anger and aggression to potentially threatening cues than others. In effect anger has become their habituated response and trigger for aggression. It is as if their brains were computers that had "anger" set as their default option; their initial reaction to potentially emotional events is always to become angry as against feeling any other emotion. Furthermore, chronically angry individuals tend to develop hair-trigger reaction mechanisms so that they become instantly angry, even enraged, in the face of stimuli that would not even set off another person's anger response. Imagine, for instance, that the anger-dominant individual is giving a talk when someone knocks on the door. Whereas most people would have either no emotional response to this event at all or perhaps feel mildly annoyed or anxious, the chronically angry person might react with fury: "I hate interruptions! Make them stop! Why are they doing that to me?" The result of this extreme reaction, unfortunately, may be that this person loses credibility and gets labeled as a hopelessly hostile individual.

Two goals emerge from the considerations above: 1) to help chronically angry clients gain better control over their angry reactions to threat; 2) to help these people develop a more flexible and versatile emotional response system. These two goals are discussed separately below.

Gaining control

Perhaps the best place to begin here is to confront the still popular myth of ventilation. This myth states that the best way to handle one's anger is to scream, yell, pound fists, throw things, etc. People are supposed to feel better after these experiences. Furthermore, their anger should be drained from their bodies so that they become considerably less angry for a long time. Unfortunately, research has not supported this theory; instead, as Tavris (1989) writes, ventilation of anger usually increases the person's anger rather than decreases it. The effect of ventilation, in most cases, is to train people to become angrier over time. Although ventilation techniques may still have value for some clients, in particular those who turn most of their anger inward, they are definitely not recommended for the aggressively angry people who attend most anger management programs.

I do want to comment on a second myth that I have frequently encountered among both clients and counselors in this field. Believers in this myth claim that anger is not a real emotion or that one can always discover a deeper emotion underneath any anger display. Sometimes the allegedly "real" emotion is fear, sometimes hurt. But whatever other emotion is named, the therapeutic goal becomes getting under the anger to this underlying feeling. The phrase often utilized with this approach is that anger is just a "cover emotion." Certainly, though, there is no physiological evidence that anger is not a real emotion or only a cover emotion. Rather, anger is a core emotion deeply rooted in the survival centers of our brains. I believe there is a grain of truth in this assertion, though, namely that the anger of very upset individuals certainly can obscure other less visible emotions. However, that is true for any strong emotion. Intense fear, for example, can temporarily prevent observers from noticing that the presenter of that fear is also ashamed or angry. Perhaps a more fitting statement would be that "anger seldom rides alone," implying that it is usually valuable to probe for the appearance of other emotions that may be somewhat hidden, especially when a client's anger display is particularly powerful. I will mention ways to help clients access these other emotions in the next section of this chapter.

Seven questions help clients challenge the myth of ventilation while directing them toward gaining better control over their anger:

1. What happens to your body when you get really mad?
2. What happens to your mind when your body feels like that?
3. What are the costs to you for losing control of your anger?
4. How important is it to you to stay in control of your anger?
5. What do you do to stay in control?
6. Have you ever tried relaxation, meditation, or any other similar ways to stay calm? If so, what happened?
7. Would you be interested in learning some new ways to relax or other ways to stay in control?

One way to help clients learn to contain their emotions is to teach exposure techniques. Kassinove and Tafrate (2002) correctly note that few anger management programs utilize systematic exposure techniques, probably because these demand rather advanced psychological training to be effective. These authors describe their exposure methods, which include trigger review, verbal exposure, combining imaginal exposure with other interventions, and *in vivo* exposure. Their goal is to teach clients to stay calm in the face of aversive stimuli, such as someone saying something critical about them, that would normally and automatically trigger a strong angry reaction.

Relaxation training is another good way to help clients learn how to contain their physical reactions to anger cues. I find relaxation particularly valuable for clients who are recognizably both angry and anxious, a combination of emotions that often leads to a rage response. Smith (1999) describes six different approaches to relaxation training, a useful reminder that it is best to fine tune each person's relaxation program to meet his or her own particular needs. I personally facilitate relaxation sessions individually for my anger clients only after getting to know them well enough to be able to utilize statements, metaphors, and descriptions of the relaxed state that match their individual vocabularies. I also emphasize that relaxation is particularly useful as a preventative tactic. Although relaxation may help people become less angry after they get upset about something, it works better in my experience when clients practice relaxation enough so that they become less likely to get angry in the first place. Learning to relax as a lifestyle works best.

The intensity of the anger experience must be contained if clients expect to gain control over their anger. One way to help clients deal with the intensity issue is to provide them with ways to gauge the importance of a situation (its threat level). The classic question "On a scale of one to ten, with ten being the highest, how serious is this event that is bothering you?" relates to the first approach. Another approach is to provide a range of words that describe various levels of anger. The use of an "anger thermometer" (Potter-Efron, 2004; Kassinove and Tafrate, 2002) in which various levels of anger are assigned specific words ("annoyed," "mad," "furious") is effective for this purpose.

Helping clients develop a more flexible and versatile emotional response system

The second major goal in the area of affective interventions is to help clients whose primary emotional reaction to any stimulus is to become angry develop a more flexible and versatile emotional response system.

Clients must realize that they have become trapped in their anger, unable to respond with any other single emotion or with a combination of emotions to life's diverse events. The general questions I ask that help them recognize this reality are these:

1. How has anger taken over your emotional life?
2. Do you ever have feelings other than anger? Which?
3. Was there a time in the past when you felt less anger? Was there a time in the past when you felt more of any other feelings?
4. What other emotions might you have if you weren't angry?
5. What feelings do you avoid with your anger?
6. How important to you is it to get back into contact with those other emotions?
7. What would it take for you to let yourself begin having those other feelings again?

A more specific question regarding a particular event is simply this: "What other feelings in addition to your anger do you have about this situation?" The purpose of these questions is to help clients realize how much their anger has taken over their emotional life.

The third question above, "Was there a time in the past when you felt less anger?" helps clients who have gradually become angrier over time to remember their more emotionally fluid past. These clients will have less trouble broadening their emotional responsiveness than clients who recall themselves as always angry, since they have a mental model already in place of themselves feeling other emotions. The fifth question, "What feelings do you avoid with your anger?" often helps clients who avoid "soft" emotions like sadness and love realize what they are doing. Finally, the last two questions, "How important to you is it to get back into contact with those other emotions?" and "What would it take for you to let yourself begin having those other feelings again?" return the initiative to the clients. The therapist's offer is to help clients retrieve or develop their other emotions. The clients then decide whether or not to accept that invitation.

Existential/Spiritual Anger Management Approaches

The existential realm has been relatively neglected in anger and aggression management. By that I mean little direct attention has been given, both in the academic literature and in my observations of anger management and domestic violence prevention programs, to such concerns as the greater meaning of their anger in people's lives, the anxiety that attends making the choice to give up the safety of an angry life for an uncertain future, the sense of isolation that often accompanies an angry or aggressive lifestyle, and, most importantly, the general misery of being chronically angry. One existential/spiritual area that has been increasingly discussed, however, is forgiveness. Please go to the deactivation section of chapter 7 for an extensive discussion of forgiveness.

Existential concerns are most critical for clients who have developed an angry lifestyle that centers on a hostile attitude toward the world. I believe the central components of attitude are these: a) the belief that most people are bad; b) the concurrent conviction that most people are also untrustworthy; c) the sense that nothing good happens in life or if it does that good will soon be overwhelmed and replaced by the bad; d) consequently, the conclusion that it is useless and too painful to hope for a good life; e) anger, especially in the forms of cynicism, sarcasm, criticism, and cutting humor is then used to push people away; f) which helps clients guard against developing what they perceive would be false hope, vulnerability to promises that will inevitably be broken, and despair. The result is that people become mean-spirited in their attitude and actions, developing an overall hostile world-view. The effect of this world-view is to negatively filter everything that happens so that the client's depressive opinions about the world are continually reinforced.

Meanness of spirit develops slowly. Clients with this condition can usually enumerate a great number of abandonments, betrayals, deceits, injustices, and undeserved wounds they have endured. Each injury warps their personality a little bit more until they become bitter in their estrangement from the world. They often describe a feeling of *impotent rage* (Potter-Efron, 2007), a feeling of utter inability to change the things that most matter to them. A parent's death, a painful divorce, being laid off from a cherished job: these losses must be protested even while the protests are useless. The result is that these people seem to be constantly shaking their fists at an uncaring universe. Some literally become angry at God, as I will describe in the case vignette below.

The questions described below help clients address the existential meaning of their anger:

1. Was there ever a time in your life when you weren't so angry?
2. What were you like then?
3. What were your goals and values?
4. How has your anger affected your spirit?
5. How has your anger changed you as a person?
6. Whom have you blamed (held responsible) for your anger? How has that affected you?
7. Who would you be if you weren't so angry?
8. What would you do with your life if you weren't so angry?

9. How would letting go of your anger affect your being?
10. How would letting go of your anger affect your connection with others?
11. How would letting go of your anger affect your work?
12. How would letting go of your anger affect your spiritual self?
13. How much do you yearn for a life free from bitterness, anger, and hate?
14. What can you do to start moving in that direction?

The first three questions in this set refer to a past that might have been much different from the present, perhaps a past filled with joy and hope. In my experience many of my most seething bitter clients are "wounded idealists," who once believed strongly that the universe was good. Then one or more disasters struck, or perhaps just a long series of disappointments, and these people gradually evolved a far more negative and hostile persona. These individuals simply cannot accept the limited reality of their current lives. They may benefit from interventions or exercises (Potter-Efron, 2001) that invite them to give up their unrealistic expectations of others, themselves, the universe, or God. On the other hand they also benefit by being encouraged to reclaim some of their discarded ideals. Perhaps, for example, a client who once was generous to others could become so again, even though several individuals did take advantage of his or her altruism. But this time the client must do so knowing well that there is no guarantee against getting ripped off again. Even so, practicing generosity again may help that person reestablish a sense of belonging with others.

Questions 4–13 above help clients assess the damage they are doing to themselves by continuing to be bitterly angry. Existential anger affects every aspect of a human being: their relationships, spirit, being, character, and personality. But it is important to ask these questions in a positive manner to these critically negative individuals. The "how would letting go of your anger affect your . . .?" points them toward a more positive future that lies within their grasp if they care to reach for it. Question 13, "How much do you yearn for a life free from bitterness, anger, and hate?," is particularly potent in helping clients find within themselves a true desire to shed their chronic hostility. Finally, Question 14, "What can you do to start moving in that direction?," reminds clients that they must take the initiative to change.

Existentially angry people often must work hard to lessen their pattern of habitual criticism. I frequently ask these clients to look at what motivates them to be so critical. Some answers include that criticism validates their negative view of life by invalidating the more positive beliefs of others; it helps keep them in a safe position of superiority and dominance; criticism helps them avoid noticing or dealing with their own imperfections; it keeps them in control by making others feel weak, dumb, or bad; criticism simply feels good to them; it is a way to hurt and punish others; and, perhaps most tellingly, criticism keeps others from getting too close to them so they will not feel so vulnerable. Some clients are willing after a discussion like this to make a commitment to abstain from being critical of others in any way for a 24-hour period. This experiment, if reasonably successful, can then lead toward helping the client make related efforts to look for the good in others, look for the spirituality of others, and to substitute praise for criticism.

Effectiveness of Anger Management Counseling

Is anger management really useful? Does it help clients reduce their overall levels of anger and/or lessen aggressive behaviors emanating from anger? DiGiuseppe and Tafrate (2007) extensively reviewed the research literature and came to these conclusions:

- Optimism is justified. Successful treatments for anger exist with adults, adolescents, and children.
- The average amount of change per treatment is of moderate to large magnitude.
- Treatment effects appear to last over time as measured by follow-up studies.
- Anger treatment also facilitates changes along other dimensions, including physiological measures, positive and assertive behaviors, and reduction of aggressive behaviors [and in this way connecting anger management with domestic violence reduction].
- Attempting to match particular clients with specific treatments did not appear to improve treatment outcomes.
- Although both group and individual therapies were successful in reducing many aspects of anger, individual therapy appeared to be more successful in reducing aggression.
- The use of manuals or other integrity checks to ensure that therapists follow the manual produced higher effect sizes than ones that did not use these checks.
- Most studies measured behavioral, cognitive, or mixed cognitive/ behavioral programs. This implies that these programs are effective but does not rule out the effectiveness of other types of programs that are less easily quantitatively studied.

CASE STUDY

A Woman Angry at the Universe

Helena, 28, describes herself as once having been a perky, naïvely optimistic, playful woman despite the early death of her mother when she was only 16 years old. By then, though, Helena's parents had instilled in her a deep religious conviction. "God only gives people as much pain as they can handle" was part of her faith. Besides, her mother had died slowly from cancer, giving Helena plenty of time to accept that reality.

Helena married when she was 21 to a hard-working and equally devout man. They had their first child two years later, a girl they named Bailey. All went well until one day Helena awoke with a sense of foreboding, realizing that she could hear no sounds coming from Bailey's room. She ran there only to discover that her beautiful daughter had died in the night. The doctors pronounced her death as the result of sudden infant death syndrome and told her not to feel guilty. It was no one's fault, they said. Her husband and relatives all gathered around to support her. So did her minister, who tried to comfort Helena by telling her that Bailey's death was God's will.

Helena could not be consoled, though. Instead, she began feeling a desperate rage growing within. "God's will!" she thought. "God's will!" This woman, who had prayed every day, gone to church at least twice a week, and devoutly believed in God's kindness and generosity, could no longer tolerate the thought of God. "God has betrayed me," she concluded. Within two years she had divorced her husband and began drinking regularly. She was placed on antidepressant medications, but they failed to alter her increasingly angry, hostile, and bitter mood. She saw two therapists as well, one faith-based and one secular, but quickly dismissed both for being "do-gooders mouthing platitudes." Helena also developed a sharp tongue, backing people away with intentionally mean words. Five years after her daughter's death, Helena had yet to return to church. "Why should I?," she argued, "I prayed my heart out and look what it got me. Nothing but heartache."

Helena was not just angry with God, though. She was angry at the entire universe and especially the people in it. She withdrew from her family and friends, calling them all "hypocrites" for failing to offer her anything more than sympathy when her daughter died. She wanted them to share her outrage, not sympathy. She did keep her job as an office manager, making life miserable for the five secretaries who worked under her supervision through a steady stream of sarcastic and critical remarks. Nobody liked Helena anymore, but that was fine with her. She chose solitude, even giving away her pet dog Sammy because he was too much trouble to take care of. But her solitude was not healing.

Then something happened that made Helena reassess her situation. A man named Norman from another department met her at a work function and, not knowing much about Helena, asked her out. Within two weeks Norm told Helena that he wanted to get serious "but why do you act so mean to everybody?" Helena heard his question and started to tell him why with all her usual bitterness. But then she stopped. She suddenly realized that she had been ruining her own life with her chronic anger. She also recognized that she and Norman wouldn't stand a chance for a decent relationship until she did something about her rage.

That is why Helena decided to give counseling one more try. The first reason, she explained, was that she wanted to give her new relationship a chance. The second reason was that Helena figured she might eventually kill herself if she couldn't feel better, either actively with medicines or passively through drinking herself to death.

Like most clients, Helena came to counseling with only one goal, namely to eliminate her "mean" behavior. Translated into behavioral terminology, that goal was listed in the treatment plan as "fewer incidents of criticism, sarcastic remarks, etc., both at work and with Norman." The positive goal that she admitted would be difficult to achieve was described as "increased incidents of praise, encouragement, etc. both at work and with Norman." As for her relationship with God, she allowed for consideration of that issue to be put on the treatment plan, but only with the clear understanding that she was under no obligation to restore or alter it.

Helena's work began at the behavioral level. She made a determined effort to reduce the number of negative remarks and to substitute praise for criticism. The place she could best practice these new behaviors was at work because her job as a supervisor gave her numerous opportunities for either praise or criticism. What amazed Helena was how firmly the habit of negativity had solidified within her. "I find myself saying something sarcastic before I even think about it. I don't like being that way." Within a few weeks Helena had altered her words to the point where the secretaries that she supervised began smiling instead of looking down when she entered their room. Norman, too, noticed and appreciated her new behavior.

The next challenge was more cognitive in nature. Helena had to confront her belief that her family and friends were hypocrites because they refused to treat Bailey's death as an outrage. Fortunately, Helena was able to understand and utilize disputation to challenge that belief. After consultation, she substituted the idea that "They offered comfort the best they could when Bailey died. I just couldn't take it in." Helena recognized with this disputation both that these people really did care and that ultimately she was responsible for her own estrangement from them. True, they had offered Helena a gift she did not want at that time, namely comfort, instead of joining her in her futile outrage, but now she could finally see the value in that gift.

Helena had issues that called for affective intervention as well. Most importantly, over the five years of her unresolved grief, she had lost track of her positive emotions. Now she could finally retrieve them. To facilitate this process we did a visualization in which Helena found herself walking down a street that had a "used furniture" store on it. Entering the store, she made her way to a chest of drawers that was oddly familiar. As Helena opened each drawer she discovered a lost emotion: sadness, joy, fear, shame, etc. The last drawer she opened was labeled "love." Each emotion was there for her to retrieve if she chose. All she had to do was take them from the drawers. And that's exactly what she did during an emotionally intense session. Helena used that experience to allow these emotions back into her life. She kept her anger as well, resisting her initial temptation to dump that emotion into the chest. Helena knew that she still needed her anger to keep her safe, especially as she dealt with her grief. That anger acted as a refuge, a place where she could retreat when the pain of her loss felt virtually unendurable.

Finally, after three months of weekly therapy sessions, it was time to address Helena's anger at God. We could have developed this theme along the lines of forgiveness. However, by now Helena had made many changes. She found herself returning to her "pre-morbid" state of optimism and joy, albeit without the naïve "If I pray to God twice a day, nothing bad will ever happen to me" quality of the past. Indeed, the key existential change Helena made was to realize that she had to renounce her formulaic belief system that revolved around the concept that God owed her a pain-free life in exchange for her loyalty. This change in her world view allowed her to develop a renewed sense of faith that didn't depend upon her understanding God's plan (Flanigan, 1992). She decided, however, not to return to her old church, a church that she believed encouraged her old beliefs, but instead found one whose minister was less formulaic. She actually found her first Sunday in church somewhat anti-climactic: "It seemed so easy, like I'd never left." God and the church were back in her life where, from her new perspective, they always belonged.

Helena's therapy entailed change in all four major therapeutic sectors: behavior, cognition, affect, and existential meaning/spirituality. Fortunately, because from earlier days she had a model of herself as a less angry and bitter human being, her changes could take place fairly rapidly. Essentially what she did was to re-connect with her past personality. Nevertheless, her path was not an easy one. Helena frequently regressed to her hostile state. However, she gradually broke her habit of anger, hostility, and bitterness.

Summary

Anger problems have been addressed with various philosophies, including ventilation, reduction, and management. The goals these philosophies suggest include helping clients prevent the development or expression of unnecessary anger, assisting them to promote the moderate expression of anger, while containing excessive ventilation of angry thoughts or aggressive behaviors, and helping them learn appropriate conflict-resolution skills.

Anger management counselors basically can pursue their task through four orientations. First, they can address the need for behavioral change, helping clients both reduce negative behavior while increasing positive actions. Second, counselors can utilize cognitive therapy techniques designed to help clients choose less anger-provoking ways to think about situations. Next are efforts to help clients contain their emotional intensity while shifting attention to other emotions. Finally, the very meaning of a client's anger may be considered at the existential/spiritual level.

The next chapter describes a specific approach I utilize to address anger problems. This approach is based on developing effective interventions at each stage of a client's typical six-step progression through an anger episode.

7

THE ANGER AND AGGRESSION CYCLE
A Therapeutic Model

I will detail in this chapter a model of an anger and aggression process. This model is applicable in many situations in which people become angry, including during episodes of domestic violence. There are six phases in this model: activation, modulation, preparation, action, feedback, and deactivation. I will describe them in linear fashion, although in reality they usually overlap considerably. I will also relate these phases to brain activity and suggest interventions at each phase to help angry and aggressive individuals function better (see Figure 7.1: Six phases of an anger episode).

This chapter describes how anger typically develops and can then lead to verbal and physical outbursts. One cautionary note: I am not proposing that all acts of aggression or domestic violence stem from anger. However, many acts of violence do begin with a feeling of anger.

Phase One: Activation

What triggers a person's anger and/or aggression? This simple question rests at the core of the activation phase. Theoretically almost anything can act as a trigger: a loud noise, a soft noise, a lack of noise, a new noise, an old noise, etc. Nor do all anger triggers reach conscious awareness. Someone may react physiologically, for example, to a slight buzzing noise, without ever sensing that sound at a conscious level. Chronically angry and aggressive individuals seem particularly susceptible to triggers. They become upset more often at more possible events than others.

One useful term for these triggers, at least consciously experienced ones, is "anger invitations." An anger invitation is anything about which you could become angry. I ask my clients to become more aware of their anger invitations by paying attention to them and by asking others for information ("My wife says I start grinding my teeth right before I get nasty"). Just as importantly, they need to learn what kinds of anger invitations they are likely to accept and which ones they refuse. Answers here

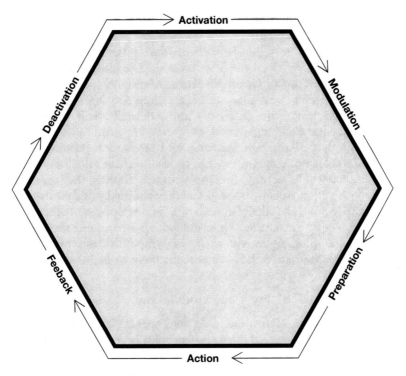

Figure 7.1 Six phases of an anger episode.

may refer to specific people ("Anything my aunt says makes me mad"), classes of people ("I start getting angry as soon as I see a cop"), physiological conditions ("I accept way more anger invitations when I'm anxious or tired"), particular words or phrases ("Don't ever call me a b ....."), perceived injustices ("I hate cheaters"), etc. The goal here is to help clients gain better control over their anger invitations. It helps to mention to them that since they do turn down many anger invitations, they certainly have the skills to decline even the ones they have been accepting. I then ask them what they say to themselves when they do decline an anger invitation.

The activation stage is where therapists face their greatest challenge in the anger cycle. This is because the anger circuitry in the brain is activated so quickly and through essentially non-conscious processes. The amygdala, as noted in chapter 1, the brain's early warning center, helps initiate a fight or flight response in far less than one second. By the time a potentially angry person becomes aware of an anger invitation, his body may have already been activated. By the time that person decides not to get angry, cortisol may already be rolling through his or her body.

In other words, he is choosing to decline an anger invitation his brain and body have already accepted!

So how can counselors best help clients during the activation stage? Prevention strategies may be the best response. The idea, basically, is to help our clients develop and maintain a sense of calmness and composure that acts as a buffer against anger and aggression. Any intervention plan that helps clients feel safe, internally and externally, will lessen that person's susceptibility to anger cues.

Breathing, relaxation, neurofeedback, and meditation training all fit this criterion. It is not enough, though, to have a client take a few deep breaths after they've already become irritated. Rather, they need to practice these skills on a daily basis so that they habitually and effortlessly can breathe deeply, relax their musculature, and self-soothe before they ever receive an anger invitation. These individuals are training themselves to operate in life more often with their parasympathetic nervous system (rest and relax) rather than their sympathetic (fight or flight) system.

Phase Two: Modulation

"How angry are you?" "How intense is your anger?" The concern in the modulation phase is all about intensity. Chronically angry and aggressive people tend to exaggerate threats to their well-being and therefore to overreact. The therapeutic challenge is to help these clients quit overreacting to these stimuli. The hippocampus is one region in the brain that clients need to utilize for this purpose. In addition to being able to place a potential threat into context ("Yes, it's a loud noise but it's just coming from kids playing"), the hippocampus sends messages to the hypothalamus to stop releasing cortisol.

A classic question in cognitive therapy is this: "On a scale from 1 to 10, how serious is this situation?" The idea, of course, is for clients to realize that they frequently have been making small problems into big ones and then to correct their thinking with phrases such as "It's no big deal. Let it go." I suggest we add another scaled question, though: "On a scale from 1 to 10, how angry are you?" This highlights the possible gap between one's conscious mind trying to calm the situation and one's highly activated unconscious mind and body. When someone says they are a "3" on the first scale but an "8" on the second, then the therapist must attend primarily to the second. I have found in many of these occasions that the client is confounding a present irritant with past, more serious incidents ("I know she doesn't mean to insult me, but when I was growing up my mother used that exact phrase to humiliate me"). If the client can separate past from present, the intensity scale will be reduced.

Taking a *time out* is the first skill I teach in anger management classes. I place time outs in the modulation stage because people need a time out when they recognize that they are at such a raised intensity level that they are in danger of not being able to control what they are saying or doing. I discourage overuse of time outs simply to avoid talking about uncomfortable topics. A good time out utilizes the Four R's: recognize, retreat, relax, and return. *Recognize* stands for learning the cues that one is losing control; *retreat* means just that – get out now; *relax* until the anger drains from your body; *return* to deal with the issue once you and the other party are able to do so without reactivating your anger. Unfortunately, taking a good time out is harder than it appears. People often fail to realize how angry they are becoming. All too often one's attempted retreat is blocked by an angry or distraught partner. People return too quickly from a time out and just become angry again. Too often the angry person returns with this line: "I'm not mad any more, but I don't want to talk about it." That philosophy almost guarantees that the argument will soon resume. In my groups we thoroughly discuss the pros and cons of time outs so clients can utilize them selectively.

One reason that chronically angry and aggressive individuals overreact to anger invitations is that their minds are biased towards negativity, suspicion, and hostility. Angry adolescents are particularly susceptible to this bias. This is at least partly because the frontal cortex of most people is not fully developed until the mid- to late twenties (Cozolino, 2010b). It is likely that cognitive development and chronic anger and aggression have an inverse relationship with each other. Bloomquist and Schnell (2002) note that adolescents who display antisocial behavior do poorly on measures of executive functioning. They also write that during social interactions aggressive children fail to attend to social interactions, pay too much attention to others' aggressive cues, interpret others' benign behavior as having a hostile intent, generate fewer pro-social and more aggressive solutions to solve interpersonal problems, anticipate fewer consequences for their actions, and expect more positive outcomes from employing aggressive solutions to solve social problems than other children. All these patterns are likely to continue into adolescence, the result of which being that relatively aggressive teens perceive the world differently, and in a far more hostile manner, than their peers. In particular, angry adolescents often harbor a *hostile attributional bias* that is triggered by ambiguous situations. One way to explain this bias is that angry people hear a positive statement as neutral, a neutral statement as negative, and a negative statement as hostile. This bias often leads angry children and adolescents to conclude wrongly that others harbor hostile intent toward them and therefore deserve to be attacked (Moeller, 2001). It is easy to exaggerate threat when someone combines this hostile attributional bias with a generally hostile world view ("Life sucks and then you die") and a generally pessimistic outlook ("Bad things will last, they will spread, and I probably did something to make them happen")

(Seligman, 2006). How can the counselor help clients with these tendencies? I have found that bringing them to a client's full awareness can be quite useful. Although clients may begin discussion by defending their negative views, they often come to realize that they have the capacity to change them if and when they so choose.

Another modulation phase intervention involves asking clients to identify other emotions they are feeling in addition to their anger. For example, a man who is furious with his drug-addicted wife may not realize he is also feeling sad and scared. Bringing these other emotions into awareness tends to distract clients from their anger, but also to help them get ready for the next phase of the cycle, namely preparation.

Phase Three: Preparation

Many individuals who commit acts of domestic violence admit to being quite impulsive. "If only I had taken the time to think I wouldn't have . . ." is a common theme. These clients need to learn to increase the gap between impulse and action. That is the purpose of the preparation stage in the anger and aggression cycle.

I tell clients that their anger is a wonderful messenger, but a lousy problem-solver. Anger tells them something is wrong and gives them energy to address the problem. However, problem-solving demands more than energy. People must be able to consider all their options before they can make good choices.

Let me ask you this question: how good were you at considering all possible action choices the last time you became really angry? If you are like most people the answer will be "poor, and the angrier I got the worse I became at it." Anger diminishes problem-solving skills. One's frontal cortex often functions badly under duress. The challenge for therapists at the preparation phase, then, is to help clients calm their emotions.

The orbitofrontal cortex is critical for problem-solving, so much so that Schore (2009) calls it the "senior executive" of the social emotional brain. The orbitofrontal cortex is part of a larger circuit that includes the caudate nucleus and thalamus and it also has strong linkages with the amygdala (Badenoch, 2008). It is necessary for impulse control, but also it is here that the brain develops an ability to appreciate the consequences of one's actions, the understanding of cultural rules, and changes in others' emotional states (Siegel, 2012). The orbitofrontal cortex therefore allows clients the opportunity to consider how others will react to one's possible behaviors. The challenge, though, is how to help angry clients actually utilize this resource.

The answer is simple: *buy time*. Even a three-second delay between impulse and action may be enough to curtail a thoughtless impulsive reaction in favor of a thoughtful considered response. Clients should be encouraged to develop habits like counting to ten and/or taking several deep breaths before saying or doing anything when they feel angry.

Additionally, let me mention the value of mindfulness practice at the preparation phase. Mindfulness encourages clients to accept their anger as part of their being but not to act upon it, thus creating a wall between the preparation and action phase of the anger cycle (Eifert et al., 2006). Additionally, clients are encouraged to envision anger as a cloud in the sky that will soon pass (Thich Nhat Hahn, 2001), essentially reminding them that what feels so tremendously important will soon be over and found to be less critical than immediately perceived. However, it is important to remind clients that they should not simply dismiss their anger but still harness its energy for thoughtful action.

Phase Four: Action

The challenge here is for clients consistently to use their anger – perhaps better stated as the energy derived from their anger – well. Another component of the later developing parts of the brain is important here, namely the dorsolateral prefrontal cortex. This area helps someone prioritize behavior, utilize verbal skills in problem-solving, and reprioritize when necessary (Olson and Colby, 2013). Just as before, angry individuals have difficulty during this phase and tend to rely upon old behavioral patterns and impulsive aggression instead of considered action.

Three simple principles can help clients improve their behaviors: a) the *moderation* principle; b) the *substitution* principle; and c) the *repetition* principle. The moderation principle states that the best response is usually a moderate one rather than the smallest or greatest possible one. For instance, a woman angry at her boyfriend for coming home late would avoid saying nothing at all (unless he was drunk) or hitting him with a baseball bat, but would instead engage him through assertive communication. My model for an assertive statement follows this pattern:

When you _____ [specific behavior]
I feel _____ [specific emotion(s)]
And I want _____ [specific changes].

Here the woman might say "When you come home more than 45 minutes late I feel angry and scared and I want you to call me ahead of time when you are going to be that late."

The *substitution* principle is absolutely critical in therapy. The idea is that it is never enough simply to stop one's angry behavior. That would be like thinking it is fine to just stop a car from going in reverse when we really want the client to learn how to drive it forward. The key question is: "What do you want to do instead of what you have been doing?"

Often this means helping clients discover socially acceptable alternatives to unacceptable behavior. Examples are exchanging giving praise for criticism, optimism for pessimism, and forgiveness for hate. This may be especially important if your client has been raised in very angry homes or perhaps in cultural settings where behaviors appreciated by middle-class society are not taught or valued.

A side note here. Anger and aggression management has inextricable connections with middle-class values. That doesn't mean that counselors must wholeheartedly endorse such values. Nor does it mean that we must insist that our clients endorse them either. What is valuable is for professionals in this field to be aware of this reality and personally decide how they want to deal with it. My own approach is to consider it my responsibility to teach clients "middle-class survival skills" with the understanding that it is totally their choice as to whether and how they will make use of them.

The *repetition* principle recognizes that our brains do not learn new behavior in one easy lesson. Clients must practice, practice, practice new actions. Eventually that practice pays off as their new behavior gets easier to do and more automatically initiated. As noted in chapter 1, with practice neural networks develop and strengthen over time.

Phase Five: Feedback (Including Empathy Training)

Accurate feedback about one's actions is crucial in adjusting one's ineffective behavior and in rewarding effective behavior. There are three main sources for feedback. First is the person's own sense of how effective his or her words or deeds were. Second is feedback from one's inner circle of family, close friends, etc. The third source is the larger society's norms, laws, and guidelines and those who represent those positions such as teachers, counselors, and law enforcement. Unfortunately, chronically angry and aggressive clients often develop flawed feedback systems. Their anger biases their ability to listen to or utilize their behavior. They may be especially reluctant to receive negative information about their anger, thus creating a "You are making me angrier by telling me I'm too angry" scenario.

I have found two interventions that help break through this defense of one's anger pattern. Both are aimed at helping clients realize that their angry thoughts and actions are ruining their lives. They improve the client's internal feedback mechanisms. These are the "Bus of your Life" analogy and the "Anger/Aggression Pie" illustration.

The bus of your life

Imagine that your life is like a bus and you are the driver of that bus. All your emotions are on it, riding along and taking turns talking to you as

148

you drive along. Now imagine that your anger stands up, grabs you by the neck, and drags you out of the driver's seat. Next he [or "she," depending on the gender of the client] kicks all your other emotions off the bus. He says you won't need them any more because now you can just get angry about everything. And then he starts aiming at every pothole in the road so you will get even angrier and pick fights with other drivers. He's picking up speed too. Looks like he plans on crashing your vehicle.

How much is your life like this? Who is driving the bus of your life, you or your anger?

How can you get back in the driver's seat of your own life? Are you ready to invite your other emotions back on the bus?

The goal of the above analogy is for clients to face up to their loss of control over their anger. Using an analogy is a good way to involve both brain hemispheres and in particular to help clients receive internal feedback about how bad this loss of control feels.

The second tool I use is called the Anger Pie (see Figure 7.2).

The goal again is to help clients receive accurate internal feedback about the costs of their anger and aggression. Here are directions for facilitating this exercise in an anger or domestic violence offender group.

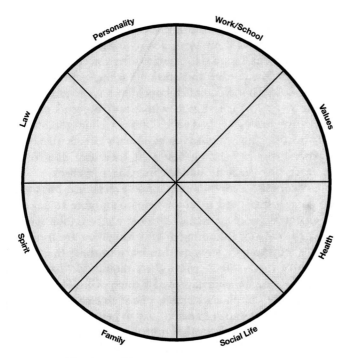

Figure 7.2 The Anger Pie.

I've drawn this circle on the board. I'm asking you to help me fill it in with the costs you personally have incurred due to your anger, aggression, or acts of domestic violence. I only want to list things that actually have happened, not possibilities.

Let's start with the *law*. What bad things have happened in this area because of your anger or aggression? [Examples: "brushes" with the law, arrests, probation, no contact orders . . .]

Now how about your *health*? What's happened there because of your anger and aggression? [Examples: broken bones, cuts, accidents because anger distracted me . . .]

Work and School? [Got fired, no promotion, walked off mad, kicked out of school . . .]

Family? [Cut offs, constant fighting, divorce, no contact with kids . . .]

Social life? [Isolation, loss of older friends, angry friends . . .]

Spirit? [Became "mean-spirited", lost faith in God]

Values? [Broke my promise never to treat my kids like I was treated, guilt and shame about what I've done . . .]

Personality? [Jekyll and Hyde changes, more depressed, hopeless . . .]

This exercise is particularly useful in groups because then the members can view the collective damage done by excessive anger and aggression. However, it is important not to end this exercise after the circle has been filled in. Clients might then leave the session feeling depressed and hopeless. Instead, ask the group how much hope they have to change this picture, to be able to fill in each section with positive events such as working steadily, reconnecting with their children, feeling good about themselves, and living up to their higher values. Usually clients then begin describing how their lives are getting better (if they are) due to the conscious decisions they've made around keeping anger in check.

Feedback from others is certainly important to everybody, but angry and aggressive people often need a lot of help to be able to take in information. The central problem is that chronic anger is like having someone with a very loud voice shouting at you while you are trying to listen to another person. Angry clients need to learn to quiet that angry voice so they can take in messages from others. Standard "listen and hear" exercises definitely help clients improve listening skills. Having two clients in a group repeat each other's words is one such technique.

Empathy training is perhaps an even better way to help clients improve their feedback skills. I spend a great deal of time teaching empathy to my angry clients because I believe failures in empathy are both a major cause of anger problems and an effect of excessive anger.

Ciaramicoli (Ciaramicoli and Ketcham, 2000) suggests two definitions for empathy: "the capacity to understand and respond to the unique experiences of another" (p. 4) and "the bridge spanning the chasm that separates us from each other" (p. 12). His focus is upon the need for individuals to abandon their egocentric position in order to be able to better see and understand others.

McCullough, Worthington, and Rachal (1997) note that there are two kinds of empathy: cognitive and emotional. Cognitive empathy could be defined as "attempting to fully understand the thoughts and reasoning of another," while emotional empathy would then be "attempting to fully comprehend the emotional experience of another." Both processes involve an active, searching, reaching out towards the other (Berecz, 2001) and a reaching inward to make connections between one's own experience and the possible experience of another (Berecz, 2001). This latter effort inevitably involves projection in that empathizer's recall experiences from their own lives that might come close to matching the experiences of another and recollect their thoughts and feelings during those times. However, no two people can have exactly the same total experience so that even the best empathic connections are doomed to be only an approximation of the other's thoughts and feelings. Indeed, Cozolino (2010b) suggests that empathy always takes the form of hypothesis formulation ("Are you angry right now?") followed by feedback ("Yes, but mostly I'm lonely") followed by another hypothesis ("So you're lonely and a little angry. Are you also scared?") as the empathizer's understanding of the other gradually increases.

The empathy circuits in the brain are quite complex. Mirror neurons form the substrate for empathy. These neurons, which are found mostly in the premotor areas of the brain (Iacoboni, 2009), react when someone observes the intentional motion of another. For example, if I were to walk in random movements, your mirror neurons would probably not fire. However, as soon as I began making a bee-line toward a book stand and reached for a book, some of your mirror neurons would indeed fire. These same neurons make up a small portion of all the premotor neurons that would fire if you were the one walking toward the book stand. In other words mirror neurons are interested in the other's intentions. This suggests that empathic inquiry revolves around three questions: "What are you thinking?" (cognitive empathy); "What are you feeling?" (affective empathy); and "What are you doing or planning to do?" (intentionality empathy). As with all things brain-related, ultimately empathy is about survival. If I can read your intentions quickly, I can better protect against dangerous ones.

Mirror neurons function unconsciously. However, empathy does involve deliberate conscious inquiry as well, and several brain regions have been identified that are involved, including the orbitofrontal cortex, the temporal parietal junction, and both hemispheres' temporal poles (Decety and Meyer, 2008). Therefore empathy is a skill that can be developed and increased with conscious effort and practice.

Here are some ways clients can improve their empathy skills.

Bring "conscious intention" to the task (Hanson, 2009, p. 139). Empathy is a learnable skill if one is willing to work consistently at it. Developing this skill is a neuroplastic exercise calling for commitment and regular practice. Eventually, when successful, individuals become more adept at empathy over time.

Become curious about others. Anger often trumps curiosity. It's as if the angry client were saying "I don't want to learn anything about him. I couldn't care less." This lack of interest is actually self-defeating at the feedback phase, since incuriosity leads to poor perception of the other's thoughts, feelings, and intentions. The exercise I use to combat disinterest is to ask each member of the group to share something about themselves that he thinks the others don't know. Group members are usually drawn into each other's lives as clients reveal hidden layers of their personality and experience.

Ask non-judgmental questions. Angry people are usually habitually critical of others. Criticism is part of their general hostility and serves to make them feel safer by keeping people at a distance. The questions they do ask often have a ring of negativity along the lines of "Why did you do that, you idiot?" Clients may need to be taught how simply to ask a neutral question. They particularly need to be taught not to follow an apparently neutral question with criticism and also to be aware of their tone of voice while asking.

Clients should be guided toward asking the three questions noted above: "What was she thinking? What was she feeling? What did she want to happen (What were her intentions)?"

Ask open-ended questions. Angry clients should also be trained to ask open-ended questions, those that cannot be answered with a simple "yes" or "no" response. This helps them reach toward the complexity of the responder's life as well as guard against judgment.

Attend to facial expressions. My anger and domestic violence group members are experts at floor watching, especially when others are sharing important emotional information. It seems that they are either not caring or fear being overwhelmed by their own emotions if they allow meaningful contact. I specifically ask members to raise their heads and make eye contact during these moments.

Practice anticipatory empathy to lessen anger activation. "Sally, you're thinking of telling Jody she's a pig because she gained a few pounds. How would you feel if somebody said that to you?" is an example of anticipatory empathy. This type of preventative approach may help cut off anger before it is expressed, essentially jumping the feedback phase in front of the activation stage in the anger cycle.

Be open to your own self-disclosure. Empathy is a mutual contact sport. In the normal course of interaction both parties progressively share information about themselves. That's why the group exercises described above are designed to get everybody involved. To me that means including the counselors. I believe that we need to be willing to self-disclose and not simply expect our clients to do the same. True, we don't want to take the spotlight off our clients. But I don't think we can teach empathy from a safe distance behind our desks. We need to be willing to enter the fray. I would suggest that the most useful type of self-disclosure involves you sharing situations during which you had strong feelings but also during which you maintained control. It is certainly acceptable, even advisable, to share one's struggles, but not a great idea to share one's defeats.

Phase Six: Deactivation (Including Forgiveness)

As noted in chapter 1, ending an anger or aggression episode often involves making a conscious effort during which regions in the frontal cortex and the hippocampus signal the hypothalamus to disengage the sympathetic nervous system's fight or flight reaction. And, indeed, when I ask clients how they let go of their anger, they often mention a conscious decision such as "I told myself to chill out" or "I remembered what we talked about in counseling and I took a long time out." Needless to add, anger seldom just vanishes. It takes a while for one's adrenalin to be reabsorbed so that calmness is restored. The decision to end one's anger, then, is more accurately a decision to turn off the anger activation system. The practical point here is that when someone says they aren't angry any more, you should ask them if that means they really don't feel any anger in their body or if they mean they are consciously attempting to quit being angry. If the latter, they are still in danger of quick reactivation and should be warned that they need more time to let their body calm down before attempting problem-solving.

Unfortunately, some angry individuals obsess about the injustices they have suffered, reviewing them endlessly while fantasizing about how they might gain revenge. One area of the brain, the caudate nucleus, might be involved here, since it acts as the brain's "gear shifter" (Doidge, 2007) and is associated therefore with obsessive thinking and compulsive behavior. Anger that cannot be deactivated easily turns first into a resentment and then into hatred.

Resentment: "A feeling of displeasure or indignation at some act, remark, person, etc., regarded as causing injury or insult" (*Random House Unabridged Dictionary*, 1993). The development of resentment is a process in which anger is stored rather than released.

153

Hatred: A dictionary definition of hatred is "To dislike intensely or passionately; to feel extreme aversion for or extreme hostility toward another; to detest" (*Random House Unabridged Dictionary*, 1993). My definition is that hatred is "an intense, long-term loathing of another person based upon perceived unrequited injuries." The development of hatred towards someone represents the end product of the resentment process, a point in which one's anger has metaphorically solidified, the result of which is that the hater develops an intense and unchanging loathing of another. Note that loathing implies that the emotion of disgust has been combined with anger, turning the hated person into something evil and less than fully human.

Although hostility in general has been a subject of psychological interest for years, secular scientists paid little attention to the development of resentments and especially to the forgiveness process until fairly recently, apparently deciding to leave that area for more religiously focused scholars. Indeed, there is a rich religious tradition in the sphere of forgiveness. Many religions, including Christianity, Judaism, and Islam emphasize the importance of forgiveness (Kassinove and Tafrate, 2002). However, forgiveness research has begun to flourish within the last two decades, producing suggestive evidence that forgiving is a positive health factor that probably lessens stress and depressive reactions (Enright and Fitzgibbons, 2000). This combination of religious and secular interest in forgiveness is certainly intellectually exciting and important for clients who too often, as is said in Alcoholics Anonymous meetings, have allowed someone to "have free rent in my brain" and now realize that their lives have been greatly diminished by their inability to let go of their resentments.

People can begin to form resentments over as small an event as a slightly thoughtless remark. Usually resenters lump one such minor insult with many others ("Well, that's not the first time she was mean to me. Just the other day she . . .") until they conclude that the other person is full of ill will towards them. Thus, the development of resentment tends to be a *progressive* and *expansive* event, gradually evolving from one piece of unfinished business to many unresolved insults. At some point free-flowing anger turns into a more hardened resentment and then resentment solidifies even further into hate, the absolute conviction that someone, the offender, is evil. A psychological split develops in which the offender becomes totally bad, while the resenter sees himself or herself as completely good – a victim of the offender's malevolence.

Dozier (2002) notes that this splitting reflects a relatively primitive "us–them" dualism centered in the survival-oriented limbic system of the brain. He describes a primitive brain system centered on the amygdala that almost instantly divides external stimuli into threatening and nonthreatening status. Hate develops when a person or group of individuals becomes associated with threat at that level and when that person or group becomes further infused with a sense of danger emanating from higher cortical areas.

There is one exception to this pattern. Sometimes a previously trusted person does something so terrible that it shatters the world view (Flanigan, 1992) of the betrayed individual. One example would be when a spouse suddenly runs off with the person's best friend. This kind of absolute betrayal is devastating, essentially throwing everything that the offended party has believed about the world into doubt. In these situations people can become almost instantly hateful toward the offender. They also demand that others ally with them against the offender and cannot understand how others fail to have the same view of that individual as they do.

Strong resentments do not necessarily fade over time. Amazingly, they even grow stronger. Indeed, some of my clients report that they are angrier and more hateful toward the offender at the time they are seeing me than when the offense occurred years earlier. All this time has been filled with endless repetitions of their victimization scenes, images that have gradually become more extreme as the resenter erases any sense of personal responsibility for his or her injuries and attributes the cause of the hostility entirely to the offender.

People who develop resentments aren't just complaining about an abstract moral injustice. Instead, they feel deeply personally wounded. Specifically, they complain about three kinds of injuries: commissions, omissions, and shortfalls. *Commissions* occur when people believe someone actively attacks them, such as by stealing their money or being unfaithful. These wounds are relatively easy to identify and are usually what brings clients into treatment. *Omissions* are more difficult to identify because this term refers to situations in which others could have but did not do good, kind, or nice things for the client. An example would be someone who complains about all the times a parent did not come to a ball game or theatrical performance in which the client was participating. Finally, *shortfalls* occur when the offender does "too little, too late." For instance, one of my clients complained that her mother had called her recently to apologize for all the mean things she had told her when she was growing up. "But now I'm a grown woman and the damage has been done. What good does this do me now? After we hung up I just felt even angrier with her." Shortfalls make people painfully aware of how much they have longed for another's love, interest, or caring, and how bitter they have become over the years because they did not receive those gifts to which they feel entitled.

The main characteristics of the resentment-building process are summarized below.

- Progressive and expansive over time.
- A deep sense of being personally wounded.
- A sense of moral injustice.
- Interference with normal life.
- Becoming stuck in the past.
- Regressive splitting pattern.
- Vengeful fantasies.
- Active search for allies.
- Tendency to expand, generalize, endure, and intensify.
- Obsessive thoughts.
- Inability to disengage.

I ask my clients to picture their resentment/hatred as a circle at the center of their being. Then I suggest four paths they could take to move away from that condition. These paths reflect four conceivable goals therapists can offer clients who want to reduce the amount of time and energy they spend resenting others.

The *first* is to find ways to *let go* of the offense and the offender so that the client can lead a more normal life focused upon the present instead of the past. The aim here is not to work through the issues that have caused the resentment, but simply to help clients get on with their lives. Clients who accept this goal usually state that they are sick and tired of carrying their resentments around with them. They want and need encouragement to do things like socializing and having fun. They may still become upset when they think about the offending party but success is measured by their report that they are thinking about that person less and less frequently.

The *second* goal is to achieve a state of *emotional indifference* toward the offender, as indicated by someone saying "I don't have any real emotional response any more when I hear that person's name. I used to get so upset, but now I don't care any more." These people tend to state that time has gradually eroded their anger. This state of indifference is usually associated with the ability of the client to achieve a good life despite past wounds, particularly in the areas where the most damage occurred ("My uncle stole my inheritance, but I more than made up for that loss within a few years. I don't need that money, so I don't think about that much anymore").

A *third* possible goal is a *physical restoration or reconciliation* of a damaged or broken relationship. This development usually demands a restoration of trust between the parties, something most difficult to achieve when there has been a serious betrayal within a relationship.

Finally, a *fourth* goal is the achievement of a state of *compassion* towards someone who has been hated. This last goal demands an end to the splitting process in that the offender is recognized once again as a human being who can be respected and loved. This transformative process normally requires energy, commitment, and hard work over an extended period of time. Forgiveness is the name for this process.

Forgiveness is a complicated process with many components. A look at two definitions of forgiveness is illustrative in that regard:

> A willingness to abandon one's right to resentment, negative judgment, and indifferent behavior toward one who unjustly injured us, while fostering the undeserved qualities of compassion, generosity, and even love toward him or her.
>
> (Enright, Freedman, and Rique, 1998, pp. 46–47)

> A motivational transformation whereby people in close relationships become less motivated to retaliate . . . and more motivated to initiate constructive responses . . . as a function of their ability to experience both cognitive and affective empathy for the offender.
>
> (McCullough et al., 1997, p. 323)

These authors, as well as Kaminer et al. (2000), emphasize the voluntary nature of the forgiveness process. It is important for therapists to keep this in mind so as not to attempt to force a client to move in that direction.

Forgiveness allows the forgiver to let go of hurt and bitterness (Berecz, 2001). The forgiver must make a personal commitment to refrain from attempting to retaliate against the offender (Freedman, 1999). Finally, when successful, the forgiver may discover that he or she has a renewed sense of caring and compassion for the offender, in essence allowing that person back into one's heart (Karen, 2001).

Forgiveness is often confused with other concepts. Therefore it may be helpful for clients to have a list available that indicates what forgiveness is (described above) and what it is not. Some important distinctions are these.

Forgiveness is NOT:

Reconciliation (although it can lead to reconciliation). Although some authors suggest that reconciliation is indeed part of the forgiveness process (Smedes, 1984; Hargrave, 1994; Coleman, 1998), I believe there is a fundamental difference between these two functions. Forgiveness, to me, fundamentally is an internal process that centers around individuals rediscovering a sense of compassion for the offenders. Reconciliation, on the other hand, is an active social process in which contact is renewed and some positive relationship redeveloped between the offended party and the offender. The key for effective reconciliation, then, would be a renewal of trust in the offender, whereas forgiveness more involves a renewal of caring.

Forgetting. Although "forgive and forget" is a popular saying, this concept probably is responsible for a great deal of the confusion that surrounds the concept of forgiveness as well as many people's reluctance to undertake the process. Simply forgetting an offense would just be a way for people to set themselves up to being hurt again in the same manner. But real forgiveness does not necessitate forgetting the offense. Rather, forgiveness is better stated to be a way of remembering without bitterness and hatred.

Excusing, pardoning, or minimizing an injustice. People who have been harmed may choose these actions as ways to end hostilities. However, they are by no means a necessary or expected part of forgiveness. Furthermore, these choices may actually conflict with forgiveness if offered too quickly or if they allow the offender to deny responsibility for his or her behavior. The message of forgiveness is "I care for you despite what you've done to me," not "It doesn't matter what you did to me because I care for you."

A loss or sign of weakness. Some clients confuse forgiveness with submission. They mistakenly believe that forgiving means giving in to the offender. But the truth is that forgiveness is a sign of strength and positive self-esteem. People need courage to confront their wounds. It is perfectly reasonable simultaneously to forgive another while making a powerful internal commitment not to allow oneself to be used or abused again by that same person. If anything, forgiveness evens the balance of power between the two parties as the wounded person renounces the role of victim.

There is one situation in which forgiveness would be a sign of weakness, however. That is when someone forgives another because of extreme pressure from that person ("I said I'm sorry so now you have to forgive me") or others such as friends, family, or clergy. These acts of forgiveness will usually prove false in the long run since they were made to appease others rather than from a sense of internal conviction.

Letting go. As noted previously, this phrase more implies choosing not to think or feel about what happened rather than working through the hurt and pain of a difficult experience. Forgiveness does help facilitate getting on with life but more by going through than just letting go of the event.

Just a decision. Forgiveness work usually takes time and energy. Indeed, it can be a lengthy process, stretching into months or years. The decision most people make is to begin this process. In other words, "I want to forgive you" precedes "I forgive you." Nor, for that matter, is forgiveness just a thought or a feeling. Forgiveness also involves altering one's behavior by declining to undertake acts of hostility towards the offender and possibly treating that person more kindly.

Possible benefits from forgiveness

DiGiuseppe and Tafrate note that "Forgiveness appears crucial to the treatment of anger because so much anger arises from condemning those who have trespassed against us" (2007, p. 360). Clearly, the forgiving process is frequently fairly long and difficult. Nevertheless, people do make this effort because they realize that they will reap many benefits if they can forgive their offenders. These benefits are:

- Healing and resolving pain from an old wound.
- Releasing long-held anger that interferes with daily functioning and emotional well-being.
- Expressing anger appropriately rather than merely complaining or aggressing inappropriately against the offender ("One cannot forgive if one cannot express and recognize their anger" – Freedman, 1999).
- Expressing anger appropriately rather than misdirecting it against others or oneself.
- Suffering less depression, hopelessness, cynicism, suspiciousness, anxiety.
- Gaining an improved ability to live in the present as against the past.
- Setting the stage for reconciliation and restoration of relationships if the other party is available and responsible.
- Achieving a sense of personal empowerment while freeing oneself from playing the role of a victim.
- Increasing psychological maturity: moving from a relatively primitive splitting process to a more integrated sense of self and others.
- Developing greater moral integrity: more specifically, gaining the ability to undertake a "supererogatory" moral task (one that is not absolutely compulsory but a positive moral choice) (Enright and Fitzgibbons, 2000).

Certainly not all clients consciously think about all these possible benefits of forgiving. But most realize that in hanging on to old resentments, something has gone wrong in their lives. They sense that they can improve their lives through forgiving their offenders. They may realize that they can never be free from the urge to commit another act of domestic violence until they forgive their partner or ex-partner for his or her transgressions. And yet forgiveness is not simply and only a gift to oneself. It is also a gift to the offending person in that forgiveness opens the possibility for reconciliation. This double-sided aspect of forgiveness reveals "the paradox of forgiveness . . . When we give to others the gift of mercy and compassion, we ourselves are healed" (Enright et al., 1998).

Conditions that improve the likelihood of successful forgiving of an offender

Forgiveness is always possible, no matter the severity of a wound. Mothers have forgiven the murderers of their children (Jaeger, 1998), spouses their partners who have betrayed them, adult children their parents who physically or sexually abused them. Nevertheless, certain conditions improve the likelihood for successful forgiveness to occur. One such condition is that the wounding event is over and not being repeated. Who, for instance, would ask a wife to forgive a wayward husband for his womanizing while that man clearly intends to continue that behavior unabated? Forgiveness can definitely be utilized with relatively fresh wounds (although some clients should be warned against fleeing from their anger by too hastily forgiving an offender before fully dealing with the wounding event and its immediate sequelae), but it is critical to help clients achieve a realistic sense of physical and emotional security before attempting to do so.

It also greatly helps when the offender expresses sincere remorse repeatedly (Fitness, 2001) and when the offender makes persistent constructive efforts to repair the relationship. For instance, one of my clients decided to confront an elderly relative who had sexually abused him years before. Expecting denial, minimization, and justification from the relative, my client was astonished when that man fully acknowledged his wrongdoing, repeatedly spoke of his great remorse for having damaged my client, and begged him for forgiveness. The offender had gone through treatment years before for his unacceptable sexual proclivities, but had been unable to locate my client to make amends. My client was still reluctant to trust his abuser, but over time was able to both forgive and reconnect with this man.

In addition, research in the area of shame and guilt (Tangney and Dearing, 2002; Potter-Efron, 2002) would appear to predict that forgiveness will be most successfully accomplished when both the wrongdoer and the injured party experience relatively little shame and the wrongdoer feels more guilt than shame. This is probably because guilt feelings tend to push people toward restorative actions that heal relationships, whereas shame leads toward interpersonal withdrawal.

Two critical processes in forgiveness: empathy and reframing

I have already described empathy in general previously in this chapter. Here I will apply it directly to the forgiveness process. Empathy certainly plays a central role in this effort (McCullough et al., 1997).

Empathy demands that the forgiver become curious about and take interest in the offender as a human being. In this regard Ciaramicoli (Ciaramicoli and Ketcham, 2000) suggests several key questions that the forgiver could ask the offender (either face-to-face or in imaginative dialogue):

Who are you?
What do you think?
What do you feel?
What means the most to you?
What can I learn from you and about you?

I would add:

How are we alike?
How are we different?
What would it feel like to be him or her?

I would also suggest two more useful empathy-increasing questions: Have you ever needed another's forgiveness for something you said or did? What was that like? These questions might help lessen the good/bad split that underlies hating another person.

Reframing is another, related process that also enhances clients' ability to forgive. Reframing has been defined as "to rethink a situation and see it with a fresh perspective" (Enright and Fitzgibbons, 2000) and as "seeing the wrongdoer in context" (North, 1998). More specifically, North (1998) suggests that reframing involves understanding the pressures the offender was under at the time of the offense, appreciating the person's personality as a result of his or her developmental history, and separating the wrongdoer from the wrong committed.

Enright and Fitzgibbons (2000) suggest that people wanting to forgive ask these questions:

What was it like for the offender growing up?
What was it like for the offender at the time of the offense?
Can you see him or her as a member of the human community?
Is he or she a child of God?
What was your relationship like other than in the context of the specific offense?
How may you have contributed to the offender's questionable behavior?

This last question must be asked cautiously, if at all. For example, it might be inadvisable to ask it of a person struggling to escape overwhelming feelings of maladaptive guilt (Potter-Efron, 2002) about participating in incest as a child. However, the question might be very relevant in situations such as a particularly nasty divorce, in which both parties became mean spirited and vindictive toward each other.

One client I worked with made use of many of these empathy and reframing questions as part of his effort to forgive his father. Melvin, a 40-year-old roofer and recovering drug addict, asked for help figuring out how to handle his actively alcoholic father, a man who had brutalized him in the past and once had literally thrown Melvin in a dumpster because "You are garbage so you belong in the garbage can." Melvin maintained a fragile relationship with his father but often felt hatred toward him as he remembered past abuses. Furthermore, his father still became verbally abusive after he'd been drinking, coming over to Melvin's house to berate Melvin and all his siblings for being ungrateful to their poor old Dad. Still, Melvin wanted some relationship with his father "because after all, he is the only father I'll ever have." I asked him the series of questions noted above over a period of two or three sessions. Here are some of Melvin's responses.

Empathy questions

Who is he? "A sad old man who hates the world."

What does he think? "That everybody hates him – and he's right. I'm the only one left in the family who even talks with him any more."

What does he feel? "Bitter. Abandoned."

What means the most to him? "His booze. That's all he has left."

What can you learn from him? "Never to go back to my drugs or I'll end up like him."

How are you alike? "We're both addicts. We're both full of hate."

How are you different? "I want to quit feeling that way, he doesn't."

What would it be like to feel like him? "Terrible. He's miserable. He's so unhappy."

Have you ever needed another person's forgiveness? "Yeah, my wife's for all the drinking and drugging I used to do."

Reframing questions

What was it like for your father growing up? "His Dad was an alcoholic too. They were dirt poor."

What was it like for your Dad that day he threw you in the dumpster? "He was drunk. He'd just lost his job. He was probably depressed too."

Can you see him as a child of God? Can you see him as a member of the human community? "I'm trying."

How may you have contributed to the offender's questionable behavior? [Not asked].

What was your relationship like, other than when he was abusing you?
"Sometimes we had a real good time together. We were fishing buddies
down at the lake near our home and we'd spend hours there just
fishing, not talking much, just being there with each other."

Melvin's animosity toward his father gradually abated as he was able to
see that man as a human being rather than a monster. His honest response
to the question about whether or not he could see his father as a child of
God or a member of the human community – "I'm trying" – was especially
poignant. Since forgiveness is usually a slowly developing state of
consciousness, many clients can only get there by trying, failing, and
trying again until they finally do achieve a true sense of forgiveness.

Stages and processes of forgiveness

Many writers on forgiveness suggest that forgiveness takes place slowly
with the forgiver gradually passing through several stages. However, each
person's experience is different. Also, few people travel through these
stages in a linear fashion. Instead, many individuals travel rather
unpredictably from one to another, back and forth, often revisiting many
times various stations on the path of forgiveness. As might be expected,
the names for the stages vary by author. Furthermore, some models
emphasize not only forgiveness but also reconciliation, while others
concentrate only upon forgiveness *per se*. Here are some of the stage
models suggested in the literature:

Berecz (2001): Either: I) Rapport; II) Reframe; III) Reconcile or
I) Rapport; II) Reframe; III) Release.
   The value of this framework is in its flexibility. Berecz allows for two
possible end products of the forgiveness process. Reconciliation can
occur under certain circumstances, which I associate with the
re-development of trust. But on other occasions the forgiver releases the
offender from further antagonism and in doing so releases himself or
herself from hate.

Enright and Fitzgibbons (2000); Enright (2001):

   I) Uncovering: insight into how injustice and injury have compromised
      life.
  II) Decision: understand the nature of forgiveness and commit to
      forgiving.
 III) Work: gain cognitive understanding of the offender and begin to
      view offense in a new light that helps produce a positive change in
      affect toward the offender.

IV) Deepening: finding increased meaning in the suffering, feeling more connected with others, less negative effect, renewed purpose in life.

This is a very detailed stage model that is further sub-divided into 20 phases. Each phase is described carefully and clients are given information as to how to understand and utilize each.

Smedes (1984): I) Hurt; II) Hate; III) Heal; IV) Coming together.
This reconciliation model is gently presented in Smede's small and easily comprehended book intended for the general public.

Hargrave (1994):

I) Exonerating Phase: The goal here is to salvage a relationship through insight and understanding.
II) Forgiving Phase: The goal here is to reconcile through giving the offender an opportunity to make compensatory efforts and with overt acts of forgiveness.

This is another reconciliation model that focuses upon the appropriate acts of contrition made by the offending person.

Coleman (1998): I) Identify the injury; II) Confront the other to confirm the reality of the injury; III) Dialogue to make sense of the suffering; IV) Forgiveness as a leap of faith and willingness to trust; V) Letting go of the wound.
The fourth stage includes both a leap of faith and a willingness to trust the offender. Therapists must be careful here to help clients delay these actions until there is some evidence that it is safe to take them.

Flanigan (1992): I) Naming the injury; II) Claiming the injury; III) Blaming the injurer; IV) Balancing the scales; V) Choosing to forgive; VI) Emergence of a new self.
Flanigan's model was developed by questioning survivors of exceptionally painful betrayers. These survivors initially believed that the offenses they had endured were unforgivable. Nevertheless, many of them did manage to forgive their offenders through stages that they described retroactively.
Although Enright's model is probably the best researched of the ones presented above, it would probably be fair to state that the names and details of forgiveness stages will continue to be elaborated and clarified over the next several years. Any of the ones presented above could be helpful for clients who need some direction.

*Exercises/helpful ideas for clients as they go
through the forgiveness process*

Clients often need help as they attempt to go through the forgiveness process, in part because there is no absolutely clear path that inevitably takes one there. Here are some suggestions that I have found useful to offer.

Make lists of the ways in which carrying one's resentments harms the client. Forgiving is not entirely self-centered in that acts of forgiveness re-create bridges between people and may lead to reconciliation. Still, the primary beneficiary of forgiving is the forgiver, since that person will be freed from his or her obsessive thinking about the offender and related compulsive behaviors. Thus it may be useful to make lists both of the ways that continuing to carry resentment hurts the client as well as of possible gains that would occur as the client forgives the offender.

Make a daily commitment to forgiveness. "Today I will try to forgive ..." Achieving a state of forgiveness takes time, during which people often vacillate between wanting to keep hating and truly wanting to forgive their offenders. For this reason the saying "trying is dying" does not apply. Instead, clients should be encouraged to try to forgive (Enright, 2001) and rewarded for that effort, even when the results are less than completely successful.

Read about forgiveness. There are many excellent books available for the general public that describe and encourage forgiveness from either a secular or religious perspective. Clients should be encouraged to read as much as they can on this topic since each volume is likely to handle the topic slightly differently.

Journaling. It is useful for some clients to keep a daily journal in which they can complete specific forgiveness assignments (Enright, 2001) as well as have a place in which to write about their desire to forgive along with the difficulties in so doing. This journal should not be used as a general diary and should only be utilized for forgiveness materials.

Forgiveness rituals. Rituals are valuable with many clients because they serve as a way to let go of the symbols of old wounds. Each ritual must be individually tailored to the needs and style of the client. Caution should be used in these rituals, however, not to increase the splitting process, for instance by burning every picture one has of the offender. Rather, a client would be better encouraged to put those pictures away for a while (to be replaced with pictures of what or whom?) until the client feels ready to allow positive feelings about the offender back into his or her thoughts.

Letter writing. No-send letters shared in therapy but not usually mailed to the offender can be very rewarding. Early in therapy these letters could describe the wounding that the client suffered because of the offender's behavior. Later, they might either offer or withhold forgiveness. These letters might include such phrases as:

"I am not ready to forgive you yet because . . ."
"I am beginning to think I can forgive you because . . ."
"I can let go of you now."
"I have begun feeling compassion toward you."
"I forgive you."

Prayer, positive visualizations, and gift-giving. The common theme of these three actions is the need for clients to move from a totally negative perception of the offender toward a more positive perception of that person as a normal human being for whom the client can feel positive regard despite the injuries that individual has caused. Praying for the offender is often useful for religiously oriented clients, especially those who have split so strongly that they have come to believe the offender is in league with the devil.

Patricia Potter-Efron developed a visualization (Potter-Efron and Potter-Efron, 1991) in which clients first visualize something good happening to themselves, such as getting hugs from all their children, and then imagine something just that wonderful happening to the person they are trying to forgive. This task helps clients feel compassion toward the offender and also helps them realize the difference between simply pitying the offender as against truly wishing them peace and joy.

Prayers and visualizations may be followed by the concrete action of giving the wrongdoer the gifts of a smile, a small present, or a few kind words. One way to approach this is to have clients develop an "as if" list (Potter-Efron and Potter-Efron, 1991) of positive things they could do with or for each person. Then they are free to do some or all of these things over time, with no insistence that any specific behavior must ever be done. This process both allows clients to stay in control of their behavior and encourages them to change what they do over time.

Develop metaphors or analogies for the forgiving process. Clients may gain a more clear sense of mission when they develop a metaphor that vividly describes a forgiving process. One person might utilize a scene in which he or she loads one's resentments onto a train and sends the train far away to dump the stuff (and then returns to be used again as needed). Another person might envision a cleansing scene such as bathing under a waterfall of forgiveness.

Discuss the difference between a wrongdoer's apparent intent and the impact of their actions. An offender, temporarily angry at his wife, shoves her out of his path as he leaves the room. Yes, he wanted at that moment to harm her. But he certainly did not realize shoving her that way would cause her to twist her back and cause a permanent injury. So should she hold him responsible for only his intent (to harm her a little) or the impact of his action (permanent damage)? What should her forgiveness work center upon? The answer is probably both, since both intent and impact are meaningful concepts both legally and morally. However, the two concepts should be separated in the client's mind and work, especially since injured parties may erroneously assume that the wrongdoer intended all aspects of the harm done to them, while the wrongdoer may confuse lack of intent to harm another with lack of damage to that party (Ferch, 1998).

Discuss times the wrongdoer needed forgiveness from others. As noted previously, this thought process helps clients lessen their tendency towards splitting that turns them into a helpless victim and their offenders into manifestations of evil.

Utilize empathy and reframing questions. These questions have been described previously in this chapter. They also are useful to lessen splitting and to increase feelings of compassion, respect, and love toward the offender.

Role-play having the client speak to or with the wrongdoer: empty chair or two-chair dialogue. Two exercises long associated with Gestalt therapy can be useful with clients seeking to work through some of their feelings toward an offender. The first simply involves imagining that the offender is sitting in front of the client in an empty chair (or one in which the client has placed a picture of the offender). This monologue would begin with a phrase such as "Here's what I want to say to you so listen carefully . . ." and the client might express any mixture of anger, rage, sadness, compassion, and love. The second exercise involves the client moving between two chairs and role-playing the imagined responses of the offender to his or her comments. This process might be particularly useful when the offender is deceased or physically unavailable.

CASE STUDY

How To Go Through the Anger Cycle Very Badly

Joseph is a 25-year-old custodian. He comes to me seeking anger management help as part of a diversion program after he got into trouble with the law for an offense even he considers "idiotic." He explains that he was walking through the check out lane of a local grocery store where he had selected a bunch of good looking grapes he planned to consume immediately. "I was hungry and tired," he adds, having just come off a 12-hour work day. He handed his money to the clerk who returned his change. Joseph counted the change and immediately became angry. "You moron," he shouted at the hapless clerk, "do you think I can't count?" He began ranting to the point that the store manager ran over to try to calm him down. Instead, Joseph went into a near rage and ended up smashing the grapes onto the counter, swearing loudly, and storming off. Unfortunately for him the manager copied his license plate and called the police. They contacted him the next day and he drove down to the police station only to become irate again at what happened and also at the police for bothering him. That's when he got charged with disorderly conduct.

And here's the quirkiest aspect of this whole affair: the clerk gave Joseph 50 cents too much change, not too little. I wonder what might have happened if she had given him back a whole dollar extra.

Let's track Joseph's mistakes though the anger cycle:

1. Activation phase. Tired and hungry Joseph enters the fray pre-triggered for battle. He immediately accepts a very minor anger invitation – receiving 50 cents too much change.
2. Modulation phase. Joseph turns a small incident into a large one by deciding the clerk's behavior constitutes a grievous insult. He treats a "2" as a "9" on both the seriousness anger scale and his emotional reactivity scale.
3. Preparation phase. The clerk and store manager try to alleviate the situation, but Joseph will have none of it. Instead of being able to think clearly about how to resolve the problem he continues to yell.
4. Action phase. Joseph springs into action by smashing the grapes onto the counter, swearing loudly, and storming off. To say the least, this violates the principle of acting in moderation. He's still too angry to care and the only principle he's following is "I'll show them not to mess with me!"
5. Feedback phase. Joseph was still angry even when contacted the next day by the police. Instead of receiving the message he needed to get, that he had done something wrong and needed to take responsibility, he simply reactivated his anger at the police station and paid the price by getting charged with disorderly conduct. Only much later, in my office, was he able to realize he had done something "stupid, stupid, stupid."
6. Deactivation phase. Joseph estimated he was really mad for at least 24 hours after the event. During that time he got into an argument with his wife and ruminated about previous times in his estimation that he had been called stupid.

Six phases of the anger cycle, six serious mistakes. The positive news, though, is that Joseph did work on his anger. We went through each stage so he could develop ways to become angry less often and with less damaging results.

Summary

There are six phases in a typical anger management cycle: activation, modulation, preparation, action, feedback, and deactivation. The earlier phases are least under conscious control but are amenable to preventative interventions such as relaxation. Later phases are more amenable to cognitive intervention. Clients can readily understand this phase model, identify which phases are problematic for them, and practice new thoughts and behaviors to give them better mastery of their anger.

8

GROUP TREATMENT
FOR DOMESTIC VIOLENCE
OFFENDERS

Three topics will be discussed in this chapter: 1) core topics that should be covered in any domestic violence offender treatment program; 2) additional highly recommended topics that improve the quality of treatment; 3) an experimental brain-change focused domestic violence treatment program the author has been running for the last several years.

Most of this chapter deals with content. However, let me begin by mentioning two important process issues. First, as with any group, the first goal should be to get members talking with each other about important aspects of their lives, including but not wholly restricted to potentially violent interactions. We begin each group with a check-in, sometimes starting with a question for each person to discuss (such as "Who do you trust more, men or women?") to get them speaking. These check-ins normally take about 10–15 minutes total, but it is not unusual for someone to bring up something truly troubling them ("I really miss my kids. My ex refused to let me see them this weekend"), which leads to extended discussions. Care must be taken, though, not to allow check-ins to become time-wasting excursions into car engines, football rivalries, etc.

Closely related to getting people talking is getting people trusting. We very carefully inform the participants about keeping confidentiality amongst them. We also tell them exactly what we must report to their probation officers and other authorities. Here facilitators must walk a fine line between guaranteeing too much ("I won't tell your p.o. anything you say, period") in order to build trust or too little ("Whatever you say here is public information and I will report you for anything you are doing against the law"). Trust generally builds slowly and is all too easily broken. Nevertheless, our experience is that most participants do gradually grow more trusting of their colleagues and counselors.

Domestic Violence Offender Treatment Program:
Educational Focus

Historically, treatment for any condition usually begins with the most extreme cases and then gradually moves toward treating people with less severe conditions. For example, alcoholism treatment began with inpatient programs in which chronically addicted patients stayed for months. Eventually, though, people with moderate alcohol problems who still had jobs and families were identified and sent into outpatient programs. The next phase occurred as the general population was "treated" through prevention programs that emphasize the dangers of alcohol even to the casual drinker ("Never drink and drive").

Similarly but much more recently, treatment for domestic violence began by targeting the worst offenders, namely extremely abusive men essentially identified as "lifers" with a long history of violent abuse, often with multiple victims. These men were basically considered hopeless and women were advised to steer clear from them. They were labeled "batterers" and "perpetrators." Incarceration and total re-education were considered the only treatment options. However, especially with mandatory arrest laws, the concept of domestic violence has steadily expanded. One result is that less violent individuals, for example a man who indeed hit his wife in an argument that got out of control but has no previous history of violence, may get sent into "one size fits all" programs designed for severe offenders. It would be better to address the needs of these people through programs specifically designed for "minimal" to "moderate" offenders. That is why we have two levels of treatment at our clinic, as described below.

Law enforcement has begun moving in this direction as well. For example, the High Point, North Carolina police department has developed four levels of intervention, ranging from "first call" warning responses to something more like "keep a close watch and be ready with powerful penalties" for those regarded as most dangerous (based on factors such as a history of violence and previous disregard of restraining orders) (Sumner, 2014).

Note also that the concept of domestic violence has expanded to include women and gay and lesbian partners. Gradually the field, and American society, has moved from "You shouldn't beat your wife" to "Nobody should ever be hit." In the same manner domestic abuse has come to include verbal aggression, "which hurts just as much or more than physical attack." These changes are generally positive but do involve the risk of over-labeling and over-treating some people.

Domestic violence treatment programs can be labeled educational or treatment programs. Educational programs tend to be shorter in duration and intended for "first timers" with no previous history of violence and

171

no or little previous criminal behavior. They are essentially designed around the concept that anyone could commit an act of domestic violence when highly stressed. The goal is to give these clients enough information to lessen the possibility that a single episode will morph into a pattern.

The following 10-week program illustrates this type of program.

Week 1: *Orientation.* Responsibilities of participants; limited confidentiality; our duty to warn; agency's relationship to other agencies regarding this program; domestic abuser laws; signed waiver of confidentiality; program expectation of full attendance and consequences of non-attendance or inappropriate participation; written contract for non-violent behavior.

An anger logbook is assigned. Clients are expected to keep track of situations in which they could have become angry or violent and to consider what they thought, felt, and did during these encounters. Each week they are expected to share this material during the initial check-in period. They are also asked to indicate how they have utilized materials presented in the sessions.

Week 2: *Negative Effects of Domestic Violence on Self.* Eight ways your act(s) of domestic violence have messed up your life. This lecture utilizes the "Anger Pie" described in chapter 7 to help clients realize how their violence is self-destructive.

Week 3: *Negative Effects of Domestic Violence upon Others.* Partner, Children, Family, Community. Victim witnesses greatly add value to this presentation.

Week 4: *Causes of Domestic Violence.* Male Power and Control model. Sociocultural basis for male violence; sexism and gender role stereotyping, etc.

Other explanatory models: genetic predisposition/brain injury/physical causes; emotional/psychological instability; alcohol/drug abuse, etc.

The Power and Control Wheel of Pence and Paymar (1993) is presented but also other explanatory models.

Week 5: *The Many Kinds of Violent and Controlling Behaviors: from Brute Force to Subtle Coercive Tactics.* Members are asked to identify ways they try to control others ranging from passive aggression and verbal abuse to life-threatening attacks.

Week 6: *Anger Management: Behavioral Interventions.* Time out; increasing your awareness of triggers, and signs of loss of control, etc. Simple tactics that help reduce the likelihood of violence are introduced and role played.

Week 7: *Anger Management: Cognitive Interventions.* Hot thoughts to cool thoughts; disputation methods; increasing flexibility, etc. Here basic cognitive therapy techniques are presented.

Week 8: *Anger Management: Affective Interventions.* Relaxation training and stress management. Recognition of full range of emotions, etc. Stress reduction is emphasized in this session with breathing exercises practiced.

Week 9: *Anger Management/Affective Interventions: Empathy Training.* Group members practice making empathic inquiries during group.

Week 10: *Anger Management: Existential Interventions.* Positive life goals etc. Group members are encouraged to utilize their strengths to move toward their life goals, thus reducing frustration and hopelessness that contribute to domestic violence episodes.

As noted above, it is very useful to find a good victim witness to explain to this group how it feels to be physically and verbally attacked by one's life partner. The following handout is useful to help participants gain empathy for the recipients of their violence. Note that I use feminine pronouns in this handout since I work primarily with men, but the questions apply to either gender.

Victim Witness Speaker: Gaining Empathy

Today I've invited a person here to speak about living in a domestically violent relationship. I ask you to listen non-defensively and non-judgmentally. Just hear what she says and try to put yourself in her shoes. That's what empathy means – to put yourself in another person's shoes so you can better understand how that person thinks and feels.

You have to become interested in others in order to develop empathy. So here are a few questions to think about while listening to the speaker.

During a Violent Episode:

- What was she feeling (Scared, terrified, angry, hurt, sad . . .)?
- What was she thinking (How to get away, wanting to fight back, making her point . . .)?
- What did she do (Fight, flight, freeze . . .) and why did she do that?

Right After a Violent Episode

- Why did she or didn't she call 911?
- How did she feel?
- What effects did the episode have on her love for her partner? For her trust of him?
- What kept her in the relationship even though she was the recipient of violence?

Longer-Term Effects

- What finally caused this person to leave the relationship for good?
- How long did it take before she began to feel safe (if ever)?
- What effects have this chapter in her life had on her self-worth and sense of self?

Questions For You:

- What would you think and feel if you were slapped, pushed around, restrained, burned, cut, beaten, or raped by someone who said they loved you?
- Have you ever been in a relationship with someone you were afraid of (maybe when you were growing up)? What was that like? How was that like this speaker's experience? How was it different?

Extended Domestic Violence Offender Treatment Program

Treatment-oriented domestic violence offender treatment programs are much longer, frequently 50 sessions in length, either meeting weekly (California) or biweekly (Wisconsin). They are targeted for relatively severe offenders of both genders. This allows more time for designated topics, but also for the introduction of new themes. The greater time frame allows members the chance to develop more trust and to practice new behaviors. For example, anger management can be extended to include topics like conflict resolution, assertiveness training, taking internal time outs, how to handle another person's anger, dealing with anger in the workplace so as not to bring it home, etc.

Here is an alphabetically arranged list of possible topics and the reasons for including them. Note they all can be presented in an educational format, while some may also be included in a therapeutic treatment program:

a) *Anger management.* Helping clients gain control of the emotion most likely to lead to acts of domestic violence.

Typical sessions: 1) Time out; 2) Fair fighting.

b) *Attachment dynamics.* Insecure attachment is highly correlated with acts of domestic violence. Clients who gain an understanding of their attachment vulnerabilities are less likely to develop dangerous patterns of jealousy and neediness.

Typical sessions: 1) Four types of attachment; 2) Bonding dynamics.

c) *Brain-change.* A brain-change oriented domestic violence offender treatment program can circumvent client oppositionality and motivate them toward personally chosen patterns of change.

Typical sessions: 1) You can change your brain; 2) Develop a brain-change plan.

d) *Causes and effects of domestic violence/legal issues.* Individual, family, group, and societal reasons for domestic abuse should be considered here. Also clients must be made aware of relevant laws and normative expectations.

Typical sessions: 1) This is the law; 2) Negative effects of domestic violence upon self/others.

e) *Cognitive-behavioral therapy.* The cognitive-behavioral approach is the best documented effective treatment for domestic violence offenders.

Typical sessions: 1) Aggression-increasing thoughts; 2) Thought-stopping.

f) *Development of trust.* Many clients actively distrust just about everybody in their world, including their relationship partner. We present a trust continuum ranging from absolute distrust (paranoia) to absolute trust (gullibility) to help clients discover and alter their "gut feelings" about their partner's and the world's trustworthiness.

Typical sessions: 1) Trust continuum; 2) Past wounds/present fears.

g) *Emotional intelligence/empathy training/victim witness.* Here the goal is to help people who may have been trained to avoid their emotions (except anger) learn how to experience a range of emotions as well as better comprehending the emotions of others.

Typical sessions: 1) Empathy training; 2) Victim witness session.

h) *Family of origin dynamics.* Domestic violence offenders may well have been the recipients of violence as children as well as witnesses to their parents' violence. Helping group members discover how their history has affected them can help them gain better control over their current behavior.

Typical sessions: 1) Violence when a child; 2) Positive family models.

i) *Gender dynamics.* Gender dynamics are at the heart of the traditional power and control model of domestic violence. The attitudes and beliefs of each gender toward the other must be considered as well as real differences between genders. Sexual violence is another important topic in this area.

Typical sessions: 1) Gender beliefs and realities; 2) Power and Control model.

j) *Grief, loss, and depression.* These problems may be hidden, especially by men who are reluctant to advertise their "weakness." Since low levels of serotonin are linked both with depression and acts of impulsive aggression, it is important to discuss these topics in group.

Typical sessions: 1) Grief and loss; 2) Depression and violence.

k) *Positive psychology.* Positive psychology places a premium upon emphasizing a client's strengths as against repairing their deficits. Helping clients identify and utilize these strengths improves self-esteem and may lower the risk for defensive aggression.

Typical sessions: 1) Character styles; 2) Being yourself at your best.

l) *Positive relationships, positive parenting, and mutual respect.* Most of our clients, male and female, want to be good parents and partners. Some just don't know how to do that since they received no modeling about positive parenting and positive relationships in childhood. The pros and cons of spanking, for instance, are discussed in group, as well as teaching non-violent disciplinary techniques.

Typical sessions: 1) 1-2-3 Magic; 2) Characteristics of a good relationship.

m) *Psychological and physical safety.* The question here is how could group members increase both their actual physical safety and their internal sense of psychological safety? The former may necessitate some participants ending dangerous relationships with partners or associates, the latter looking deep inside oneself to find an internal "place of safety." Education about psychological trauma could be included.

Typical sessions: 1) Feeling safe; 2) Ending dangerous relationships.

n) *Rage.* Rage is an extreme emotional state characterized by behavioral loss of control, intense feelings, and frequently partial or total blackouts. Rages are associated with the most violent and vicious domestic assaults (Potter-Efron, 2007). As such, it is imperative that group members be screened for a history of rage.

Typical sessions: 1) Rage Questionnaire; 2) Loss of control.

o) *Self-care and "codependency."* Many domestic violence offenders stay in dangerous relationships because of a belief system in which taking care of others, even at considerable self-sacrifice, is morally necessary and perhaps the only reason to justify one's existence. Although this behavior is certainly understandable, facilitators must help participants balance caring for others with self-care.

Typical sessions: 1) Aspects of self-care; 2) When "good enough" is enough.

p) *Shame, guilt, and pride.* Social emotions are less hard-wired than primary emotions such as anger and fear. Social emotions demand that someone understand that "I exist, you exist, and you can judge me." They do not become activated until approximately the eighteenth month of age (Potter-Efron, 2002). Social emotions tell people if what they are doing is acceptable to the society. Essentially shame tells people that they have not done enough, guilt that they have gone too far (transgressed), and pride that the society is pleased with their performance. An excess of shame is particularly likely to contribute to acts of domestic aggression. Guilt is more likely to stop such acts or prevent them from happening in anticipation of punishment, while I believe that healthy feelings of pride ("I did this and I did it well") can be a major contributor to redirecting clients away from self-destructive behaviors and toward self-promoting ones.

Typical sessions: 1) Shame and guilt; 2) Healthy pride.

q) *Stress management/meditation/mindfulness.* Participants who commit acts of domestic violence often suffer from acute and chronic stress conditions. Lessening stress could reduce aggression.

Typical sessions: 1) Breathing exercises; 2) Introduction to mindfulness.

r) *Substance abuse and process addictions.* Although clients should not be allowed to dismiss responsibility for their actions on the grounds they were intoxicated, still the reality is that many acts of domestic aggression would have been curtailed or been less brutal if the individuals were sober. Process addictions such as sexual addiction also may play a role in some people's violence.

Typical sessions: 1) Relation between violence and addiction; 2) Addiction as psychological need, physical chemistry, and habit.

We utilize the following questionnaire at the beginning of closed-groups, both to elicit information that helps us plan our curriculum and to increase client involvement in the agenda:

Possible Topics for New Domestic Violence Group

We'd like to ask your assistance in planning the agenda for this group. We have many topics to cover but some choice about how much time we spend on each area. Please rank the following subjects by how important they are to you (right now and also to help prevent another act of domestic violence).

Your name _____

Score each area from 1 to 5 where   1 = not important to me
    3 = somewhat important
    5 = very important.

_____ Anger management (why and how you get angry and how to stay in control)

_____ Stress management (calmness, relaxation, mindfulness meditation)

_____ Causes and types of domestic violence (power and control, subtle forms of domestic violence including verbal aggression, ending domestic violence)

_____ Self-care and self-esteem work (learning to feel better about yourself)

_____ Changing the way you think (cognitive therapy – challenging negative thought patterns)

_____ Relationship skill-building (negotiation, listening better, respect, differences between men and women, gender equality)

_____ Dealing with family of origin problems (parental abuse or violence, neglect, etc. that still affect you)

_____ Parenting (how to be a positive role model to your children)

_____ Substance abuse (past and present – help from group to stay sober)

_____ Jealousy and general distrust (learn to trust when trust is deserved)

_____ Developing positive directions in life (setting new goals and carrying them out)

_____ Finding ways to deal with difficult people (ex-partners, probation officers, etc.)

_____ Emotional intelligence (learning how to have and share feelings, learn how to understand other people's feelings better)

> _____ Accepting responsibility for your own life (vs. blaming others, denial and minimization, passivity, drifting through life)
>
> _____ Other (What?) _____

So how should you choose from this wide array of topics? One highly recommended way is to utilize interventions and approaches that have stood up well during testing, so-called "evidence-based" interventions (I prefer the term "statistically supported" interventions since the concept of "evidence" seems excessively optimistic at this stage of research). John Hamel (2014), the editor of the journal *Partner Abuse*, is the leading advocate for this approach in domestic violence offender treatment and he has led a massive effort – a series of meta-research studies called PASK, the Partner Abuse State of Knowledge Project (Hamel, 2014) – in which leading scholars have reviewed thousands of domestic violence studies. These studies have been published in several volumes of the journal *Partner Abuse*. Some of the Hamel group's findings are noted in chapter 5.

Another approach that complements the one above is for you to craft a program that best utilizes your particular skills and interests. For instance, if you are deeply involved in cognitive therapy, then you might spend up to 50% of the sessions on cognitive interventions. Your enthusiasm for your approach will certainly be noticed by group members and may well increase their interest. Furthermore, as noted in chapter 5, Eckhardt et al. (2013) report in their meta-survey of domestic violence treatment programs that a strong therapist–client relationship and group cohesion appear to improve program efficacy. Of course I'm not suggesting you design a program around a very esoteric subject that only you understand (astral projections are out), but do not fear advancing your best ideas, activities, and interventions into this still poorly understood field.

Women's Domestic Violence Offender Treatment Groups

There are far more similarities than differences between men and women in their motivations, risk factors, and rationales for domestic violence (Hamel, 2014). Therefore, treatment programs that treat women tend to be similar to those for men. John Hamel, describing his center's programs, states that: "We have found that the issues of concern to men and those of importance to women are quite similar. Both genders present with similar motives for their violence and use similar defense mechanisms" (2014, p. 131). Still, there are some differences worth mentioning that could affect the relative amount of time and effort devoted to certain topics and procedures. For example, Hamel notes that women find role-playing less threatening than males do and that women more readily describe process issues such as their feelings about other group members (Hamel, 2014). This situation may be a mixed blessing, however. Bowen notes that in her experience: "female abusers . . . are infinitely more verbal and more psychologically fragile. They are more likely to view female relationships with fear and competition, and to act out in group. For example, women have taken offense to questions posed by other group members and have retaliated with terroristic threats" (Bowen, 2009, p. 12). This tendency might be related to the well-documented reality that women must usually "act out" far more dramatically than men to get arrested for domestic violence (Hamel, 2014). If so, they are likely to bring this dramatic flair into group.

It is important to consider some practical issues when developing a treatment program for female domestic violence offenders. For instance:

- Many female participants will have *multiple problems*. It is not unusual to work with women who have these simultaneous concerns:
    - a history of sexual assault/incest;
    - past and current physical abuse;
    - alcohol/drug abuse;
    - defiant oppositionality;
    - extreme anger/rage;
    - borderline personality disorder;
    - practical problems: poverty, transportation, child care, etc.

  As mentioned before, it is difficult to change when you don't feel safe and women with these multiplicative problems hardly ever feel safe. Keeping their heads above water constitutes a major challenge for these women. Just getting to group without transportation may create a major difficulty.
- Child care may be a major issue. Women participants may legitimately have trouble arranging child care to get to groups. Ideally both women's and men's groups should offer child care at their facility, but this is unlikely to occur. A worse case scenario plays out when the woman is facing the threat of losing her children – either to the father's efforts to obtain custody or to a human service department's warnings about previous child neglect or abuse incidents. "You say I have to come to group, but if I come here I have to leave my kids and then they'll say I can't keep them safe! Not only that, but the human service lady is telling me I have to attend a parenting group that takes place when I work. If I go there I'll get fired and we'll be homeless. What can I do?" This threat of loss may understandably get demonstrated as apparently defiant behavior in group.

Cultural Diversity: LGBT and Ethnic Minority Groups

It is reasonable to assert that domestic violence offender treatment considerations are mostly similar in any program in the United States. Still, cultural positions vary widely in such areas as what would be considered "normal" relationship behavior, what behaviors would be considered abusive or violent, how much local police and other authorities could or should be involved, etc. For example, a survey of literature and conversation within the lesbian/gay/bisexual/transsexual (LGBT) community quickly demonstrates an unwillingness to report abuse because of the shared sense that they will not be protected by a prejudiced society. Similarly, some members of ethnic minorities such as Native Americans, African Americans, and Latinos may function better in groups in which they feel less isolated and better understood. It is certainly advisable whenever possible to encourage the development of a wide range of domestic violence offender programs within larger communities as well as to have cultural diversity (as well as gender diversity) among the counseling staff.

The reality is that most domestic violence offender groups will engage a wide range of racial, ethnic, religious, and class-differentiated participants. It is the job of the therapy team to help make the treatment setting safe for everyone.

Here are some concepts that should be taken into consideration with culturally diverse groups.

- Loyalty to a minority community may trump calling for help. For example, members of the ultra-orthodox Jewish community resist reporting both sexual and physical abuse, believing that these are private matters that should be handled (or ignored) within the community.
- Norms within groups, especially recently arrived groups, may ignore or condone domestic violence. In my region, people who are first-generation Hmong refugees have had to be educated to American norms prohibiting domestic violence.
- Poverty, alcoholism, etc. may increase the probability of domestic violence episodes while decreasing ability to escape bad situations. Again in my area, Native Americans struggle with these concerns that tend to increase incidents of domestic violence.
- Negative experiences with mainstream authorities may limit willingness to seek help. Perhaps the best example in American society of this tendency resides within the African-American community, where many people maintain a deep suspicion of the white-dominated police and courts. Members of the LGBT community also frequently cite the animosity of authorities as reasons not to pursue legal protection.

- Language barriers may impede support, protection, and treatment for offenders. Hispanic groups represent a strong presence here. I have had the interesting experience of facilitating, with the help of a translator, domestic abuse offender groups for Spanish-speaking individuals.
- Illegal immigrants may be fearful of seeking help and/or treatment services.
- Some minority members may prefer or do better with ethnically/ racially matched counselors.
- Outreach and advocacy services may not reach into minority neighborhoods.
- Greater isolation within the LGBT community.
- LGBT people also cite the general homophobic environment creating "heterosexist" control in which one partner threatens to "out" their partner.

Brain-Change Model for Domestic Violence Offender Treatment

I have previously described (see chapter 5) several models for domestic violence treatment. Here I detail an experimental brain-change model for domestic violence offender treatment that I devised and have been using with groups over the last several years. I will first describe the rationale for this model and then its mechanics. I will also include a 50-session outline of course topics and provide examples of work done by participants in the program.

Please note that at this point fewer than 100 people have completed the program. Because of this and also because we have not had time to follow clients for over three years after completion, I am not offering statistical evidence of the effectiveness of this program.

Rationale

"I've been through a dozen anger management and domestic violence classes. They're all the same. I could lead the lectures on power and control, fair fighting, time outs, you name it. None of that stuff works. If it did, I wouldn't be here."

I run a program for domestic violence offenders sponsored by our regional corrections department. Almost all the people who enter this program are men in their twenties and thirties with a long history of crime. Most of the crimes are relatively petty – offenses such as drunk and disorderly conduct. However, there usually is a history of violence, sometimes severe. Although the norm is that this is their first conviction specifically for a domestic aggression incident, they readily admit that they could have been charged with that offense many times over if their victims had called the police. Perhaps half of these men are convicted felons with significant prison time. Almost everyone has done time in local jails. A few have spent well over half of their adult years behind bars. All who enter the program come under the watchful eyes of their probation officer. Completing this program is a condition for getting off probation.

Many of these men got into trouble while intoxicated and have been through several alcohol/drug treatment programs. Most have been through anger management and domestic violence prevention classes as well, up to seven times or more. They enter our program unwillingly, shuddering at the idea of having to attend 50 sessions at a twice a week rate for the next six months. They walk in with a negative attitude that I would summarize as "Show me what you've got that I haven't seen (and defeated) before."

These clients present us with a three-fold problem. First, they have already been educated with regard to classic anger management and domestic violence prevention concepts. They probably know how to use a time out or fight fair. They understand the concept of gender equality. I certainly do ask each man what they've learned from past programs and encourage them to use the skills they best remember. The reality is, though, that they seldom try to utilize this information and when they do use these tactics they report that they don't work.

Second, and even more relevant, most new participants begin with a deeply rooted sense of cynicism toward the entire criminal justice system in general and specifically toward "do-gooder" counselors. They totally believe that our program will be a gigantic waste of time. To them they are receiving punishment, not rehabilitation. Beyond these beliefs is a more general sense of hopelessness and despair. Many of these men feel locked into an endless cycle of poverty, petty crime, addiction, arrest, jail, and violence. Several of them have commented about how they see others escape this horrible cycle, but they have not and perhaps cannot do so. Yes, they have committed acts of domestic violence for which they must accept responsibility and our program must be geared in that direction. However, we will probably fail to help them if we only offer a set of skills. Rather, I believe a domestic violence offender treatment program must direct attention to the client as a whole person, someone who has been overwhelmed and defeated by life's challenges.

Third, the cynicism of these men is encased within a general oppositional psychological stance. I define oppositionality as a tendency to fight against whatever others say or suggest, no matter how sensible their comments. Adult oppositionality probably is rooted in the child's need to develop autonomy by saying "no" to parents. "No" seems to mean "I exist and have a mind of my own" to a two-year-old. "No" creates space to develop one's core personality. Most adults refine their oppositional instincts, though. They learn to harness that drive unless they are really pushed to do something against their best interests. Although some people tend to react with "no" more quickly than others, those with a healthy, limited sense of oppositionality also have the capacity to say "yes."

Habitual oppositionality is different. Here individuals characteristically recoil against all advice and directions, in particular against would-be authority figures. Children who develop in this manner defy authority for defiance's sake. As adults "You can't make me . . ." becomes a key phrase as well as a centerpiece of their sense of self. This automatic behavior is an example of neural plasticity, but unfortunately people with habitual oppositionality have overdeveloped a neural network that ultimately damages them. They become locked into defiance. They then bring that "You can't make me . . ." attitude into their treatment programs, spending much of their mental effort proudly refusing to learn or change their behavior. They challenge counselors to win them over in a "You can try, but it won't work" game.

The worst thing most counselors could do is to make a frontal assault on oppositionality. Our clients are simply better at it than we are. Rather, we must strive to avoid useless "pissing contests." Instead, we must gradually build trust to the point our clients will actually consider our suggestions.

The brain-change focused program presented here represents an effort to fully engage clients while sidestepping their boredom, cynicism, and oppositionality.

To put this material into a positive framework, the question becomes this: Could we come up with an alternative program that a) is interesting and doesn't repeat all the ideas clients have been offered before and b) motivates them to participate actively with the sense that they can really change their lives?

Motivational researchers describe five stages of motivation: precontemplation, contemplation, preparation, action, and maintenance (Bowen, 2009). We have begun to utilize the Safe at Home Questionnaire (Begun et al., 2008) to measure our clients' level of motivation at the beginning and end of treatment. Our working assumption, though, is that almost every new participant enters at the precontemplation stage because of the issues noted above. However, a minority of entrants do begin at the contemplation or action stages. It is not uncommon, for instance, for someone coming in to have become an active participant at their church or at Alcoholics Anonymous. These individuals may be in the middle of making big changes in their lives. Nevertheless, the majority of new clients are poorly motivated and determined to stay that way.

Brain-change focused domestic violence treatment program

You may recall from chapter 1 that brain-change involves three alterations in neuronal networks: myelination, long-term potentiation, and
arborization. Myelination speeds up electrical transmission of signals
within a cell's axon; long-term potentiation increases the amount of
neurochemicals that are transmitted across the synaptic gap between
neurons; arborization increases the density of dendritic arbors, which in
turn creates more neural receptors that capture neurochemicals.

I have roughly translated these highly technical terms into three goals:
1) *build* a network (myelination); 2) *improve* the network (long-term
potentiation; 3) *expand* the network (arborization). My colleagues
(Patricia Potter-Efron, Chastity Drake, and Dennice Janz) and I challenge
our participants to develop their own brain-change plan based on this
model. First, we explain how the brain actually changes and that the
brain can change throughout life. This explanation attacks their sense of
hopelessness and despair, their doubt that they can actually create a
better life for themselves. Second, we suggest that only they can know
what changes they could make in their brains that would really
help create a better life. This approach makes them the expert on
themselves and relieves us from the role of expert/authority that they so
dislike. It also suggests that we are not interested in punishing them for
their past misdeeds but are allying with them to help them have a better
future.

New participants are given approximately two to three weeks to
develop and defend their own brain-change plan. Clients must name their
plan, show how they will build it initially and how they hope to improve
and expand the plan over time. Below is a handout that clients receive to
help them understand what this opportunity to change their neural
networks could mean for them.

Changing Your Brain Means Changing Your Life

Here's what we know about how you can change your brain, your
behavior, and your life.

Brains change by building huge networks of millions of neurons
all working together. Normally this happens unconsciously,
but sometimes people deliberately choose to build a network.
We are giving you an opportunity in this group to change
your brain by creating a new network or by improving a weak
one.

Here's what you need to think about when you choose your brain
plan.

---

1. *Make a Careful Choice.* This plan could be the most important thing you will do over the next 5–6 months in this group. So take some time to think about this question: How do I really want my life to be different and what steps do I need to take to make that happen?
2. *Set Positive Goals.* Don't just design a plan around what you want to stop doing. Make sure you know what good things you want to say, do, or think. That way you are a double winner: you stop old bad habits while you build new ones.
3. *It Takes Steady Effort to Change Your Brain.* Brains are creatures of habit. They like doing what they've been doing. You will need to remind yourself every day about the changes you want to make and then practice making those changes.
4. *Expect Gradual Change.* The principle here is "Neurons that fire together wire together." The more often you practice your new behavior (which may be words, actions, or even thoughts), the stronger the new network becomes.
5. *Eventually These Changes Will Become Easier and Easier.* You're actually forming new habits – ones of your own choosing. Habits are mostly triggered unconsciously – you're doing something before you even think about it. So as you practice your new thoughts, feelings, and actions, they will become more and more automatic.
6. *Don't Stop Once Things Start Going Right.* The principle here is "Use it or lose it," meaning over time even new brain habits you have developed will weaken unless you keep practicing them.
7. *One Good Thing Leads to Another.* Brain networks connect with each other. As you make this single important change, you might find that other good things are starting to happen too.

Bottom Line: How Much Do You Want A Better Life Than You Have Had?

We give participants many sample plans to look through, although we expect them to develop their own unique proposal. The box below contains a list of sample brain-change plans.

Clients then bring their proposals to the group, where members question the proposer to find out how well he or she has thought out their plan and how motivated they are to proceed. Questions include:

- How important is this plan to you?
- How committed are you to following through with this plan? What will keep you motivated to keep developing this plan over the next six months?
- If you succeed, how do you think your life will change?
- How will these changes help you be less likely to commit an act of domestic violence and/or keep you out of trouble with the law?
- Who could help you make this plan work?
- How might you sabotage your effort – How could you make yourself fail?
- Who else might oppose your goals? How and why? What can you do to stay on track in the face of opposition?
- Have you already taken any steps to succeed in your plan? What are they?
- To whom do you intend to tell your plan? Not tell? Why?
- How can the members of this group help you?
- What's the first thing (or next thing) you need to do to get going on your plan? If that works, what would come next?

Examples of Neuroplastic Change Processes

There are three components to any long-term brain changes. First, you must *build* a neural network (or at least find one that has been neglected) and make a strong commitment to building it. Second, you need to *improve* the network by steadily practicing what you are trying to learn or change. Third, you must keep *expanding* the net by making new connections that keep it developing and growing. Here are several examples of this process relevant to anger management and domestic violence prevention:

1. *Become significantly less negative and more positive and optimistic.*
   Build: First recognize and challenge your immediate and automatic negative thought pattern.
   Improve: Design and carry out one activity/choice a day based upon an optimistic outlook.
   Expand: Develop a set of optimistic beliefs you regularly share with others.

2. *Move from allowing anger to dominate your emotions to having all your emotions available.*
   Build: Identify at least one other feeling you have in anger-promoting situations.

Improve: Consciously focus upon these other emotions to strengthen their impact.

Expand: Identify emotions you have avoided and consciously develop them (such as going to sad movies to develop your ability to feel sorrow).

3. *Develop skills for treating members of the opposite gender with respect.*

   Build: Gather a list of ways you've been disrespectful of the other gender and commit to change at least one area immediately.

   Improve: Keep adding new ways to demonstrate respect.

   Expand: Regularly get feedback from members of the opposite gender and change your actions if necessary.

4. *Take a leadership role in helping your entire family end violent interactions.*

   Build: Inform your family that you will no longer be violent with any of them and encourage them to be nonviolent as well.

   Improve: Patiently demonstrate ways to be nonviolent with each other and consistently reward such behavior.

   Expand: Help your family become verbally nonaggressive as well as physically nonviolent.

5. *Commit to becoming more interested in and more empathic toward others.*

   Build: First focus upon listening without interrupting.

   Improve: Ask open-ended and nonjudgmental questions to get others to tell their stories.

   Expand: Practice acts of caring/kindness/compassion (empathic caring).

6. *Moving from the habit of criticism to the habit of praise.*

   Build: Commit to four-step program; select single person to give praise to one time a day.

   Improve: Give praise a total of six times a day to two or three people.

   Expand: If needed, learn to give self-praise, and/or to take in praise from others.

7. *Learn to fully practice relaxation to lessen stress.*

   Build: Commit to a daily stress reduction program beginning with breathing exercises.

   Improve: Significantly change daily habits/actions to lessen stress.

   Expand: Take yoga and/or mindfulness classes to redesign neural networks.

8. *Become less controlling and more accepting of others.*
Build: Commit to tolerating (not trying to prevent) specific things you've had trouble accepting that your partner or other family members do.
Improve: Through empathy learn to accept others for who they are rather than for whom you want them to be.
Expand: Begin encouraging their differences rather than just tolerating or accepting them.

9. *Move from feeling insecure and jealous to secure and trusting in your relationship.*
Build: Act "as if" you are secure in specific situations (such as your partner taking a trip).
Improve: Practice cognitive therapy principles to challenge jealous and suspicious thoughts.
Expand: Get therapy to deal with old abandonments/betrayals that interfere with your ability to feel secure in your current relationship.

10. *Develop the ability to be patient and to plan your actions rather than commit impulsive mistakes.*
Build: Institute a five-second delay between impulse and action.
Improve: Rank the seriousness of an issue on a 1–10 scale before considering action.
Expand: Plan in advance for how you will handle predictable anger-provoking situations.

11. *Build a workable daily living sobriety plan if you've used alcohol or mood-altering chemicals (or behaviors such as gambling) to run away from reality.*
Build: Commit to abstinence as the most important goal in your life.
Improve: Develop a sobriety plan that includes people who will help you face life.
Expand: Learn to move toward challenging situations rather than away from them.

12. *Let go of resentment and hate and move toward acceptance and forgiveness.*
Build: Study the concepts of forgiveness and letting go of resentments.
Improve: Begin acting "as if" you had let go of your resentments with one person.
Expand: Let go of other past resentments and learn ways to keep from building more.

We tell participants that brain change doesn't come quickly or easily. However, with steady effort and lots of practice they can make significant alterations in their thoughts, feelings, actions, and sense of self. It helps greatly that participants who are farther along in their plans offer support and model these changes. We then review each individual's brain change monthly with the group. Clients occasionally throw out their original plans, sometimes commenting that they were just producing a document to placate the staff but then realized they were wasting their time while others were actually making important changes in their lives.

Approximately 20–30% of the group's time is spent on brain change. The rest of the program is more traditional in scope.

Here is the form we give clients to develop and present their personal brain-change plan.

Personal Brain-Change Program

Your name and date: _____

Build your network. Improve the network. Expand your network. That is how real change takes place both in your actions and in your brain.

Here is your opportunity to create and pursue your own personally designed program for significant change. You will be in charge of this program. Only you can make it happen. However, you will receive help and advice from your co-participants and from us. We will regularly ask you to present your program to the group for feedback, support, and encouragement. Your goal should be to demonstrate to the rest of us that you are indeed improving your life in exactly the ways you most want.

Please use the rest of this page to write out your plan. We will go over your proposal in group next week. Expect your plan to be challenged. You may have to change parts of it.

Also we will review your progress regularly in group, at least once every two weeks.

Name your plan: _____.
Why is this plan important to you? _____

_____.

How will this plan help keep you from committing an act of domestic violence?

_____

_____.

Build your network. What will be the first steps you will take to start carrying out your plan? Note: you must be able to name *specific* behaviors here. For example, "I'll talk nicer to my girlfriend" is not specific. "I will compliment my girlfriend at least three times a day" is specific.

_____

_____

_____.

Improve your network. Over time you should add new specific goals and steps so the network becomes larger and stronger. For instance, "In two or three weeks I will begin doing at least one unrequested positive thing each day for her, such as making dinner or putting the kids to bed."

_____

_____

_____.

Expand your network. The idea here is to connect your new network with other good ones. For instance, "Next I will try to improve my communication pattern with my girlfriend by listening carefully without interrupting." You may not know yet exactly how you will expand your network, but consider here some possibilities: "Maybe I could . . ."

_____

_____

_____.

After clients present their brain-change plan, we follow-up regularly by reviewing their plan five times during the next four months. Follow-up sessions after the first one suggest new challenges. We introduce the idea of improving the plan by adding new tasks in Review #2, getting feedback from others in Review #3, and linking the emerging network to other networks (such as adding being more generous) to an initial brain-change plan centered upon being respectful to others in Review #4.

191

CASE STUDY

Domestic Violence Offender Brain-Change Program*

Alan is a 35-year-old Caucasian male in a long-term relationship with a woman named Danielle. They have three children aged 2, 5, and 6. They have lived together, with occasional separations, for seven years. Alan is intelligent but poorly educated. He works six days a week as a farm hand, a job that includes everything from milking cows three times a day, which he dislikes, to fixing heavy duty farm machinery that frequently breaks down during cold Wisconsin winters. He is a wiry man with a good sense of humor. Like most members of the group, he prefers talking about actions over emotions. However, he is capable of empathic understanding of others, including Danielle. Also like many of the men, he is deeply concerned for his children, wanting them to have a better, and safer, life then he had during childhood. Alan's father was "a good man and a hard worker but he was a mean, mean drunk." Alan witnessed his mother being beaten by his father and was the recipient of many "whuppins" in his youth.

Alan was arrested two years ago when a neighbor called police after hearing what he described as a "hellacious argument." Indeed, when the authorities arrived they found Alan and Danielle screaming at each other. They continued to argue even after the police tried to separate them, with Danielle attempting to strike Alan while being held back by two officers. Meanwhile, Alan kept shouting at Danielle that he'd had enough of her "b . . . s . . . games" and he was moving out right then. After determining that Alan had thrown several objects in Danielle's direction, he was arrested and a mandatory 48-hour restraining order was imposed. This was Alan's first arrest for domestic violence, although he had been cited at least twice previously for disorderly conduct. Alcohol was involved on all three occasions, but Alan had never officially been diagnosed as alcoholic or chemically dependent. Danielle also had a history of disorderly conduct citations. Beyond that, Danielle had actually herself gone through an anger management program that was imposed upon her as an alternative to incarceration after a previous altercation between her and Alan.

Danielle quickly allowed Alan back into their home. She told the district attorney that they were simply a "highly emotional couple" who got after each other too loudly from time to time. She said she didn't fear that Alan would try to hurt her "and if he does I'll kick his scrawny ass." She apparently hadn't learned a lot in anger management or, if she had, she showed no interest in utilizing those communication skills.

Alan spent a few days in jail and then agreed to plead guilty to a domestic violence misdemeanor. One result was that he was court ordered to the domestic violence prevention program at my clinic. He began the program approximately six months after the incident. He noted in his first session that he had never completed probation before without being revoked and had never completed a program that he had been court ordered to attend. "They tell me what to do and then I do what I want. Nobody has the right to order me around." He initially expressed disdain for the court, contempt for his probation officer, and disinterest in the class. Nevertheless, he fit in easily with the group and didn't directly challenge our authority. Indeed, he rather quickly became involved in what we were doing. The brain-change concept particularly intrigued him because "You aren't telling me what I should change. You're letting me decide."

Alan was given a couple weeks to become acclimated to the group. We explained the core brain-change concept to him, gave him the appropriate handouts, and asked him to return with a proposal within seven days. In the meantime he heard other clients describe their particular plans during our daily check-ins and during more official brain-change reviews. Alan did return with his plan the next week.

The name of Alan's plan was "Be more positive to my family." He explained that "I've been an a . . . h . . . to Danielle and the kids all this time. I don't want to be an a . . . h . . . no more." His sincerity was obvious, as was his determination to make real changes in his life. When the group asked him how he would begin, he told us that he had decided to quit saying the "f" word in front of his kids. The positive direction he would take would be to listen to what they said and not to find fault with them ("the way my parents did to me"). As for Danielle, he said he would not respond to her frequent "anger invitations," times when she deliberately said incredibly demeaning things to him (such as "You are a worthless piece of trash I should have thrown away years ago"). Here the group became doubtful, asking Alan how long he could just sit there and take it when she was bad mouthing him. He replied he didn't know, but he would probably find out.

Alan maintained his plan throughout the 50-session program. He steadily discovered new ways to be a positive influence in his family. For instance, he began spending more time doing things with his children. He learned to sit quietly instead of immediately over-reacting to their chatter. However, the group's concern was well founded. About four months into the program Alan reported that he had "had enough" of Danielle's continual attacks. Rather than striking out at her, though, he had abruptly packed a bag and left home, intending not to return. A week later he was back, but only after receiving a promise from Danielle that she would minimize her verbal attacks. Apparently she has kept her promise, at least enough so that Alan feels relatively safe in her presence.

Here is what Alan offered in his last review:

a) *Build the plan.* "I give praise every day to my children. I'm swearing a lot less, not just at home but everywhere."

b) *Improve the plan.* "I look to make them smile." In addition, Alan remarked that he was getting along with his often cranky boss – "I used to antagonize him intentionally to see him get mad, but I don't do that anymore." He also noted that he was getting along very well with his probation officer, certainly the first time he could ever make that claim.

c) *Expand the plan.* "I've quit drinking and that really helps." Furthermore, "Even Danielle isn't calling me names. We ain't at each other so much. She don't have that snarly face so much." He adds: "Now they're not so shocked by my new behavior. They're used to it, and I'm getting used to it too." However, he adds that his new behavior has yet to become so automatic that he doesn't have to think about it – the ultimate goal for a brain-change program.

Alan finished his last brain-change summary in this way: "My life is so good now I hope it won't change back." That certainly is our hope for him, and for all the clients who participate in the brain-change oriented domestic violence prevention program. We did remind Alan that he would have to keep using his plan or it would eventually fail, following the principle of "use it or lose it."

---

* This case study was originally published in *Partner Abuse* 5(2) and is reproduced here with permission from Springer Publishing.

Summary

As the field of domestic violence offender treatment expands, there is a concurrent need to develop a variety of programs that address a varied audience. I have presented here a brief educationally focused group plan for minimal offenders as well as the basis for a 50-session program for more severe offenders. I've also included a description of the program I facilitate, a long-term domestic violence offender program centered upon brain change. My suggestion, though, at this time of limited wisdom about the treatment effectiveness of domestic violence programs, is for therapists to develop their own programs that blend the best current knowledge with their own skills and interests.

9

ALTERNATIVES TO GROUP THERAPY FOR ANGRY AND DOMESTICALLY VIOLENT PEOPLE

Individual, Group, and Family Therapy

Group work is the norm in anger management and domestic violence offender treatment. Its main advantages over other modalities are that group work gives clients the opportunity to share their stories, learn positive behaviors and attitudes from their peers (although they may also learn negative behaviors and attitudes), and give each other mutual support. A practical advantage is cost efficiency, a very important consideration in this era of diminishing funding. Also, in the realm of domestic violence treatment same-sex group treatment has been considered the only appropriate modality and couples counseling has been specifically disallowed (to be discussed later in this chapter).

There are reasons, however, to explore other ways to treat anger and domestic violence problems. Here I will present arguments for individual counseling, couples work, and family counseling.

Individual Anger and Domestic Violence Counseling

I suggest that for many reasons (described below) more consideration ought to be given to individual anger management and domestic violence offender treatment. However, I do not mean that angry clients should only receive individual therapy. What is critical is that each client's needs be assessed separately; that every client will be perceived as having a unique set of angry and aggressive behaviors, beliefs, and concerns; and that the treatment for each person will consist of the best possible balance of individual, group, couples and family therapy as befits his or her situation.

That being said, I now want to make a case for individual counseling in anger and aggression management. In particular, I will discuss some of the advantages specifically of individual therapy over group counseling. However, I want to state clearly that my goal is not to advocate for replacing groups with individual treatment but to have both modes of intervention, along with couples and family therapy, readily available so that the needs of clients can be well met.

One size does not fit all

Please imagine that you have been asked to treat the following eight individuals *and* furthermore that you are to form them into a single group:

Hector: 25, a mechanic, married. Hector has been arrested for beating his wife. He's done it before. He's also been arrested on several occasions for assaultive crimes. He was kicked out of high school after attacking a teacher. Hector hates authority.

Melanie: 17, high school junior. Melanie's parents say that she hasn't been herself for about a year now. Melanie agrees, stating that she just can't seem to control her anger. She flies into rages at the slightest affront, first swearing at her parents or teachers, then yelling and pounding her fists and occasionally slapping her boyfriend, and then bursting into sobs. She desperately hopes the people she's angry at won't leave even while she's pushing them away. There is a history of depression and mental illness in her family.

Gaylord: 62, a retired executive going through his second divorce. This man is chronically hostile, critical, and cynical. Most people, even professionals, try to avoid him because of his incessant negativity. Two of his four grown children refuse to have anything to do with him. He's volunteering for counseling because he wants to learn how to be "less of a pain in the ass before I lose the rest of my family."

Sharika: 35, a medical secretary who was physically and sexually abused from age nine to fourteen by her father. She is tired of hating him and by extension all men. She needs to learn how to forgive so she can get on with her life.

Jorge: 40, an attorney who keeps running into trouble at work because of his short fuse. Jorge can be volatile at home, where his periodic outbursts are anticipated and tolerated. However, that same behavior is not well received at the office. He's been told that he will never make partner in the firm until he learns to treat people more respectfully.

Theodore: 50, whose wife has demanded he get treatment for his passive aggressive behavior. Theodore totally frustrates his wife by forgetting important things, not finishing jobs, refusing to talk about what's bothering him, and, above all, by saying he's not angry when she knows that he is fuming inside.

Erika: 35, a real-estate sales person. Erika only seems to have an anger problem when she's been drinking. Unfortunately, lately she's been doing that a lot. Every day. Several hours a day. The more she drinks, the nastier and more physically aggressive she gets.

Charity: 28, a woman with a dissociative disorder. One of her alters is nicknamed "The Madman" and appears to be the depository for the entire system's anger. The Madman rages when he comes out, sometimes physically attacking anybody in sight but equally frequently cutting or burning Charity's body.

Your job is to design one set of lectures and activities that will apply to all eight of these highly differentiated clients. But how can you possibly do this? True, every one of the clients named above can claim to have an anger and/or aggression problem. However, each person's anger problem is so radically different from the others that it would be virtually impossible to construct a single group that would suit them all.

Some of the individuals above are violent and really should be in "aggression management" or domestic violence offender groups rather than anger management. Others have psychological problems that probably cannot be properly addressed within a group educational context. Some of these potential clients have impulse control problems while others are dealing with the build up of long-term resentments. Group work, though, functions best when the participants are relatively similar in primary concerns, age, education, etc. It is simply unproductive to throw together a disparate collection of individuals who have little in common. And it is unlikely that groups could be designed for all the people described above. At least some of them will need to be treated individually if only because their problems are relatively uncommon.

Individual treatment encourages more specific goals and methods

There are three primary goals in anger management and domestic violence work: *prevention of unnecessary anger and aggression*; containment of anger and aggression so as *not to lose control*; and *resolution of ongoing conflict* (Potter-Efron, 2001) in order to reduce the build up of more anger. Individuals have greatly differing needs with regards to these goals. The man who suddenly "snaps" seemingly without warning will need to be guided strenuously towards greater awareness of the build-up cues that predict these explosions. Thus, prevention will need to be emphasized. Another client, though, says that she knows perfectly well that she's ready to explode. The problem is that she then chooses to keep going, perhaps because she gains a certain excitement from the action. This woman will need much work in the arena of containment. Finally there is the person who fundamentally believes in the principle that once somebody gets on his "s . . . list," he should never let that individual off it. The bulk of treatment for this client will be in the area of resolution. Individual therapy permits the design of a treatment plan that allots time proportionate to need.

Similarly, it is possible to identify at least four different intervention methods in anger management and domestic violence offender treatment. These are *behavior, cognitive, affective,* and *existential/spiritual* interventions. The *behavioral* emphasis describes how clients develop a habit of anger and aggression, teach basic tools such as how to take a time out, and offers help in developing positive, pro-social modes of communication. *Cognitive* interventions help clients understand how their "irrational" assumptions about the world, beliefs about people or themselves, and interpretations of others' words and deeds create excessive anger and prepare the way for harmful actions. *Affective* interventions are directed at teaching individuals to relax instead of becoming agitated and to locate other emotions instead of or in addition to anger that they have been disregarding. Lastly, *existential/spiritual* interventions attempt to place the client's anger and aggression into a larger perspective such as the meaning of aggression within that person's life, the role of despair or impotent rage, and anger as a signal that some important need that has been ignored must now be addressed.

My point here is once again that individual treatment permits a much greater flexibility in selecting from among these four approaches. While one client will benefit primarily from behavioral and cognitive approaches, another will do far better with affective interventions, while a third might mostly need existential or spiritual assistance.

Specialized issues demand specialized treatment

There are some areas of anger management and domestic violence treatment that stand apart from others because of their uniqueness. These areas are somewhat specialized and are best approached by therapists with appropriate training and experience. Four that I will briefly describe here are: 1) the dissociative episodes of individuals with dissociative identity disorder and post-traumatic stress disorder; 2) the self-mutilative and self-destructive behaviors of individuals who habitually direct fierce anger inwardly against themselves; 3) the rageful outbursts that emanate from clients with significant attachment insecurities, some of whom may be diagnosed with borderline personality disorder; 4) the seething anger, spitefulness, and vengeance-seeking of those who hate and cannot forgive.

Clients like this might benefit somewhat from group therapy. Hopefully they will gain an improved ability to take time outs, combat anger-provoking thoughts, utilize fair fighting tactics, and become more accepting of their partners. Realistically, though, these individuals need much more help. Many of these people will quickly lose the skills they learned in group if they fail to receive extra care, while others will only be able to utilize them at work or in otherwise less threatening situations. Without individual care the dissociative person will still blindly defend himself against illusory attacks; the self-mutilator will "stuff" her external anger only to increase the number and intensity of attacks against herself; the person with attachment insecurities will be unable to control irrational bouts of jealousy; the person who hates will continue to turn away with disgust from past friends and family members while bathing in the pain of remembered insults.

I advocate a "both/and" or two-tier approach to anger management and domestic violence offender treatment with these difficult and seriously impaired individuals. If possible, these clients should receive both group and individual counseling. However, if that proves impracticable and a choice has to be made between the two formats, I would advocate for individual therapy over group work. In each of these situations these chronically fearful and suspicious people need to learn how to trust another human being. The gradual development of trust allows stronger and more effective challenges to the deeply held irrational belief systems that underlie the anger and aggression these clients display.

Essentially, clients with these deeper pathologies must learn to manage their anger at two levels. First, they need to learn some basic skills that allow them to participate relatively safely in the world around them. Then they must discover the links between their anger and aggression and the core insults to their honor, integrity, sense of self, spirit, wholeness, and ability to achieve a sense of belonging and intimacy with others. Individual counseling may be the key to this second tier of learning. Once achieved, many of these clients will be able to practice anger management not as a set of skills to be applied mechanically but as a way to heal their troubled lives at the level of soul and core self. Only then will they be able to substitute positive thoughts, beliefs, emotions, and experiences for the negative ones they have now.

An individual counseling focus allows treatment for anger and aggression as a symptomatic, secondary, or complementary issue

The treatment of anger management and domestic violence, as presently conceived and practiced in group counseling approaches, usually stands alone as a separately targeted phenomenon. However, there are many situations in which an individual's anger and aggression might better be treated as part of a larger problem or more compelling issue.

One example concerns clients whose anger or aggression is secondary to a major depressive disorder. True, these individuals certainly have anger problems. They frequently make negative, cynical, disparaging, and hostile remarks for seemingly little reason; they offend people by avoiding them unnecessarily; they report that they feel continually irritable and consequently short-tempered; they are pessimistic and even paranoid in their interpretations of the words and actions of their associates; they appear ready to pick fights just to ensure that everybody around them feels as bad as they do. Anger management and domestic violence counseling can help these people curtail some of these activities, especially the most visible and public ones. However, that treatment must be folded into a larger discussion of the client's depression so that the client can be steered toward medical assistance and/or cognitive depression therapy.

Alcoholism and drug addiction is another area in which anger and aggression concerns become commingled with another major or even primary issue. Sometimes the causal connection seems fairly obvious: a person only becomes verbally aggressive or physically violent under the influence of copious amounts of an intoxicant or someone who is already angry gets drunk in order to release inhibitions against expressing that anger. At other times the relationship seems to circle or spiral so that it is impossible to separate the individual's use of mood-altering substances from his or her anger issues. This is particularly likely with people who harbor long-term resentments. These people may say they drink in order to forget their misery, but the reality is that their drinking only compounds their pain and increases their sense of victimization. Then there are also clients who utilize various substances, not infrequently marijuana, in an attempt to contain their anger. Newly abstinent, these individuals may find themselves overwhelmed with floods of anger that had been effectively held off through addictive processes.

So what comes first, alcohol and drug abuse treatment or anger management? Traditionally, trained addiction experts emphasize addiction treatment, believing that the anger issue is symptomatic and secondary. Anger management specialists might argue that the client needs that service in order to be willing to participate in addiction treatment. Probably the best answer is that both issues need to be treated in whichever order the client will allow, including simultaneously. Individual therapy may well be more efficient and timely than having the client undergo months of group counseling in both areas.

Working individually with exceptionally angry and domestically violent individuals does have its drawbacks. Perhaps the worst problem is the potential lack of honest or realistic feedback from the client about how well he or she really is doing in containing anger and aggression. I suggest the following guidelines to minimize this problem:

1. Be sure to get signed releases immediately from these clients (while assuring them of their privacy rights and negotiating with them, if necessary, as to what the therapist can and cannot reveal; if at all possible, one release should be to allow communication with the client's relationship partner.

2. Regularly check with these people as to the client's success with anger and aggression containment.

3. When clients report successes, ask for specific details. See if they can discuss differences, both behavioral and cognitive, between how they responded in these immediate situations as against what they would have done before in similar circumstances.

4. Frequently ask clients what they are doing right when they report the absence of aggression or anger. That helps them realize that change happens because they are substituting new behaviors for old.

5. Regularly inquire as to whether anyone else has commented on either their changes or lack of changes since beginning treatment. Lack of confirmation may be a sign that clients think they are making more changes than they really are (or an unwillingness to give them credit for changing by angry, doubtful, or distrusting significant others).

CASE STUDY

A Man Who Benefited from Both Group and Individual Counseling

Hector, a 25-year-old male, was sent to my domestic violence offender group by his probation officer even though he was actually still in jail at the time. Hector had a lengthy history of relatively petty crime (convictions for cigarette theft and disorderly conduct) and domestic aggression (an example of which was a situation in which he reportedly pushed his way past his wife Tammy when she tried to keep him from leaving during an argument, resulting in her falling to the ground but not being injured. A talk with Tammy confirmed this report). He was nearing the end of a six-month sojourn in jail for writing bad checks and faced another year of probation.

Hector did well in the group, becoming a leader on the first evening when he disputed another member's claim that nobody wanted to be there. "Well, I do," he said. "I'm tired of being angry all the time." He steadily reported success with his anger, except in one area: jealousy. No matter how hard he tried, he found himself sitting in his cell at night wondering what Tammy was doing, with whom she might be speaking, if she was planning on leaving him, and, worst of all, if she was already having sex with another man. Although we discussed jealousy in the group, Hector simply could not quit obsessing. Consequently, he asked for and received permission (and funding) from the department of corrections to attend twelve individual sessions with me, six sessions before and six after he was released from jail.

202

Hector revealed things in individual therapy sessions he had not talked about in the group. Most significantly, he described the day he stumbled upon his father having intercourse with a family friend. His father swore Hector to secrecy. But his mother became suspicious and asked Hector if he knew what his Dad was up to. Hector was caught in the middle. He lied to her but felt terribly guilty. Hector believed his jealousy problems began right then. It didn't help that these events took place just as he was entering puberty. "I guess I've always believed that married people cheat on each other, just like Dad did to Mom."

Why hadn't Hector discussed these things in group treatment? The reason, he explained, was that he was too ashamed of his family of origin. Besides, he pointed out, despite confidentiality agreements you could not count on the group members, all young men with honesty problems, to keep quiet.

Hector made good progress during individual therapy. He came to realize that the generalization he had made – that since his father cheated on his mother, then anyone might cheat on their partner – was far too generalized and certainly not an inevitability in his marriage. He claimed gradually to be coming more trusting of her, a statement validated by his wife, who told me she had been thinking of leaving him just because of his jealousy problems before he started changing.

Hector gained anger management skills in both his group and individual therapy experiences. His group supplied support, general information, and motivation. Then individual counseling helped him with his personal issues that had kept him jealous and insecure despite his overall improvement.

Couples Counseling with Angry or Violent Couples

Couples counseling is a fairly common adjunct to anger management counseling, both approached serially or concomitantly. The one thing I want to emphasize here is that anger management counselors should check carefully for hidden physical aggression, including sexual violence, within the relationship. Each party should be asked about this concern privately. I also suggest that since many couples are initially unwilling to admit the presence of physical violence that the counselor should inquire about it several times over the course of therapy.

The issue of couples counseling is particularly complex when there is evidence of physical aggression within a relationship. Traditionally, couples counseling is ruled out in these situations because of the risk that things said in counseling will be used as an excuse for further violence by the perpetrator. Additionally, as noted previously, couples counseling violates the norms of the Power and Control treatment model. Instead, the couple gets split into a victim and victimizer duality, with each treated separately (and often the victim is urged emphatically to leave the victimizer).

Many counselors judge the risks as too great to merit couples counseling with violent couples. Certainly that is a legitimate concern. The emotional volatility of couples counseling might increase rather than decrease the risk for violence, especially in the period immediately after a session. Furthermore, some clients could be intimidated from being truthful during discussions if they believe they will be punished for their honesty. An additional risk is that physically violent individuals will attempt to use counseling sessions to convince themselves, the spouse, and the counselor of the correctness of their behavior.

Nevertheless, a case for couples counseling can be made. Automatically ruling out couples counseling because of any history of relationship aggression can become a rigid ethos rather than a considered decision. Some couples might benefit from counseling as long as there is a clear understanding that the therapist retains the right to curtail counseling if what is said during sessions is misused or appears to worsen the situation. Also note that the most common form of domestic violence is mutual, not unilateral aggression. Treating one party entirely as perpetrator and the other as victim denies this reality.

Couples counseling within the field of domestic violence has been recommended by several authors. Neidig and Freidman (1984) detail an extensive anger management program they developed for couples in which acts of domestic violence had occurred. They cite six major principles upon which their program is based: 1) The primary goal is to eliminate violence in the home; 2) although anger and conflict are normal elements of family life, violence in the family is never justified; 3) abusiveness is a learned behavior; 4) abusive behavior is a relationship issue, but it is ultimately the responsibility of the male to control physical violence; 5) abusiveness is a desperate but ultimately maladaptive effort to effect relationship change; 6) abusiveness tends to escalate in severity and frequency if not treated. They chose to work with couples because they concluded from their work with military men that most acts of abuse occur during periods of exceptional stress and were related to specific deficits in the areas of anger control, stress management, and communication.

Tucker et al. (2000) discuss the use of in-session "meta-dialogue" between co-counselors in couples therapy with domestic abusers and their spouses. The work they describe is an add-on to a male batterers program in which the male has perpetrated mild to moderate violence.

Their goal is to attend systematically to marriage concerns while still insisting that the perpetrator of violence accepts responsibility for that behavior and also assure the safety of both partners.

Holtzworth-Munroe et al. (2003) distinguish couples in which there is "common couple violence" characterized by relatively mild to moderate physical aggression, often by both partners, from a more severe husband-only aggression in which the male's violence serves to control his partner. They suggest that couples counseling might be appropriate only for the former group. They also recommend conjoint treatment primarily for "family-only" male perpetrators, men whose violence is linked with stress and skills limitations that periodically predict physical aggression during escalating marital conflicts. These men are remorseful about their aggression, have low levels of psychopathology, and maintain generally positive attitudes toward women. In contrast, they do not recommend couples work with dysphoric/borderline batterers or with generally antisocial males. Couples counseling should be considered even with couples in which violence has been manifested.

More recently, several authors have developed well-designed couples counseling programs with violent couples. All approach couples work cautiously. For example, Vetere and Cooper (2001, 2007) place safety first. To help ensure safety they have both parties sign a non-violence contract, get releases to include a "stable third" individual who can provide regular feedback about how the couple is doing, initially see each partner separately, and only accept clients who take responsibility for their violent behavior. These therapists utilize an attachment model in which a major goal is to help relationship partners learn to self-soothe and to comfort each other.

O'Leary and Cohen (2007) treat couples whose domestic aggression is primarily psychological and with infrequent and mild levels of physical violence. They state that these individuals usually are only physically aggressive against their partners as against being more generally violent and that the aggression pattern is usually mutual. They argue that couples counseling can help these couples not escalate their conflicts into more severe violence. They seek to have each partner accept responsibility for escalation of angry interchanges into physical aggression. Their eventual aim is to have each partner treat the other with respect.

Hamel (2014) utilizes a systems model in couples counseling with violent couples. He notes that violent relationships tend to be self-perpetuating and highly resistant to change. He describes a three-phase program to break into and change this dysfunctional pattern. First, he brings new information into the system by teaching about relationship dynamics and basic relationship skills. Next, he moves toward second-order change as both partners incorporate new beliefs about relationships and consequently alter their behavior. Hamel emphasizes the need for both parties to make these changes. It is likely, given a system's strong tendency to return to the *status quo*, that regression will occur if both partners aren't willing to make changes. Third, he then promotes deeper therapy to help each person deal with family of origin dynamics to resolve childhood issues.

The box below provides a summary of reasons for and against undertaking couples counseling with domestically violent couples.

The Pros and Cons of Doing Couples Work When There is a History of Domestic Violence

Cautions with regard to considering the use of couples counseling when there is a history of domestic violence:

- Couples counseling is inconsistent with the patriarchal domination model of domestic abuse that emphasizes on one hand *individual responsibility* of the male ("No matter what your partner says or does, you are fully and solely responsible for your aggression") and *cultural influence* on the other ("Men beat women because they are explicitly and implicitly encouraged to do so in a society that advocates male supremacy, power, and control").
- Couples counseling might actually increase the risk for violence.
- Some violent individuals may view counseling as an opportunity to convince the therapist that the partner is to blame and so try to avoid personal responsibility for their actions.
- Some individuals have severe pathologies (antisocial personality disorder, paranoia, etc.) that might make couples counseling untenable.
- Partners of domestically violent individuals may feel too intimidated to speak truthfully during couples sessions.
- Clients may believe that agreeing to couples counseling means that the therapist believes or promotes the idea that they must stay in the relationship at all costs.

Reasons to consider couples therapy in situations where there is a history of violence:

- Couples counseling is consistent with systems therapy, communications models, and attachment theory perspectives.
- When both parties may specifically request and desire couples counseling.

- When one or both partners may have already worked at the individual level and made significant progress in minimizing their anger and aggressive tendencies.
- When the level of violence is fairly infrequent and low-level (no or minor injuries).
- When neither partner demonstrates any tendency to leave the relationship even when repeatedly advised to do so because of violence.
- When hostile feelings, angry communications, and aggressive behaviors have infiltrated the couples and/or family system to the point that it will take a mutual effort to reduce them.
- With "nothing to lose" couples in which their interactions have become so dangerous that not attempting couples counseling only leaves the survival of one or both partners to chance.

If couples counseling is to be considered seriously when there is a history of domestic violence, two serious objections must be answered: 1) that couples counseling may shift responsibility from the perpetrator of the violence onto the partner; 2) that couples counseling might increase the risk for violence.

The first objection is related to the strong and appropriate movement in the United States over the last 30 years to protect women from their battering male partners. Mandatory arrest, the creation of numerous anger management groups specifically for male domestic abusers, and a strong emphasis upon women's right to safety in their own homes reflect this deep commitment. Women's rights advocates have noted that all too often it is the female victims of abuse who have been told by church personnel, family members, counselors, and even the courts that they are responsible for the violence against them. "None of this would be happening if you were just a better wife" are words that all too many women still hear today. However, both the male aggressor and the female survivor are now likely to be told almost the diametrically opposite statement: "No matter what the provocation, no matter what the woman's behavior (up to and including her violence, which is characteristically justified as defensive in nature), it is solely and completely the man's responsibility." Couples counseling, then, is contraindicated from this perspective since the violence that occurs is solely the responsibility of the man.

There is a counter argument, though. Systems theory in general, and attachment theory more specifically, posits that a marital relationship is an interactive system in which each person's behavior is highly influenced by that of the other person in an unending series of feedback mechanisms.

Marital discord and even domestic violence is not an exception to this process. Indeed, "From an attachment perspective the underlying cause of marital distress is the lack of accessibility and responsiveness of at least one partner and the problematic ways in which the partners deal with their insecurities" (Johnson and Sims, 2000, p. 172) and "an assaulter's abusive episodes can be seen as an adult's version of protest when attachment needs are not satisfied" (Bartholomew et al., 2001, p. 60) by his or her partner. The attachment model implies, furthermore, that attachment insecurities are mutually created by the couple and therefore not entirely within the province of the male: "The problem-solving skills that people in violent relationships lack are spouse-specific" (Roberts and Noller, 1998, p. 342). A particularly strong argument for this perspective is expressed by Bartholomew et al. when they state that: "Contrary to the dominant feminist perspective . . . we believe that relationship abuse is best understood within a dyadic or relationship context" (2001, p. 57).

A reasonable "both/and" approach that utilizes these apparently contradictory theoretical approaches is certainly possible. First, strong emphasis must be placed upon insisting that all perpetrators of domestic aggression take full responsibility for their actions. No "She (or he) made me do it" excuses can be accepted, no matter what the specific treatment modality. Second, couples can be seen together to help them work out how they can maximize threat-reducing and safety-enhancing behaviors by both parties. Essentially the goal is to help violent individuals arrive at this thought: "I am fully responsible for everything I say and do, especially my acts of aggression. I must make a commitment to cease being violent no matter what my partner says and does. And I will meet in counseling with my partner to help us both learn how to make our relationship as safe, caring, and loving as possible." These statements are applicable for both genders so that female-initiated violence and same-sex aggression can be addressed in addition to male-initiated violence.

The second objection, that couples counseling might actually increase the danger of physical aggression between the partners, must be taken seriously. Certainly learning from a client that he or she was accosted "because of what you told the counselor" or was verbally attacked by someone using the information disclosed in therapy is a terrible, hope-shattering experience for client and therapist. Furthermore, clients conceivably could take a therapist to court for providing couples counseling that goes badly in this manner. For both these reasons counselors should think very carefully before engaging in couples work with physically abusive or abused people. The "default option" should be individual counseling for each partner unless and until there are clear reasons to justify couples work.

What might these reasons be? The first reason is the simplest: the couple has asked for this kind of counseling. Each partner, whether abuser, perpetrator, or both, expressly states that he or she desires couples counseling and gives specific reasons for this request. Given that it is made without coercion (and this needs to be checked carefully by discussing the matter in private with each person), it would seem cavalier for the therapist categorically to deny this request. It is more reasonable to consider each request carefully, discussing with the individual or pair the pros and cons of couples counseling before coming to a decision that could involve immediate or deferred mutual counseling, or a clear decision to avoid that venue.

A second reason for undertaking couples therapy occurs when the aggressor(s) in the relationship has/have worked diligently at the individual level, taking full responsibility for his or her actions and strongly committing to nonviolence in the relationship. A new round of therapy, with that person's partner, may be quite appropriate so that the client can more fully make amends, gain improved awareness of the partner's needs, etc. Couples counseling in this setting could help restore trust and accelerate reconciliation if the couple has separated.

A third reason for couples work occurs when a couple has a long history of fairly low-level violence (such as pushing and threatening, but not closed-hand punching) and neither partner appears to have any real intention of leaving the relationship. Given the low degree of danger, the option of couples counseling may offer these people a new way to address their issues. Alternatively, some couples who seek counseling after an act of marital aggression display what Roberts and Noller (1998, p. 319) label "ordinary couple violence." This violence is generally mild (pushing and shoving rather than punching), relatively infrequent, and equally frequent for men and women. The participants in such altercations feel remorseful, as against the remorseless pattern of more violent antisocial batterers. Roberts and Noller mention that the presence of this pattern of marital aggression is often missed because researchers tend to gather their statistics on violent episodes from hospital emergency rooms and police reports, both of which describe generally more violent marital situations.

Finally, and most controversially, there are the "little to lose" clients. These couples engage in strong unidirectional or mutual violence, to the point where they inflict serious harm such as broken bones, burns, etc. They frequently have a history of police intervention. They also usually have been urged repeatedly by family, friends, attorneys, clergy, criminal justice representatives, and professional counselors to leave the relationship before one or both of them are killed. And yet they stay together, perhaps because their unresolved attachment needs make it impossible for them to part. It is definitely a gamble to attempt couples counseling here. Things could go very wrong. However, not attempting couples counseling may be even worse, in effect eschewing utilizing a systems approach that might help save someone's life. Survival odds are literally a concern in this situation: is someone more or less likely to die because of couples therapy or because that kind of therapy was not pursued?

Five guidelines are helpful in directing couples work with violent couples:

1. Couples counseling must be accompanied by a strong commitment on the part of each partner to accept full responsibility for everything that individual says or does.
2. The therapist reserves the right to curtail couples counseling temporarily or permanently if it appears that such counseling is becoming too dangerous or is ineffective.
3. The first and most important goal is the creation of a place of mutual safety, a safe haven as free as possible from acts of physical and verbal aggression. This safe haven begins in the therapy session, but must be extended to real-life situations for it to be considered effective. The safe haven may develop gradually as the frequency, intensity, and level of injury of incidents decrease.
4. As this safe haven develops, the couple can better use their relationship as a secure base with which to establish mutual intimacy.
5. Specific attachment problems, such as the fear of abandonment of the preoccupied partner and the fear of intimacy of the dismissive person, should be addressed, challenged, and amended within the framework of the couple's unique relationship.

It is also important to recognize that there are differences between couples in which violence is primarily unidirectional, when only one partner physically assaults the other, and those in which both partners are regularly violent. With regard to unidirectional aggression, the difficult therapeutic task is to firmly stand against the physical aggression of the attacker while maintaining a stance of empathy for both partners. That means the psychological vulnerability and needs of both partners must be addressed, not just those of the apparent victim. However, I believe that the recipient of violence should be offered individual therapy sessions to ensure his or her freedom of speech and safety. It would usually be advisable for that individual to receive individual counseling from a different therapist who can act as an advocate when necessary. Meanwhile, the physical aggressor may need extra time and special training in communication and empathy.

With regard to bi-directional domestic violence, one important effort must be to distinguish between a partner's defensive violence and truly mutual aggression: e.g., pushing someone back who has just hit you is defensive violence, while striking out against someone for past insults or attacks is part of a mutual aggression pattern. This distinction may be difficult to make, especially when both parties claim that they only strike defensively. I believe it is important to study each episode of aggression carefully, free from any assumptions. Counselors should get clients to discuss which situations lead to one person's aggression, the other partner's aggression, or to simultaneous aggression.

It is also necessary to recognize the reality that the stronger person's aggression is more dangerous than the weaker person's. Practically, that usually means that a male's violence is more dangerous than that of a woman. However, some women are physically quite capable of inflicting serious bodily damage to their partners with their fists and of course all individuals can cause lethal damage when armed.

If both partners are angry, there is a good chance that any children in the system are also angry and violent. I will address family work next.

Family Therapy Addressing Anger and Violence

The treatment of angry and aggressive families presents all the challenges and difficulties previously described for doing couples work. Systemic approaches, especially those that incorporate an attachment perspective (Thomas, 2007), offer perhaps the best therapeutic model for this pursuit.

I define an angry family as one in which at least two individuals from two generations regularly display excessive anger and in which anger has become the dominant emotion displayed within family interactions. A simple saying clarifies this concept: "Angry people live in angry families." Similarly, an aggressive family passes aggression down through the generations and "Aggressive people live in aggressive families." Of course this statement does not apply universally. Some individuals are uniquely angry within the family unit. But in these cases anger does not typically dominate the ongoing life of the family unit. For example, a very angry and sulking adolescent may carry on that behavior for months even while the family as a whole has little anger, the situation perhaps being defined as "Not to worry. He's just going through a stage." Even when one angry and violent person terrifies the others in the family, that dominance may be somewhat limited and not totally overwhelming: "Now kids, Dad's coming home so now we have to get real serious. We'll finish the game after he leaves for the bar." Nor do I label a unit as an angry family if only the couple is engaging in mutual hostilities, if somehow the children are carrying on their lives without excessive anger.

The box below indicates many of the patterns of chronically angry families (Potter-Efron, 1996).

211

People in Angry Families Do This:

1. One or more parent often gets angry
2. One or more child often gets angry
3. Anger drowns out other feelings
4. Lots of anger and arguing is "normal" (expected)
5. Nobody listens until someone gets angry
6. Family members try to solve problems with anger
7. Family members teach each other to be angry
8. Negative, critical, hostile feelings are common
9. People hit, push, shove, pinch, slap, hold, and threaten each other
10. Everybody blames each other
11. Everybody is easily hurt (thin-skinned), hyper-vigilant, and defensive

---

It is helpful when working with angry families to go over these characteristics in detail.

One or more parent often gets angry. One or more child often gets angry. "It never fails. Just when things are starting to go well, we have another blow up. Fight, fight, fight, that's all we do around here." Frequently that anger emanates from one or more angry adults who sets the tone for the entire family. These parents may have many reasons for being angry: bad jobs, financial stress, health concerns, marriage difficulties, etc. They may themselves have grown up in an angry home, since angry people often come from angry families. Whatever the reasons, these angry adults set the tone for the family. They model anger for the children, in effect saying "Go ahead and get angry. I do."

Meanwhile, at least one child has become habitually angry, irritable, and actively oppositional. Sibling rivalries abound, more extreme and longer lasting than in less anger-dominated families. Day in and day out, children are at each other's throats, often playing off parental divisions to gain advantage while developing mutual hostilities that will endure a lifetime.

Anger drowns out other feelings. Anger has become the dominant emotion in chronically angry families. Anger takes control of the family like a visitor who came to stay a few days but now refuses to leave. Tension is constant as almost everything that anyone says or does may precipitate a battle. There simply is no room left for "softer" emotions and behaviors like love, caring, and nurture. Sadness and fear are banished because they are signs of weakness. Joy, happiness, and contentment also become rare events in chronically angry families and cause for immediate condemnation: "Hey, you, wipe that smile off your face right now. What do you think is so funny? Now get to work." The choices of family members become limited to two states: they can be angry or neutral.

Lots of anger and arguing is "normal" (expected). Anger can become as much a part of a family's routine as breakfast. Family members come to expect and predict anger ("Don't tell me you're going to be good at Grandma's. I know better. You're going to get in trouble again like you always do"). Indeed, a day without anyone getting angry would be considered quite unusual. In essence anger has become the "default option" for these families, always set "on" unless consciously turned off.

Nobody listens until someone gets angry. Furthermore, as family members become habituated to this pattern, there is a definite possibility that the frequency and intensity of the anger episodes will increase to offset the members' building tolerance toward anger. One adolescent I worked with succinctly described this pattern: "I used to pay attention to Mom when she yelled loud. Now I ignore her until she starts throwing things at me." Mere irritability builds toward verbal anger outbursts, which gradually may be replaced by minor physical displays, which themselves are replaced by full-fledged rage episodes.

Family members try to solve problems with anger. Anger and aggression can be effective ways to get what you want and to deter others from undesired behavior. Learning this reality over time, some members of these chronically angry families intentionally work themselves into rages in order to get what they want. However, the benefits of such behavior tend to be short term and unfortunately the use of these bullying tactics forces out normal conflict management skills such as compromise and negotiation. Also, moral development for children in these families may be delayed at the pre-conventional level when the working model of the unit is "Might makes right." Angry families already have too much anger within them. They need to learn to reward each other for controlling their anger rather than exploding with it.

More generally, the members of angry families seem not to have learned a very important lesson about anger: although anger is an excellent signal that something is wrong, the mere display of anger does not solve any problems. Unfamiliar with studies that demonstrate the ill effects of excessive ventilation, they frequently voice the opinion that letting off steam is both healthy and useful. What they mean is that sometimes they feel a little better after they explode, although the reality is that often they feel worse because they have lost control and because they have precipitated yet another in a seemingly endless series of family arguments.

Family members teach each other to be angry. Anger begets anger. Children who watch their parents yell and scream at them and each other learn that getting angry is normal and expected. Furthermore, they notice that non-angry interactions are frequently ignored, while angry behavior receives more attention. In addition, parent–child interactions take on a coercive pattern, in which parents display harsh and inconsistent discipline, poor monitoring and supervision, low levels of warmth and nurturance, and high levels of negative verbalizations directed toward the children (Bloomquist and Schnell, 2002). Children in these families then tend to respond with anger, avoidance, and oppositionality. Each person's negative behavior elicits a negative reaction from the other family members. The result is a family mired in negativity.

Negative, critical, hostile feelings are common. "Fight, fight, fight. That's all we ever do. I'm so sick of the fighting that I can't wait to go to work." This kind of statement is common in angry families. As this pattern of negative interactions builds, family members give up hope that they will ever be happy together. The family as a whole seems to become depressed and despairing. Nor do family members give each other much praise, since praise would break the pattern of almost unremitting negativity. The ultimate result is that everyone over time becomes more defensive, bitter, angry, and hostile.

People hit, push, shove, pinch, slap, hold, and threaten each other. Although by no means inevitable, physical violence may be a serious problem in chronically angry families. Negative verbal interactions within these families can easily spiral toward violence over time. Grumbling turns into shouting and then shouting converts to threatening, threatening changes into shoving, shoving becomes slapping, and slapping finally yields to hitting. While not necessarily everyone in the family becomes physically violent, still everybody is deeply affected by the aggression. Adults who become violent often feel guilty and out of control of themselves as well as the family. Nonviolent spouses often feel scared and helpless. Children can be traumatized when witnessing parental violence or when they themselves become the recipients of harm. They can also learn in this manner that violence is an acceptable form of communication, something they can do either right away or when they grow up to their own partners and children.

Everybody blames each other. Members of chronically angry families seldom take responsibility for their own actions. Instead, they blame other family members, essentially playing a game of "It's not my fault." After all, who would want to admit that he or she is contributing to making everyone miserable? But people in these families will only begin to change when each person does take personal responsibility for their share of the family's anger, resentments, quarrelling, and complaining. Each person will have to make a personal commitment to contain his or her own anger and anger-provoking behaviors before the family as a whole can change.

Everybody is easily hurt (thin-skinned), hyper-vigilant, and defensive. Although one might expect family members to become distant and thick-skinned under these circumstances, my experience is that just the opposite frequently occurs; instead, family members become exceptionally sensitive to attack. They often become hyper-vigilant, ready to spring to their own defense, and all too often misinterpreting as attacks the neutral or even positive remarks of other family members. They may repeat this behavior outside their homes as well, taking a hair-trigger reactivity to threat with them into work, school, dating, and friendship situations. Certain of the inevitability that others will become hostile towards them, these habitually defensive individuals may attack first, thus gaining the reputation of being dangerous, troublesome, and erratic.

Working with angry or violent families

The three goals of anger reduction apply with angry families: to reduce the number of angry episodes, their intensity, and the damage done during these episodes. With this in mind, my first effort is to *strongly encourage parents to minimize their use of corporal punishment* as a disciplinary technique. There are many reasons to do so, since research indicates that parental use of corporal punishment is correlated with increased child oppositionality, the delayed development of empathy and an internalized conscience, and reduced self-esteem (McKay et al., 1996). However, it is quite important to remember that many parents believe strongly in the value and indeed the necessity for corporal punishment. It is critical to attempt to enter into a dialogue with these parents around the topics of when, why, and how they use corporal punishment. Hopefully, counselors and parents can at least come to some mutual understanding that protects children from unnecessary parental aggression.

It is apparent from a systems perspective that a single counselor will usually not achieve very much if the main people in the family become or stay totally opposed to the three anger reduction goals stated above. For that reason counselors should make every effort to *recruit parents as allies* during the therapeutic process. One way to do so is to share the list of angry family characteristics noted previously so that they can better recognize the pattern and realize that their own family is displaying those behaviors. Another way is to explain to the parents that you need their help in order to help their children become less volatile. Feeling respected and appreciated by the counselor, parents may be far more eager to join in the change process than if they believe that they are being coerced.

What does it mean practically when at least one parent agrees to be an ally in the name of bringing peace to the family? Although the actual role varies with each parent, in general the parent will remind other family members about this goal, begin modeling the ability to contain his or her own anger, help family members utilize fair fighting methods, engage the children in more effective problem-solving techniques, and demonstrate a willingness to respect and appreciate each member of the family.

A third point is to *help families learn how they train each other to get and stay angry*. This can be done by going through "Here we go again" repeated family cycles of anger and aggression in which each family member both instigates and reacts to the other members' anger. The goal here is to help each family member make commitments that break the cycle, such as Dad not immediately threatening to spank the children or Mom allowing her son to take a time out instead of shouting "You aren't going anywhere. You just sit down and listen to me."

A fourth step in working with angry families is to *dethrone anger*, by which I mean that anger must no longer be the only or primary emotion expressed within the family. Instead, therapists should encourage family members to notice and share both positive emotions such as happiness and love but also other negative emotions like shame and sadness. All family members will need encouragement to express these emotions as well as practice in receiving them, instead of converting all emotions immediately back into the more familiar terrain of anger.

It may be important also to *help angry families find hope that their lives could get better*. One woman I worked with, a mother of four in an amazingly chaotic and angry family, stated this yearning: "I wish we could just have one night when we could eat dinner without anyone yelling, screaming, cussing, or fighting." That goal was eventually accomplished, becoming evidence that the family was indeed improving.

When setting goals, though, it is wise to *begin with small goals that can lead to immediate success*. Angry individuals are notably impatient people; angry families are also impatient and so need quick proof that they can change. In most cases it is better to have each person make a commitment to one small change, such as an adolescent agreeing not to use one particularly nasty swear word at the table as against asking that teenager not to swear at all.

Finally, it is critical to *substitute praise for criticism* in habitually angry families. Most members of these families are poor at both giving and receiving praise. For instance, one mother I worked with made the following statement when I asked her to praise her daughter: "Missy, I liked it when you did the laundry all by yourself last night BUT you left the clothes in the dryer too long, they got all wrinkly, and now I'll have to do them all over again." Angry family members need to learn to look for things to praise (activities, accomplishments, effort, appearance, etc.), then to give praise directly to the person, and finally how to receive that praise without either shrugging it off or converting it into perceived criticism.

Summary

Individual, couples, and family therapy represent three alternative approaches to group counseling. Each has its value and difficulties. Individual therapy allows therapists to access the unique aspects of each person's anger and violence but isolates the client and helper from the client's environment. Couples therapy addresses the system but carries with it intrinsic factors that could increase the risk of violence. Family therapy may be productive but is difficult to develop and sustain. Still, all three modes of treatment should be included in anger management and domestic violence offender treatment to create the most inclusive and effective programs.

10

ANGER AND AGGRESSION
TURNED INWARD

What is "Anger Turned Inward"?

The topic of anger turned inward is a relatively neglected area in today's anger management field. That was not always the situation, however. In the 1980s, for instance, popular books like Harriet Lerner's *Dance of Anger* (1997) emphasized the need for people and in particular women to accept the reality of their anger and to utilize it appropriately as against "stuffing" it. Gestalt therapy (Polster and Polster, 1973), with its emphasis on ventilating one's emotions, was exceptionally popular then as well and also served to give clients permission to express their anger. But the emphasis in anger management changed gradually from helping overly inhibited clients get angry to helping overly demonstrative clients contain their anger. A related effort to curtail domestic abuse added to this tendency. Although clients are certainly still encouraged to express their feelings (in moderation) and to take assertive actions when appropriate, the concern with anger turned inward has become so subordinate in most anger management programs that it is not even covered in the agenda.

My definition of anger *turned inward* is wide-ranging, referring to "any conscious or unconscious process in which an individual: a) becomes angry but suppresses direct expression of that anger toward the perceived offender; b) becomes angry at another but redirects that anger upon oneself; c) regularly expresses anger at oneself because of perceived inadequacies, failures or transgressions." Thus, anger turned inward (as I am using it) includes but is not limited to suppressed anger. I define anger *suppression* as "a conscious effort not to express felt anger behaviorally or verbally." Anger turned inward may be a conscious effort, as above, or an unconscious one, in which case the proper term is anger *repression*: "an unconscious blocking of angry sensations from the consciousness of the angered individual so that he or she is unaware of being angry."

Individuals may also consciously or unconsciously redirect their anger toward themselves in situations in which others would express their anger outwardly, sometimes in relatively minor ways such as accepting blame for something gone wrong instead of accusing others, but sometimes in such pathological forms as banging one's head into a wall rather than allowing oneself to feel or express rage against another person. As I will discuss later in this chapter, there are many reasons to do so, not the least of which is the fear of being harmed if one expresses anger outwardly.

I include passive aggression in this chapter because, although the person's anger is ultimately directed at the target, it is done in ways in which one's anger is never fully acknowledged to oneself or others. In addition, clients who strongly endorsed passive aggression items in the Anger Disorders Scale (DiGiuseppe and Tafrate, 2007) also scored high on anger turned inward items, indicating a close correlation between these two concepts.

Please note that my usage of "anger turned inward" is more inclusive than Spielberger's (1999) concept of "Anger-In" as measured in the State-Trait Anger Expression Inventory—II, previously discussed. Spielberger defines Anger-In as the frequency that anger is suppressed after anger has been experienced and so focuses exclusively upon consciously suppressed anger. He also measures "Anger Expression Control-In," a scale measuring the frequency that an individual tries to lessen the *intensity* of felt anger by calming down or cooling off, another exclusively conscious effect.

DiGiuseppe and Tafrate developed an Anger-In scale as part of their Anger Disorders Scale (DiGiuseppe and Tafrate, 2004). They also used cluster analysis to distinguish 13 separate anger patterns. Of these, five are of particular interest in this chapter:

1. "Average anger and passive aggression," whose hallmark is becoming totally non-cooperative with the target of their anger.
2. "Subclinical, enduring anger with behavioral control," whose generally low level of anger is characterized by rumination, resentment, suspicion, and a desire for retribution.
3. "Ruminating, high arousal, enduring anger-in," whose anger is triggered by social rejection, social disappointments, or failures to receive attention from others. These people hold their anger in and fail to express it.
4. "Low-intensity, hostile attitudes, and anger-in," whose members were relatively low in anger but who scored somewhat higher on anger-in and resentment and suspicion than other scales.
5. "Extreme anger and aggression." These individuals were very high on many scales and had the highest overall scores on the Anger Disorders Scale. They also happened to have the highest average anger-in scores, higher than the four previous groups that would be

more commonly associated with anger turned inward. The possible implication is that this particular group of people is very angry at everybody, including themselves.

It seems evident that domestic violence episodes could develop from the above patterns. For example, the passive aggressive person who becomes totally non-cooperative with others may eventually lash out at a partner. In addition, the partner of a passive aggressive individual may become frustrated enough to lose control and strike out physically.

DiGiuseppe and Tafrate note that many people with anger-in patterns score generally low enough on anger to be excluded from being diagnosed with an anger problem. However, this is not to say they are free from anger-related symptoms. They found, for instance, that "when people hold their anger in, the desire to express anger leads to other forms of expression . . . people who hold their anger in may not be so innocent, and they get revenge through a failure to cooperate [those in the passive aggressive cluster] . . . clusters with high Anger-in scores have high scores on the Indirect Aggression subscale . . . Thus, anger-in may occur alone, with hurtful physical aggression, verbal expression, or with more indirect or passive-aggressive behaviors" (DiGiuseppe and Tafrate, 2007, p. 310).

Domestic Violence and Anger Turned Inward

The "extreme anger and aggression" cluster located by DiGiuseppe and Tafrate is indicative of the reality that someone can score highly on both anger-in and aggression. The authors state that these individuals (74% were men) score at the 95th percentile on the subscales of impulsivity, physical aggression, relational aggression, and physiological arousal. These people seem quite likely to become members of domestic violence offender groups.

Another likely connection occurs when people engage in what I call "stuff and blow" explosions. These clients often report that they knew they were becoming more and more angry, but kept trying to "shove it down" until "I couldn't take it anymore." They then committed impulsive verbal and oftentimes physical behaviors they soon regretted but couldn't undo. Feeling bad and guilty they then resolved to keep suppressing their anger even more, instead of realizing they needed to express their anger more frequently, directly, and in moderation.

It is unusual for domestic violence offender treatment programs to include the varieties of anger turned inward I have mentioned. I would suggest that therapists give serious consideration to exploring this material with their clients, though, since unexamined it could well contribute to violent recidivism.

Below is a questionnaire that helps identify individuals with strong tendencies to suppress their anger, respond to their anger with passive aggressive tactics, and/or primarily target themselves with their anger. This instrument has not been scientifically normed, however, so it should only be utilized in an advisory fashion. Nevertheless, it is helpful both to gather information and to educate and motivate clients. It is useful to discuss with clients any single item that they have scored at least 3 points on. Also, I suggest that a score of 15 points (an average of 3 points per item) per area is indicative of some anger turned inward issues, while a score of 20 points (an average of 4 points per item) is indicative of a definite tendency toward excessively turning anger inward in that area.

Anger Turned Inward Quiz

How often and how much do you turn anger inward? Here's a quick checklist. Please score each item from 1 to 5 points, where:

1 = That's not what I do at all
2 = I only do that once in a great while
3 = I do that fairly often
4 = I do that a lot
5 = I do that all the time

1. ____ I feel angry with someone but don't say anything.
2. ____ I indirectly let people know I'm angry by pouting, sulking, etc.
3. ____ I become so angry with myself that I call myself names like stupid, ugly, etc.
4. ____ I'm afraid others will be angry with me if I show anger.
5. ____ I often "forget" on purpose things people want me to do.
6. ____ I am full of anger at myself.
7. ____ I "stuff" my anger and then get headaches, a stiff neck, stomach aches, etc.
8. ____ I'm good at frustrating people by not doing what they want.
9. ____ Others don't realize how angry I get at myself.
10. ____ I put on a good front by smiling and looking happy even when I'm angry.
11. ____ I ignore people when I'm angry at them.
12. ____ When I get mad at myself, I physically attack my body (scratching, biting, burning, head banging, etc.).
13. ____ I tell myself I should never get angry, no matter what the provocation.

14. ____ The saying "Don't get mad, get even" fits what I do when I'm angry.
15. ____ I am more likely to get mad at myself than at other people.

Guidelines:
Items 1, 4, 7, 10, and 13 are indicative of suppressed anger.
Items 2, 5, 8, 11, and 14 are indicative of passive aggression.
Items 3, 6, 9, 12, and 15 are indicative of self-directed anger.
Any item scored 3 or higher should be discussed.
Any area with a score of 15 or higher indicates possible clinical concerns in that area.
Any area with a score of 20 or higher indicates probable clinical concerns in that area.

Suppressed Anger

It is certainly appropriate for people to occasionally suppress anger. However, some individuals seem to have lost a sense of choice in this matter: they automatically redirect anger inwardly that could safely be expressed outwardly. These people could benefit from treatment for anger with the stated goal of helping them achieve a better balance between the two poles of turning anger in and out. Needless to say, the optimum end state is someone who can express their anger in moderation, not someone who travels from excessively turning anger against the self into someone acting out long-restricted vengeful fantasies.

Clients with strong tendencies toward suppressing their anger have many identifiable patterns of behavior. These patterns frequently emanate from a central prohibition against directly expressing anger against others. Many of these people have essentially renounced their anger. They believe that good people do not and should not get angry very often, if at all. Thus, they attempt to suppress any negative feelings they have toward others. If they cannot do that all the time, so that they have to admit to themselves that they are really upset about something, they can at least make a commitment not to let others know that they are angry. Thus, many of these people become habitual anger and conflict avoiders, tending to handle conflict more through avoidance and accommodation than through negotiation, compromise, or collaboration. Compromise and collaboration cannot be pursued because they are activities in which people must address and promote their desires, raising the possibility for anger and aggression. Over time, though, some "anger stuffers" recognize that they are far angrier than they want anybody to realize. Still, they rigorously attempt to maintain and display a "public self" even within their families that is very different from their own sense of self. They loyally play the role of a happy, never angry person but know that is not their real self. Some of these clients come to therapy smiling and laughing even while seething with undisclosed fury against the world. They feel rageful inside but refuse to disclose their feelings to anyone, least of all those who have offended them.

Sometimes anger suppressors allow their stifled anger out in sudden and unpredictable "stuff and blow" episodes. These individuals suddenly become extremely and disproportionately irate over seemingly small problems. Their thoughts on these occasions usually approximate the idea that "I couldn't take it anymore" when they finally blow up. Unfortunately, such dramatic ventilations seldom prove useful because they do not lead to effective problem-solving. Indeed, these people are likely to conclude from them only that they made a mistake by getting mad and in this way reinforce their tendency to direct their anger inwardly.

Since clients whose anger is primarily directed inwardly are poor communicators who have difficulty directly addressing their grievances, they tend to hold grudges. Letting go of old insults, much less truly forgiving the offender, is hard when people cannot even acknowledge to others, and sometimes themselves, how truly angry they are.

All these patterns are destructive to an individual's health. Suppressed anger has been linked with proneness toward anxiety, depression, somatic complaints, and heart disease (Martin et al., 1999; Begley, 1994; Lisspers, Nygren, and Söderman, 1998). Begley (1994) notes that people who turn their anger inward often feel very responsible for others even though they are angry with them. This combination of high anger turned inward and high responsibility for others is particularly associated with anxiety, depression, and somatic complaints. This combination of thoughts translates to "I'm angry with you right now, but if I expressed my anger I would hurt you, so I can't do that because I also feel responsible for you. That means I must keep my anger at you to myself." Interestingly, I observe this pattern regularly with my domestic violence offender clients. Alcohol or drug abuse may also develop as individuals utilize these substances either to help them contain their anger or to become disinhibited enough to express anger at others (Tivis, Parsons, and Nixon, 1998).

Finally, Martin et al. (1999) mention that many people who do not disclose anger are generally emotionally inexpressive. These individuals don't experience and/or don't express other emotions as well as anger. Thus, such people will need therapeutic help to express the entire range of their emotions, not just anger, during counseling.

Reasons why anger may be suppressed

There are several possible reasons, described below, that promote the tendency to suppress one's anger. The more of these justifications that are endorsed by a particular individual, the stronger is the belief that anger should or must be suppressed.

- **Fear of harming others.** As just noted, one reason people suppress their anger is a strong sense that they are responsible for the feelings of others. Not wanting to hurt anyone, even when angry, they choose instead to keep quiet even at the cost of their own emotional, mental, and physical well-being. Although counselors promote the expression of anger as necessary and even beneficial in relationships, some individuals believe that expressing anger is almost inevitably harmful, causing immediate or long-term damage to the target of the anger. Turning anger onto oneself then deflects the damage onto oneself, a decision that would be viewed as a better moral and practical choice.

  Some individuals with a history of violence, general or family-centered, legitimately fear loss of control if they ever become angry. One man I worked with who had an exceptionally violent history said this: "I know I stuff my anger all the time but I'm afraid I'll kill someone if I don't."

- **Compliance with learned moral training.** Closely related to the point above, some people learn in childhood that they *should* suppress their anger instead of expressing it in ambiguously frustrating situations. Thus, suppressing one's anger is morally superior to lashing out with it. The painful and unacceptable cost of expressing one's anger here is guilt. On the other hand, these individuals may feel a certain pride in suppressing their anger, a sense that they are doing a socially valued and morally correct thing.

  Some men in my groups have been raised with a moral claim that one should never strike a woman no matter what she says or does to them. These men may find themselves in relationships with women who regularly initiate violence. They cannot easily leave such women since in their minds they should not be upset with these acts of aggression. Eventually, though, they do "defend" themselves, often getting charged with domestic violence as a result.

- **Disavowal of protest.** Suppressed anger turned inward may be linked with early childhood socialization in many ways. Beyond simply being discouraged from getting angry or from expressing emotions in general, some families specifically reject the right of children to object to perceived injustices. As Robert Karen writes, "One of the most devastating things we experienced [as children] was the rejection of our protests – they were dismissed as wrong, irrational, illogical, rude, insulting, disloyal, ungrateful, and so on" (Karen, 2001, p. 89). When children are taught that they should never protest, they may instead suppress their anger or even attack themselves whenever they sense an angry impulse in order to quash that impulse before it is exposed.

- **Fear of punishment.** Sometimes protests may be more than just discouraged. They may instead be severely punished through physical attack, loss of love, and verbal aggression. In these situations it may be too dangerous for children to direct their anger at someone else, even when that other person is the cause of their anger.

- **Relationship maintenance.** Expressing anger can be immediately disruptive to the smooth flow of relationships. Normal routines become disrupted when someone's anger "rocks the boat," causing disruption and "wasting" time and energy. Needs, vulnerabilities, wants, and desires become exposed when anger is expressed, sometimes bringing with them the threat of impending chaos. Given these risks, some individuals decide that suppressing their anger is better than risking the potential loss of a relationship.

General therapeutic concepts and guidelines: treating suppressed anger and aggression

There are many opportunities for therapeutic intervention with clients who suppress their anger. Several of these possibilities are described below.

Help clients recognize the signs and signals that they are getting angry

The line between suppression and repression of one's anger is indistinct. Clients may not be fully aware of how often they decline opportunities to become angry. Consequently, clients may need to become more aware of the signs they are becoming angry and/or directing their anger at themselves. Some of these signs include: relatively direct physical cues such as making fists or aggressively scratching themselves; suggestive somatic symptoms such as headaches or fatigue; thought patterns that predict or precede "stuff and blow" episodes in which clients suddenly lose control of their anger; behavioral cues such as avoidance of others or diving harder into work that occur when clients are nearing the limits of their ability to contain their anger; emotional symptoms such as increased depression or anxiety that might be related to the existence of suppressed anger; and existential or spiritual symptoms including hopelessness and despair. Of course the mere appearance of these behaviors is not positive evidence for anger turned inward. Patterns of behavior and cognition need to be established that repeatedly correlate these events with inwardly focused anger.

Help clients recognize indirect expressions of anger

Some clients who primarily direct their anger inwardly, especially those who very consciously suppress their angry feelings towards others, may come to realize during counseling that their anger "leaks out" in relatively subtle fashion. Typically, they frequently make slightly cynical, suspicious, or negative remarks (for instance, "Oh, really. I would never have thought of that" in the face of someone's obvious statement). This pattern is related to passive aggression but usually less consciously perceived.

Discuss positive and negative aspects of internalizing one's anger

Internalized anger has its rewards. It is essential to discuss these payoffs with clients in order to discover which of these advantages is most relevant to them. There are practical advantages such as lessening the risk of harming others with one's anger, avoiding retaliation, and avoiding perhaps unnecessary conflicts. Additionally, there are cognitive and conceptual advantages including the sense that suppressing one's anger is morally appropriate or consistent with the client's self-concept. But there are also significant negative results when people primarily internalize anger. These include such practical disadvantages as non-resolution of conflictual issues because legitimate concerns are not addressed, needs not getting met because they are not expressed, the eventual resultant build up of resentments, loss of self-esteem, the health risks mentioned previously, and the possibility of eventual violence. Equally significant may be the client's invalidation of his or her emotions ("No, I'm not angry") and excessive guilt at the mere thought of expressing anger ("It's not OK to feel angry"). Finally, individuals with chronic patterns of suppressed anger, especially when combined with excessive shame, may develop self-damaging patterns of behavior that will be described later in this chapter.

Selected specific therapeutic interventions and exercises

I have found the following discussions and exercises useful because they help clients recognize the extent to which they utilize anger turned inward and also the consequences of doing so.

First, have clients describe in detail how, when, where, and with whom they suppress their anger, including their justifications for doing so. The "Anger Turned Inward Quiz" presented earlier in this chapter is quite useful in developing this dialogue, as is this series of questions:

1. Is the suppressed anger best described as anger that: a) the client has completely not perceived, or b) the client knows about but minimizes its intensity, or c) the client is aware of but doesn't want to express outwardly?
2. How intense or powerful is this anger?
3. How *important* is it to the client to contain this anger?
4. How *difficult* is it for the client to contain this anger?
5. What does the client think might happen if he or she were to express anger outwardly more often? Would it be dangerous?
6. What are the gains and costs to the client when he or she suppresses anger?
7. To what extent does the client want to a) quit being as angry with his or her self and/or b) redirect the anger towards external targets?

With regard to this last question, I believe it is important that the counselor generally acts as a neutral party who helps clients to decide when to continue internalizing anger and when to change its direction. However, on occasion it may be appropriate to become an advocate for expressing anger, for example in situations where the client is clearly being misused or abused by others. Here the therapist can become an advocate for action by giving clients permission and encouragement to express anger directly to others.

Motivation to redirect anger externally may be insufficient, though, if clients have not developed the requisite skills. Therefore counselors may need to teach specific skills, such as making "I" statements, saying "no" to unreasonable or excessive requests, effective assertiveness, conflict management techniques, and negotiation tactics, all of which serve to help build both the client's competence and confidence. Role-playing expressing and receiving anger with clients is another way to improve their ability to direct their anger outwardly. These role-plays can be graded by beginning with the therapist acting the part of someone quite willing to be confronted ("Jackie, I'm really glad you told me that my coming home late bothers you. I didn't know that at all."), but evolving into people who are initially defensive ("What are you talking about? I'm not coming home late") or outright aggressive ("Who the Hell are you to tell me what to do? I'll come home whenever I want!").

Another useful set of interventions are questions designed to help clients recognize their choices. Three of these questions are: "If your anger had a voice, what would it be saying to you?" "What is the message in your anger that you need to act upon?" "If your anger at yourself is appropriate, then what do you need to do to become less angry at yourself?"

Finally, a Gestalt therapy two-chair dialogue in which clients alternate between the part of themselves that suppresses anger and the part of themselves that would prefer expressing it can be quite effective in helping individuals to validate both aspects of themselves so that they can more effectively select the best action to take in the varied situations they face.

CASE STUDY

The Lady Who Quit Smiling

Jenni Calloway, 45, comes to counseling after a strange, out-of-character incident that has left her shocked and confused. This woman describes herself as generally quiet, unassuming, conflict avoidant, and over-responsible for others, the kind of woman who can always be counted on to bake a cake for the church fund drive even if she baked three for the one just last month.

Jenni wears a constant smile, even while discussing distressing events. She explains that when she was growing up her mother always told her that people only like you when you smile. Lately, though, life has been hard for Jenni. Her husband Paul has suffered a serious back injury that put him out of work and quickly developed an addiction to pain medications. Her oldest daughter Sue accused Jenni of being selfish because she asked to have Christmas at Sue's house instead of her own due to Paul's condition. Furthermore, people at work have been taking advantage of Jenni by dumping unpleasant duties on her.

Jenni admits that she "stuffs" her anger a lot: "I'm like that old saying about a pressure cooker that keeps gaining pressure until it blows up." But actually she never had exploded until the week before she came to counseling. Then, in a single day she swore at one of her work colleagues, told Paul to "get off that stinking couch and do something with your life," and blasted her daughter over the phone. Shaken, she signed up for therapy. True to form, she told the counselor that her goal was to get back to being someone who could smile again.

A mixture of shame and maladaptive guilt emerged as her dominant emotion, since she was usually either feeling guilty about her alleged transgressions (especially "selfishness") or desperately trying to please others so as to avoid shame. This emotional mixture prevented Jenni from setting appropriate boundaries with others because saying "no" to anyone, however unreasonable their request, made her feel terrible.

The combination of suppressed anger and excessive guilt made treatment difficult and slow. The first step was to help Jenni recognize what she was doing with her anger and its relationship to her maladaptive guilt. Some family of origin work around the family myths and belief systems that supported Jenni's continual smiling was necessary. However, the bulk of work was present-oriented with emphasis on her right and ability to make choices, say "no," and set boundaries. Jenni read books on assertiveness and practiced confronting her work colleagues during role-plays in the office. She eventually decided exactly what single specific action to contest: a co-worker's habit of dropping off work on Jenni's desk as that woman headed out the door. Jenni stopped that person, told her to take that work back, and handled her inevitable guilt by reminding herself she was doing the right thing even though it felt bad. After her success at work, Jenni spoke with her husband and daughter about how she was changing. She told them she was not going to smile quite as much as they were used to. She also stated that she might even get angry from time to time. Fortunately, her family supported her efforts once they realized that a more assertive Jenni might also be a more truly loving Jenni.

Jenni still feels guilty frequently. But now she uses that guilt in a new way: "Whenever I start to feel guilty, I ask myself what I am angry about. When I figure that out, I ask myself what I want to do about it. And then, if I can, I talk directly to whomever I need to about it." In other words, Jenni has learned to direct her anger outwardly instead of constantly suppressing it.

Passive Aggression

I often call passive aggression "sneaky anger" (Potter-Efron and Potter-Efron, 2006) with my clients. The term refers to how clients with strong passive aggressive traits demonstrate their anger in ways that are especially difficult to recognize. It also refers to the quiet sense of victory passive aggressive clients often feel when they "defeat" their antagonists with passive behaviors.

The key to understanding passive aggressive clients is to understand their behavior as a weapon used by relatively weak individuals (or at least people who feel relatively weak) against those who are stronger by weight of position or personality. These stronger individuals inevitably attempt to assert their power and authority upon the client, who then feels both overpowered and resentful. Passive aggressive clients do not feel confident enough to directly express their anger and resentment, however. Instead, they resist authority and display their anger more through inertia than direct protest. While some passive aggressive people don't consciously recognize their anger, others know full well that they are upset with people but cannot give themselves permission to say so directly. Instead, they continually frustrate their partners, family, work associates, and anyone else whom they believe wants to have power over them. They may admit, with gentle prodding, that they derive a definite sense of pleasure from defeating their foes in this manner.

Passive aggressive behavior is likely to occur in couples where one partner is generally dominant. The partner, feeling weak and ineffective, may resort to passive aggressive behaviors in an effort to retain some sense of autonomy. In a worst case scenario such behavior will infuriate the dominator and lead to more violence.

Passive aggressive clients exhibit an astoundingly creative range of behaviors or non-behaviors. For instance, they may:

Forget things on purpose. Everybody forgets, of course, some more than others. But passive aggressive clients are experts at forgetting exactly what is really important to someone else. One example would be a partner who "forgets" to place an ad in the paper giving away a batch of kittens just because his wife refused to neuter the mother cat months ago.

Make promises with no intention of carrying them out. "Yes, honey" (or "boss") "I'll do that by Friday for sure." Internally the passive aggressive client is angered about being asked to do more and more work, but rather than say anything he or she simply ignores the job.

Make a thousand excuses. I call this the "yeah but" game. "Yes, I'd walk to the store, but my feet hurt too much;" "Sure I'd love to go to the play, but you know Friday is my bad day," etc. The goal is eventually to frustrate others enough that they quit asking for anything.

Use stalling tactics. One frustrated wife's passive aggressive husband had managed not to finish a bathroom project for over two years, forcing the family to use an inconvenient bathroom in the basement. Needless to say, he took offense when his family complained, saying they always wanted more from him than he could do.

Play dumb or helpless. I once had a client who explained that he couldn't get home on time because he was bad at reading clocks. He was, however, an advanced level computer programmer for a time efficiency organization.

Isolate themselves. Basements seem to be favorite hangouts for people with passive aggressive tendencies. Their theory seems to be that if nobody can find them, then nobody can order them around.

Pout and sulk. Some passive aggressive clients do allow hints of their dissatisfaction to leak out, announcing their anger through pouting and sulking (Forgays et al., 1998). When asked what they are upset about, they may well refuse to say, making others play a guessing game.

Display sudden bursts of anger. The "stuff and blow" pattern mentioned with anger suppressors also appears with passive aggressive individuals. The only difference is that it often appears with a distinct "Nobody appreciates all I do around here" theme. Passive aggressors often feel overworked and underappreciated even while others see them as under-working and over-rewarded.

There is a central theme to all these behaviors: "You can't make me." This leads to a repeated pattern of mini-dramas, tugs of war between demanding spouses, children, employers, colleagues, and all authority figures against seemingly overmatched, resentful but resourceful individuals determined to maintain their autonomy.

I believe that at the extreme some passive aggressive people develop their identity around "You can't make me." This pattern creates a negative identity best expressed as "I won't be who you want me to be." My clients often agree wholeheartedly with this statement. What puzzles them, though, is if I ask them to tell me who they are rather than who they refuse to be. In other words much more of their energy and identity centers on defiance. They are so busy, and from a brain perspective so habituated, doing this that they have little concept of a positive self striving to meet one's own goals in life.

Interventions for passive aggression

First, it is important that these clients better recognize and acknowledge their anger. Although some passive aggressors do fully understand their actions, many do not and tend to see themselves as hapless and defeated but not particularly angry people. It is important to explain how their actions and inactions are indeed manifestations of anger. It is important to explore empathically the client's positive feelings about this behavior before moving on to its many costs.

Second, these clients must be challenged to exchange passive aggressive tactics for more assertive behaviors. Bear in mind that some of these clients are in relationships with relatively powerful partners who may tend to be aggressive and demanding. Also note that such behavior may be just as much a reaction to the passive aggressor's tactics "driving me crazy" as their natural style. Having clients practice clearly saying "yes" and "no" out loud helps them get a feeling for the simple power of these words. This goes along with helping them make active choices about positive goals. They also need to tell people out loud when they feel pushed around rather than grumbling about it.

Third, longer term self-concept work might be needed since assertive behavior is not likely to succeed if accompanied by a sense of weakness and incompetence.

Anger Directed at Self

Not all anger directed at oneself is intrinsically bad. Some anger at self may be an appropriate response to a personal mistake or transgression. Getting angry with oneself may be perfectly reasonable in certain circumstances, especially when someone has done something that has caused harm either to themselves or others. This response may lead to reparative efforts in the same way that anger against others may lead to altered social interactions. The appropriate therapeutic question here, then, is "How can you use your current anger at yourself to make things better?"

However, many clients who direct their anger at themselves are afflicted with great amounts of shame. Deeply shamed individuals may have powerfully internalized an abiding sense of badness, worthlessness, incompetence, etc. that leads to chronic, continuing self-condemnation. Turning their anger onto themselves is a way of endorsing their internal sense of defectiveness. This response occurs when individuals believe they should punish themselves after making a mistake or transgression. These attacks are not reparative because the nature of the problem is not addressed. The reasoning process is somewhat primitive: "I did something bad so I must hurt myself." Sometimes this pattern has developed in situations of extreme external threat, as with parental physical abuse. In effect the child develops a habit of punishing himself or herself before the parent does so, at least partly to maintain a limited sense of control over a life-threatening situation.

The combination of excessive levels of anger and shame may result in a variety of self-damaging behaviors. The result of excessive shame is that clients often think they are no good, not good enough, unlovable, that they believe they do not belong anywhere, and that in the extreme they should not exist (Potter-Efron and Potter-Efron, 1989). Meanwhile, the simultaneous presence of high levels of anger turned inward may result in a tendency toward self-punishment. Combined, shame and anger turned inward predicts a variety of self-damaging attitudes and behaviors, as illustrated in the pyramid below. The behaviors at the base of the pyramid are the most common but least damaging, while those at the top are least common but most destructive.

Self-neglect

Shame most commonly drives people to withdraw from whatever causes their shame (Tangney and Dearing, 2002; Potter-Efron, 2002). When

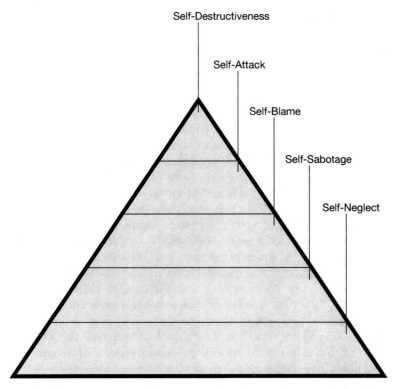

Figure 10.1 Pyramid of self-damaging thoughts and behaviors.

that source is the self, then shamed individuals may flee from self-awareness and self-attentiveness. The result is self-neglect, defined as "disinterest in and inability to attend to oneself." Although not essential to the pattern of self-neglect, these individuals are also likely to fail to recognize and express their external anger, especially if those individuals also feel shameful enough to believe they are not or good enough to merit attention, and if they believe they are less valuable in general than others. Given that combination of elements, anger at others may be redirected toward oneself in the relatively passive form of self-neglect.

One of the characteristics of self-neglect is that individuals may appear to be disinterested in themselves while being highly focused on the welfare of others. Clients may justify this pattern of self-neglect on moral grounds, arguing that they are taking care of others while neglecting themselves because that is the morally correct thing to do. Their message is "Let me take care of you because that is the right thing to do," but the underlying theme is really "Let me take care of you because I myself am not worthy of care." Nagged by this mostly unconscious conviction, self-neglecting people often fail to notice or attend to their basic wants and needs, such as making doctor appointments, getting exercise, and finding time to sleep. Furthermore, they will have difficulty and feel excessively guilty saying "no" to others even when angry about those people's expectations or demands. These individuals have difficulty either listening to their anger as it signals a problem ("Something's wrong here!") or to utilize the energy that accompanies anger in order to change their environment.

One cost of self-neglect is that individuals who are unable to attend to their own needs and are over-responsive to others may periodically collapse when overwhelmed by their responsibilities. Even then, though, they will be reluctant to receive help from others, and they will make every effort to restore the equilibrium as quickly as possible.

The treatment for self-neglect must address both helping clients gain better awareness of their anger and challenging the internalized shame that keeps them from addressing their needs. In particular they must become much more comfortable saying "no" to others and "yes" to themselves, a pattern diametrically opposed to their self-neglecting tendencies. That means discovering and listening to their inner self-nurturing voice, but to do so they first must become more curious about and interested in themselves as human beings worthy of attention.

Self-neglecting people must be challenged to question the absolute moral correctness of giving priority to others instead of themselves. "Who told you that?" is often a good starting place for this challenge, especially if they received strong family of origin messages to take care of others first, last, and always. Naturally the idea is not to turn such individuals into totally hedonistic self-centered egotists, but to help them balance their care for others with self-care. Doing so will help prevent the periodic collapsing burn-out pattern described above.

Self-sabotage

Self-sabotage is the second self-damaging combination of anger turned inward and shame. Self-sabotage is essentially passive aggression turned inward. Here anger against the self is displayed through a variety of failure patterns. For example, clients often demonstrate an inability to finish projects even when they say they personally desire to do so, they don't get around to making personally important phone calls, etc. Driven by a combination of shame and self-directed anger, these clients fail at least partially in order to exact punishment against their inadequate selves.

Passive aggression against others represents a quiet rebellion against authority, control, and being told what to do. Similarly, I believe self-sabotage may represent the client's perpetual rebellion against internalized demands. The client says "You can't make me" not to others but to an internalized voice that demands achievement and success. The result, unfortunately, is the creation of an abiding negative routine in which clients seemingly destroy almost every opportunity they have for personal happiness.

The treatment for self-sabotage involves helping clients challenge their internalized "I don't deserve to succeed" messages. These messages must first be identified, then linked with shame and anger turned inward, and then challenged through standard cognitive therapy approaches such as disputation. It is also important to discover and challenge the personal failure patterns and rituals of such clients. That is because people usually fail repeatedly in the same manner. For instance, one of my clients developed a highly predictable pattern of carrying through with great success on a number of projects just until the very last step, such as turning in the final paper for a college class. That's when he simply stopped working, as if he were paralyzed by the threat of accomplishment. Identification of this pattern helped this client begin to break this routine. In this case it was helpful to treat the ongoing failures of this client like a phobia, setting small goals so he could take small steps toward success.

Self-blame

Whereas the presence of shame and anger turned inward might have to be inferred in self-neglect and self-sabotage, that is hardly the case with self-blame. Here clients are more than ready consciously to attack themselves, almost as if they lived by the slogan "When in doubt it must be my fault." Shame-bound (Kaufman, 1996), the working model of these people is that they are to blame for everything that goes wrong because they possess an irrational sense of being responsible for all problems. Metaphorically, these clients seem to possess an internalized scolder and flaw seeker, a part of themselves that continually scans the environment looking for things they have done wrong. Quick to blame themselves, their anger turned inward takes the form of blistering verbal accusations: "Dummy, why did you do that?" "What's wrong with you anyhow?" "How could you think anybody would ever love you?"

Treatment for self-blaming begins with helping clients challenge the idea that they are always to blame for everything that goes badly ("Who told you that?"). They need to recognize the connections between their self-blaming reproach and the existence of internalized shame. That in turn might allow them to quit taking excessive responsibility for others and to exchange their negative scanning pattern for more neutral or positive scanning patterns. Eventually they may learn to see themselves in a more positive light so that they can give themselves praise as well as criticism as befits the actual situation.

It may also be useful with self-blaming clients to have them describe and externalize their internalized scolder and flaw seeker, perhaps by writing their imagined critic a letter to be read and discussed in therapy or by engaging in a two-chair dialogue in which clients alternate speaking on behalf of the critic ("I'm only telling the truth. You are really a pitiful excuse for a human being") and the part of themselves that wants to accept the self ("Leave me alone. I'm a good person and I'm tired of feeling ashamed of myself all the time").

Self-attack

The fourth form of self-damaging behavior occurs as clients increase their verbal aggression and add physical aggression to their attack against the self. By now the anger turned inward has become rageful. It is as if these individuals possessed an internalized punisher. This intropunitive agent, often primitive in thought, sometimes literally demands blood, triggering episodes of self-mutilation in which the primary message becomes "I am bad. I deserve pain. I must suffer. I must hurt myself to demonstrate my badness to everyone." This behavior may signal others not to attack since the self-attacker is already at work, especially with those individuals who have been badly verbally, physically, or sexually abused as children.

Interpersonally, some clients mired in self-attack may tend to attract punishing partners. These abusive partners externalize the client's internal attack; in response to their internalized statement "I am a bad person who deserves punishment" their partner responds with "Yes you are and I will be the one who hurts you." However, I want to state that this interpretation must be used very cautiously around clients who are in abusive relationships. No matter what the internal cognitive state of the recipients of abuse may be, abusive partners must not be given an excuse to perpetuate their actions.

Treatment for self-attacking clients begins with helping them make a commitment to lessening the frequency and intensity of self-attack episodes, in particular self-mutilation events. However, before they can do this some clients may need to describe the characteristics of their internalized punisher, including sensed age, gender, most common thoughts, etc. Gathering this information helps clients contest the need to be punished and sometimes, when the internalized punisher is found to be an introjected form of a punishing parent or other significant figure, clients can then begin to externalize and reject the internalized figure. In other situations, those in which clients are diverting rage against others onto themselves, they must learn to listen for the underlying message in their physical aggression against themselves. For instance, a client who engages in butting his head into a wall may really just want to smash through an adversary or, less obviously, that client might desperately want someone important to step in and stop his or her suffering. Finally, but critically, self-attacking people must learn to select non-punitive friends, employers, and partners. Self-attackers can only thrive in the presence of others who fully appreciate their goodness and who refuse to join in with the person's internalized punisher.

Self-destructiveness

Self-destructiveness is the most extreme combination of anger turned inward and shame. The internalized shame message is "I should not be" (Potter-Efron and Potter-Efron, 1989), a message that strongly promotes suicidal ideation. In addition, clients develop a powerful splitting process that places their selves into an "all bad" (evil) category while practically everyone else is good. The result is a sense of hopelessness and despair that serves to prevent these individuals from taking in praise, comfort, or love. Internally, it is as if these people were haunted by the presence of "internalized annihilators" that produce within themselves a sense of inevitable doom. Life can only be bad for these individuals, so what sense is there in living?

The long-term treatment for self-destructiveness lies in helping clients convert their "I should not be" messages to messages that simply state "I am." This usually represents a long and difficult journey because clients must learn to bypass their shame and internalized anger, to quit trying either to prove they should or should not exist, and instead learn how to view themselves without judgment, approval, or disapproval. Some of these people could benefit by learning about the concept of splitting and how their particular splitting process makes them appear totally bad and evil to themselves. Therapists will certainly need to help self-destructive clients voice and gently challenge their despair, being careful to check for the presence of a major depressive condition in the process. Those clients closest to suicide will need to remember and take in the love of others even when in despair and to acknowledge how others would be affected by their death. It may also be useful to help these clients get in touch with their inner self-preserver, the part that wants to survive and that brings them to therapy.

What if Clients are High on Both Anger Turned Inward and Outward?

Spielberger's (1999) findings from research with the State-Trait Anger Expression Inventory—II was that Anger-In and Anger-Out are relatively uncorrelated and that some individuals can be high on both Anger-In and Anger-Out, while others may be low on both variables. I believe this double situation may reflect people who stay continually very angry even while they frequently express themselves loudly and clearly. Their anger does not go away no matter how often they use it and it may not be used for the purpose of getting something specific. These could be individuals for whom their anger simply begets more anger. These people may be likely candidates for committing acts of domestic violence, given their continuing anger, suspiciousness, and hostility.

I also speculate that many of these clients are habitually and chronically angry at both others and themselves. Their anger directed inwardly, though, may be missed in traditional anger management and domestic violence offender programs that by necessity focus upon anger and aggression against others. One result may be that clients confuse "stuffing" their anger, i.e., redirecting it inwardly, with learning how to express their external anger appropriately. Furthermore, untreated inner-directed anger may actually sabotage clients' efforts to contain their externally directed anger, since they still have not fundamentally altered their relationship with their anger. If anger remains the dominant emotion in someone's life, that individual is unlikely to be able to maintain a commitment to non-aggression.

Once it is recognized that clients are high on both directions of anger, it is important to address the problem primarily as an excess of anger rather than a directional issue. Clients need to be encouraged to make a commitment to lessening the totality of their anger. That means setting goals of becoming angry at both the self and others less frequently and decreasing the intensity of both anger experiences. The alternative is to experience and express anger in moderation in both spheres.

Therapists can help their clients discover what circumstances are most likely to trigger turning anger inward, outward, or in both directions. For example, a client may regularly turn anger inward with a spouse but direct it outwardly towards children (or vice versa). Clients who can learn to identify their key trigger thoughts in response to anger invitations from the environment may discover that some issues trigger internal attack ("I did it again. I'm worthless"), while others trigger external aggression ("Nobody can say that to me!"). Another related therapeutic task is to find out how the messages clients give themselves when turning their anger upon themselves are similar or different to the messages they give others when their anger is directed outward.

Should one direction of anger be treated first? My preference is to allow the client to set initial priorities on which anger direction to treat, but to continually address both issues and their relation to each other. However, externally directed anger containment may have to be the initial focus if the client is extremely hostile or violent. If so, it is still critical that the client receive treatment for both directions of anger.

Clients who are high in both anger directions will need help generally developing a compassionate attitude towards themselves, significant others, and the world. Love, caring, empathy, and kindness must find more room in the client's mental universe. Otherwise they will continue to be besieged with angry thoughts, feelings, and behaviors.

Summary

Anger may be turned inward in several ways: it may be suppressed, converted into passive aggression, or directed against the self in such forms as self-neglect, self-blame, self-shaming, self-attack, and self-destruction. Anger turned inward may replace anger directed outwardly, but may also exist along with anger-out. The goal in any case is to help clients identify how and why they turn their anger inward and to then help them reduce these behaviors while either assisting them to appropriately express their anger (as with assertiveness counseling) or become less generally angry.

REFERENCES

Alberti, R. & Emmons, M. (2001). *Your perfect right* (eighth edition). Atascadero, CA: Impact Publishers.

Alcoholics Anonymous (1976). *Alcoholics Anonymous Big Book*. New York: A.A. World Service.

Amthor, F. (2012). *Neuroscience for dummies*. Mississauga, ON: John Wiley & Sons Canada.

APA (2014). *Diagnostic and statistical manual of the American Psychiatric Association*. Washington, DC: American Psychiatric Association.

Babcock, J.C., Costa, D., Green, C.E., & Eckhardt, C.I. (2004). What situations induce intimate partner violence? A reliability and validity study of the proximal antecedents to violent episodes (PAVE) scale. *Journal of Family Psychology*, 18(3), 433–442.

Badenoch, B. (2008). *Being a brain-wise therapist*. New York: W.W. Norton.

Bartholomew, K., Henderson, A., & Dutton, D. (2001). Insecure attachment and insecure intimate relationships. In C. Clulow (Ed.), *Adult attachment and couple psychotherapy* (pp. 43–62). London: Brunner-Routledge.

Baumeister, R.F., Smart, L., & Boden, J. (1996). Relation of threatened egotism to violence and aggression. *Psychological Review*, 103, 25–33.

Beck, A. (1976). *Cognitive therapy and the emotional disorders*. New York: International Universities Press.

Beck, A. (1999). *Prisoners of hate: The cognitive basis of anger, hostility and violence*. New York: HarperCollins.

Begley, T. (1994). Expressed and suppressed anger as predictors of health complaints. *Journal of Organizational Behavior*, 15(6), 503–516.

Begun, A., Brondino, M., Bolt, B., Weinstein, B., Strodthoff, T., & Shelly, G. (2008). The revised Safe at Home instrument for assessing readiness to change intimate family violence. *Violence and Victims*, 23(4), 508–524.

Berecz, J. (2001). All that glitters is not gold: Bad forgiving in counseling and preaching. *Pastoral Psychology*, 49(4), 253–275.

Berman, W. & Sperling, M. (1994). The structure and function of adult attachment. In M. Sperling & W. Berman (Eds.), *Attachment in adults* (pp. 1–30). New York: Guilford Press.

Berman, W., Marcus, L., & Berman, E. (1994). Attachment in marital relations. In M. Sperling & W. Berman (Eds.), *Attachment in adults* (pp. 204–231). New York: Guilford Press.

240

Berns, G. & Atrin, S. (2012). The biology of cultural conflict. *Philosophical Transactions of the Royal Society: Biological Sciences, 367,* 633–639.

Bloomquist, M. & Schnell, S. (2002). *Helping children with aggression and conduct problems.* New York: Guilford.

Bowen, E. (2009). *Domestic violence treatment for abusive women.* New York: Routledge.

Bowlby, J. (1969). *Attachment and loss: Vol. one. Attachment.* New York: Basic Books.

Bowlby, J. (1973). *Attachment and loss: Vol. two. Separation: anxiety and anger.* New York: Basic Books.

Bowlby, J. (1980). *Attachment and loss: Vol. three. Loss: sadness and depression.* New York: Basic Books.

Bushman, B., Baumeister, R., & Stack, A. (1999). Catharsis, aggression and persuasive influence: Self-fulfilling or self-defeating prophecies? *Journal of Personality and Social Psychology, 76,* 367–376.

Buss, A. & Durkee, A. (1957). An inventory for assessing different kinds of hostility. *Journal of Counseling Psychology, 63,* 452–459.

Campbell, J. (1995). *Assessing dangerousness: Violence by sexual offenders.* Thousand Oaks, CA: Sage.

Capaldi, D.M., Knoble, N.B., Shortt, J.W., & Kim, H.K (2012). A systematic review of risk factors for intimate partner violence. *Partner Abuse, 3*(2), 231–280.

Ciaramicoli, A. & Ketcham, K. (2000). *The power of empathy.* New York: Dutton.

Coleman, P. (1998). The process of forgiveness in marriage and the family. In R. Enright & J. North (Eds.), *Exploring forgiveness* (pp. 75–94). Madison, WI: University of Wisconsin Press.

Cowan, P. & Cowan, C. (2001). Attachment theory and the therapeutic frame. In C. Clulow (Ed.), *Adult attachment and couple psychotherapy* (pp. 62–82). London: Brunner-Routledge.

Cozolino, L. (2002). *The neuroscience of psychotherapy.* New York: W.W. Norton.

Cozolino, L. (2006). *The neuroscience of human relationships.* New York: W.W. Norton.

Cozolino, L. (2009). "Fire or don't fire". Personal communication.

Cozolino, L. (2010a). *The neuroscience of psychotherapy* (second edition). New York: W.W. Norton.

Cozolino, L. (2010b). "Empathy as hypothesis formation." Personal communication.

Damasio, A. (2000). A second chance for emotion. In R. Lane & L. Nadel (Eds.), *Cognitive neuroscience of emotion* (pp. 12–23). New York: Oxford University Press.

Damasio, A. (2003). *Looking for Spinoza: Joy, sorrow, and the feeling brain.* Orlando, FL: Harcourt.

Dearing, R. & Tangney, J. (2011). *Shame in the therapy hour.* Washington, DC: American Psychological Association.

Decety, J. & Meyer, M. (2008). From emotion resonance to empathic understanding: A social developmental neuroscience account. *Development and Psychopathology, 20,* 1053–1080.

Deffenbacher, J. (2003). Anger disorders. In E.F. Coccaro (Ed.), *Aggression, psychiatric assessment and treatment* (pp. 89–111). New York: Marcel Dekker.

Desmarais, S.L., Reeves, K.A., Nicholls, T.L., Telford, R., & Fiebert, M.S. (2012a). Prevalence of physical violence in intimate relationships – Part 1: Rates of male and female victimization. *Partner Abuse*, 3(2), 140–169.

Desmarais, S.L., Reeves, K.A., Nicholls, T.L., Telford, R.P., & Fiebert, M. (2012b). Prevalence of physical violence in intimate relationships – Part 2: Rates of male and female perpetration. *Partner Abuse*, 3(2), 170–198.

Diamond, D. & Blatt, S. (1994). Internal working models and the representational world in attachment and psychoanalytic theories. In M. Sperling & W. Berman (Eds.), *Attachment in adults* (pp. 72–97). New York: Guilford Press.

DiGiuseppe, R. & Tafrate, R. (2004). *Anger disorders scale: manual*. Toronto, Ontario: Multi Health Systems.

DiGiuseppe, R. & Tafrate, R. (2007). *Understanding anger disorders*. New York: Oxford University Press.

Dispenza, J. (2007). *Evolve your brain*. Deerfield Beach, FL: Health Communications.

Doidge, N. (2007). *The brain that changes itself*. New York: Penguin Books.

Dozier, R. (2002). *Why we hate: Understanding, curbing and eliminating hate in ourselves and the world*. Chicago, IL: Contemporary Books.

Dutton, D. (1998). *The abusive personality*. New York: Guilford.

Dutton, D. (2007). Thinking outside the box: Gender and court-mandated therapy. In J. Hamel & T. Nichols (Eds.), *Family interventions in domestic violence* (pp. 27–58). New York: Springer.

Dutton, D., Van Winkel, C., & Landolt, M. (1997). Jealousy, intimate abusiveness, and intrusiveness. *Journal of Family Violence*, 11(4), 411–423.

Eckhardt, C., Murphy, C., Whitaker, D., Sprunger, J., Dykstra, R., & Woodard, K. (2013). The effectiveness of intervention programs for perpetrators and victims of intimate partner abuse. *Partner Abuse*, 4(2), 196–231.

Eifert, G., McKay, M., & Forsythe, J. (2006). *Act on life, not anger*. Oakland, CA: New Harbinger.

Ekman, P. (2003). *Emotions revealed*. New York: Henry Holt.

Ellis, A. (1962). *Reason and emotion in psychotherapy*. New York: Lyle Stuart.

Ellis, A. & Harper, R. (1975). *A new guide to rational living*. Hollywood, CA: Wilshire Books.

Ellis, A. & Tafrate, R. (1997). *How to control your anger before it controls you*. Secaucus, NY: Carol Publishing.

Enright, R. (2001). *Forgiveness is a choice*. Washington, DC: American Psychological Association.

Enright, R. & Fitzgibbons, R. (2000). *Helping clients forgive*. Washington, DC: American Psychological Association.

Enright, R., Freedman, S., & Rique, J. (1998). The psychology of interpersonal forgiveness. In R. Enright & J. North (Eds.), *Exploring forgiveness* (pp. 46–62). Madison, WI: University of Wisconsin Press.

Evans, D., Hearn, M., & Saklofske, D. (1973). Anger, arousal and systematic desensitization. *Psychological Reports*, 32, 625–626.

REFERENCES

Felsten, G. & Leitten, C.L. (1993). Expressive, but not neurotic hostility is related to cardiovascular reactivity during a hostile competitive task. *Personality and Individual Differences*, 14, 805–813.

Ferch, S. (1998). Intentional forgiving as a counseling intervention. *Journal of Counseling and Development*, 76, 261–270.

Fitness, J. (2001). Betrayal, rejection, revenge and forgiveness. In M. Leary (Ed.), *Interpersonal rejection* (pp. 73–101). New York: Oxford University Press.

Flanigan, B. (1992). *Forgiving the unforgivable*. New York: Macmillan.

Forgays, D., Spielberger, C., Ottaway, S., & Forgays, D. (1998). Factor structure of the State-Trait Anger Expression Inventory for middle-aged men and women. *Psychological Assessment*, 5(2), 141–155.

Fraley, R.C., Davis, K., & Shaver, P. (1998). Dismissing-avoidance and the defensive organization of emotion, cognition and behavior. In J. Simson & W.S. Rholes (Eds.), *Attachment theory and close relationships* (pp. 249–279). New York: Guilford Press.

Freedman, S. (1999). A voice of forgiveness: One incest survivor's experience forgiving her father. *Journal of Family Psychotherapy*, 10(4), 37–60.

Gladwell, M. (2005). *Blink*. New York: Back Bay Books.

Graham-Kevan, N. (2007). Power and control in relationship aggression. In J. Hamel and T. Nichols (Eds.), *Family interventions in domestic violence* (pp. 87–108). New York: Springer.

Green, R. (1998). *MMPI-2: An interpretive manual* (second edition). New York: Allyn and Bacon.

Groetsch, M. (1996). *The battering syndrome*. Brookfield, WI: CPI Publishing.

Hamel, J. (2007). Domestic violence: A gender-inclusive conception. In J. Hamel & T. Nichols (Eds.), *Family interventions in domestic violence* (pp. 3–26). New York: Springer.

Hamel, J. (2014). *Gender-inclusive treatment of intimate partner abuse* (second edition). New York: Springer.

Hamel, J., Jones, D., Dutton, D., & Graham-Kevan, N. (in press, 2015). The CAT: A gender-inclusive measure of abusive and controlling tactics. *Violence and Victims* 30.

Hanson, R. with Mendius, R. (2009). *Buddha's brain*. Oakland, CA: New Harbinger.

Hargrave, T. (1994). *Families and forgiveness*. New York: Brunner/Mazel.

Harway, M. & Hansen, M. (2004). *Spouse abuse* (second edition). Sarasota, FL: Professional Resource Press.

Hauck, P. (1974). *Overcoming frustration and anger*. Philadelphia, PA: Westminster.

Holmes, J. (2001). *Attachment, intimacy, autonomy*. Northvale, NJ: Jason Aronson.

Holtzworth-Munroe, A., Marshall, A., Meehan, J., & Rehman, U. (2003). Physical aggression. In D. Snyder & M. Whisman (Eds.), *Treating difficult couples* (pp. 201–230). New York: Guilford.

Iacoboni, M. (2009). *Mirroring people*. New York: Picador.

Jacobsen, N. & Gottman, J. (1998). *When men batter women*. New York: Simon and Schuster.

243

Jaeger, M. (1998). The power and reality of forgiveness: Forgiving the murderer of one's child. In R. Enright & J. North (Eds.), *Exploring forgiveness* (pp. 9–14). Madison, WI: University of Wisconsin Press.

Johnson, S. (2003, March). Negative emotions. *Discover*, 31–39.

Johnson, S. (2009). Extravagant emotion: Understanding and transforming love relationships in emotionally focused therapy. In D. Fosha, D. Siegel, & M. Solomon (Eds.), *The healing power of emotion* (pp. 257–279). New York: W.W. Norton.

Johnson, S. & Sims, A. (2000). Attachment theory: A map for couples counseling. In Terry Levy (Ed.), *Handbook of attachment interventions* (pp. 169–191). San Diego, CA: Academic Press.

Jordan, C., Nietzel, M., Walker, R., & Logan, T.K. (2004). *Intimate partner violence*. New York: Springer.

Kaminer, D., Stein, D., Mbanga, I., & Zungu-Dirwayi, N. (2000). Forgiveness: Toward an integration of theoretical models. *Psychiatry*, 63(4), 344–357.

Kandel, E., Schwartz, J., Jessell, T., Siegelbaum, S., & Hudspeth, A.J. (2013). *Principles of neuroscience* (fifth edition). New York: McGraw-Hill.

Karen, R. (1994). *Becoming attached*. New York: Oxford University Press.

Karen, R. (2001). *The forgiving self*. New York: Doubleday.

Kassinove, H. & Tafrate, R. (2002). *Anger management*. Atascadero, CA: Impact.

Kaufman, G. (1996). *The psychology of shame* (second edition). New York: Springer.

Klohnen, E. & John, O. (1998). Working models of attachment: A theory-based prototype approach. In J. Simson & W.S. Rholes (Eds.), *Attachment theory and close relationships* (pp. 115–142). New York: Guilford Press.

Knobloch, L., Solomon, D., & Cruz, M. (2001). The role of relationship development and attachment in the experience of romantic jealousy. *Personal Relationships*, 8, 205–224.

Kring, A. (2001). Emotion and psychopathology. In T. Mayne & G. Bonanno (Eds.), *Emotions: Current issues and future directions* (pp. 337–360). New York: Guilford.

Kuhn, T. (1996). *The structure of scientific revolutions* (third edition). Chicago, IL: University of Chicago Press.

Lane, R. & Nadel, L. (Eds.) (2000). *Cognitive neuroscience of emotion*. New York: Oxford University Press.

Langhinrichsen-Rohling, J., Misra, T.A., Selwyn, C., & Rohling, M.L. (2012). Rates of bi-directional vs. unidirectional intimate partner violence across samples, sexual orientations, and race/ethnicities: A comprehensive review. *Partner Abuse*, 3(2), 199–230.

Langhinrichsen-Rohling, J., McCullars, A., & Misra, T.A. (2012). Motivations for men's and women's intimate partner violence perpetration: A comprehensive review. *Partner Abuse*, 3(4), 429–468.

Lazarus, R. (1991). *Emotion and adaptation*. New York: Oxford.

Leary, M., Koch, E., & Hechenbleikner, N. (2001). Emotional responses to interpersonal rejection. In M. Leary (Ed.), *Interpersonal rejection*. New York: Oxford University Press.

LeDoux, J. (1996). *The emotional brain*. New York: Touchstone.

REFERENCES

LeDoux, J. (2002). *Synaptic self*. New York: Viking.

LeDoux, J. & Damasio, A. (2013). Emotions and feelings. In E. Kandel, J. Schwartz, T. Jessell, S. Siegelbaum, & A.J. Hudspeth (Eds.), *Principles of neural science* (pp. 1079–1094). New York: McGraw-Hill.

Lerner, H. (1997). *The dance of anger*. New York: Quill.

Levine, A. & Heller, R. (2010). *Attached*. New York: Penguin.

Levy, T. & Orlans, M. (2000). Attachment disorder as an antecedent to violence and antisocial patterns in children. In T. Levy (Ed.), *Handbook of attachment interventions* (pp. 1–25). San Diego: Academic Press.

Lisspers, J., Nygren, A., & Söderman, E. (1998). Psychological patterns in patients with coronary heart disease, chronic pain and respiratory disorder. *Scandinavian Journal of Caring Sciences*, 12(1), 25–31.

Maiuro, R.D., Cahn, T., Vitaliano, P., Wagner, B., & Zegree, J.B. (1988). Anger, hostility and depression in domestically violent vs. generally assaultive men and nonviolent control subjects. *Journal of Consulting and Clinical Psychology*, 56(1), 17–23.

Margolin, G. & Wampold, B. (1981). Sequential analysis of conflict and accord in distressed and nondistressed marital partners. *Journal of Consulting and Clinical Psychology*, 49(4), 554–567.

Martin, R., Wan, C., David, J., Wegner, E., Olson, B., & Watson, D. (1999). Style of anger expression: relation to expressivity, personality and health. *Personality and Social Psychology Bulletin*, 25(10), 1196–1207.

McCullough, M., Worthington, E., & Rachal, K.C. (1997). Interpersonal forgiving in close relationships. *Journal of Personality and Social Psychology*, 73(2), 321–336.

McKay, M., Davis, M., Paleg, K., & Landis, D. (1996). *When anger hurts your children*. Oakland, CA: New Harbinger.

Medeiros, R. & Straus, M. (2007). Risk factors for physical violence between dating partners: Implications for gender-inclusive prevention and treatment of family violence. In J. Hamel & T. Nichols (Eds.), *Family interventions in domestic violence* (pp. 59–86). New York: Springer.

Mikulincer, M. & Florian, V. (1998). The relationship between adult attachment styles and emotional and cognitive reactions to stressful events. In J. Simson & W.S. Rholes (Eds.), *Attachment theory and close relationships* (pp. 143–165). New York: Guilford.

Miller, M., Drake, E., & Natzinger, M. (2013). *What works to reduce recidivism by domestic violence offenders?* Olympia, WA: Washington State Institute for Public Policy.

Moeller, T. (2001). *Youth, aggression and violence*. London: Lawrence Erlbaum Associates.

Neidig, P. & Freidman, D. (1984). *Spouse abuse: A treatment program for couples*. Champaign, IL: Research Press.

Niehoff, D. (1998). *The biology of violence*. New York: Free Press.

Norden, J. (2007). *Understanding the brain*. Chantilly, VA: The Teaching Company.

Norlander, B. & Eckhardt, C. (2005). Anger, hostility and male perpetrators of intimate partner violence: A meta-analytic review. *Clinical Psychology Review*, 25, 119–152.

North, J. (1998). The "ideal" of forgiveness: A philosopher's exploration. In R. Enright & J. North (Eds.), *Exploring forgiveness* (pp. 15–34). Madison, WI: University of Wisconsin Press.

Novaco, R. (1975). *Anger control: The development and evaluation of an experimental treatment.* Lexington, MA: D.C. Heath.

O'Leary, K.D. & Cohen, S. (2007). Treatment of psychological and physical aggression in a couple context. In J. Hamel & T. Nichols (Eds.), *Family interventions in domestic violence* (pp. 363–380). New York: Springer.

Olson, C. & Colby, C. (2013). The organization of cognition. In E. Kandel, J. Schwartz, T. Jessell, S. Siegelbaum, & A.J. Hudspeth (Eds.), *Principles of neuroscience* (fifth edition) (pp. 392–411). New York: McGraw-Hill.

Panksepp, J. (1998). *Affective neuroscience: The foundations of human and animal emotions.* New York: Oxford University Press.

Panksepp, J. (2009). Brain emotional systems and qualities of mental life: From animal models to implications for psychotherapeutics. In D. Fosha, D. Siegal, & M. Solomon (Eds.), *The healing power of emotion* (pp. 1–26). New York: W.W. Norton.

Panksepp, J. & Biven, L. (2012). *The archaeology of mind.* New York: W.W. Norton.

Parrot, W.G. (2001). The emotional experiences of envy and jealousy. In W.G. Parrott (Ed.), *Emotions in social psychology* (pp. 306–320). New York: Taylor & Francis.

Pence, E. & Paymar, M. (1993). *Education groups for men who batter: the Duluth model.* New York: Springer.

Pittman, F. (1989). *Private lies.* New York: W.W. Norton.

Plutchik, R. (2001). The nature of emotions. *American Scientist*, 89(July–August), 344–350.

Polster, E. & Polster, M. (1973). *Gestalt therapy integrated.* New York: Vintage.

Porges, S. (2009). Reciprocal influences between body and brain in the perception and expression of affect: A polyvagal perspective. In D. Fosha, D. Siegel & M. Solomon (Eds.), *The healing power of emotion* (pp. 27–54). New York: W.W. Norton.

Porges, S. (2011). *The polyvagal theory.* New York: W.W. Norton.

Potter-Efron, R. (1991). *Anger, alcoholism and addiction.* New York: W.W. Norton.

Potter-Efron, R. (1996). *Help for the angry family.* Self-published, Eau Claire, WI.

Potter-Efron, R. (2001). *Stop the anger now: A workbook for the prevention, containment and resolution of anger.* Oakland, CA: New Harbinger.

Potter-Efron, R. (2002). *Shame, guilt and alcoholism* (second edition). New York: Haworth Press.

Potter-Efron, R. (2004). *Angry all the time: An emergency guide to anger control* (second edition). Oakland, CA: New Harbinger.

Potter-Efron, R. (2005). *Handbook of anger management.* New York: Haworth Press.

Potter-Efron, R. (2007). *Rage: A step by step guide to overcoming explosive anger.* Oakland, CA: New Harbinger.

Potter-Efron, R. (2012). *Healing the angry brain.* Oakland, CA: New Harbinger.

Potter-Efron, R. & Potter-Efron, P. (1989). *Letting go of shame.* Center City, MN: Hazelden.

Potter-Efron, R. & Potter-Efron, P. (1991). *Ending our resentments.* Center City, MN: Hazelden.

Potter-Efron, R. & Potter-Efron, P. (2006). *Letting go of anger: The eleven most common anger styles and what to do about them* (second edition). Oakland, CA: New Harbinger.

Power, M. & Dalgleish, T. (1997). *Cognition and emotion: Order to disorder.* Hove: Psychology Press.

Random House unabridged dictionary (second edition). (1993). New York: Random House.

Ratey, J. (2002). *A user's guide to the brain.* New York: Vintage Books.

Rholes, W.S., Simpson, J., & Stevens, J. (1998). Attachment orientations, social support, and conflict resolution in close relationships. In J. Simson & W.S. Rholes (Eds.), *Attachment theory and close relationships* (pp. 166–188). New York: Guilford Press.

Roberts, N. & Noller, P. (1998). The associations between adult attachment and couple violence: The role of communication patterns and relationship satisfaction. In J. Simson & W.S. Rholes (Eds.), *Attachment theory and close relationships* (pp. 317–352). New York: Guilford Press.

Rodgers, J. (2014, April). Go forth in anger. *Psychology Today,* 72–79.

Sapolsky, R. (2005). *Biology and human behavior: The neurobiological origins of individuality.* Chantilly, VA: The Teaching Company.

Saunders, D. (1992). A typology of men who batter: three types derived from cluster analysis. *American Journal of Orthopsychiatry,* 62(2), 264–275.

Schacter, D. & Wagner, A. (2013). Learning and memory. In E. Kandel, J.H. Schwartz, & T.M. Jessel (Eds.), *Principles of neuroscience* (pp. 1441–1460). New York: McGraw-Hill.

Schneider, C. (1977). *Shame, exposure and privacy.* Boston, MA: Beacon Press.

Schore, A. (1994). *Affect regulation and the origin of the self.* Hillsdale, NJ: Lawrence Erlbaum Associates.

Schore, A. (2009). Right brain affect regulation: An essential mechanism of development, trauma, dissociation and psychotherapy. In D. Fosha, D. Siegel, & M. Soloman (Eds.), *The healing power of emotions* (pp. 112–144). New York: W.W. Norton.

Schwartz, J., Barres, B., & Goldman, J. (2013). The cells of the nervous system. In E. Kandel, J. Schwartz, T. Jessell, S. Siegelbaum, & A.J. Hudspeth (Eds.). *Principles of neuroscience,* fifth edition (pp. 71–99). New York: McGraw Hill.

Seligman, M. (2006). *Learned optimism.* New York: Vintage.

Shapiro, F. (1995). *Eye movement desensitization and reprocessing.* New York: Guilford.

Sharpsteen, D. & Kirkpatrick, L. (1997). Romantic jealousy and adult romantic attachment. *Journal of Personality and Social Psychology,* 72(3), 627–640.

Siegel, A. (2005). *The neurobiology of aggression and rage.* Boca Raton, FL: CRC Press.

Siegel, D. (2011). *Mindsight.* New York: Bantam Books.

Siegel, D. (2012). *The developing mind* (second edition). New York: Guilford.

Smedes, L. (1984). *Forgive and forget.* San Francisco, CA: Harper and Row.

Smith, J. (1999). *ABC relaxation training.* New York: Springer.

Spielberger, C. (1999). *Manual for the State-Trait Anger Expression Inventory—2.* Odessa, FL: Psychological Assessment Resources.

Spielberger, C. (2001). "Relationship between anger-in and suppressed anger." Personal correspondence.

Stearns, P. (1994). *American cool.* New York: American University Press.

Straus, M., Hamby, S., & Warren, W.L. (2003). *The Conflict Tactics Scales handbook.* Los Angeles: WPS.

Sumner, M. (2014). Personal conversation with Chief of Police, High Point, NC.

Tafrate, R. (1995). Evaluation of treatment strategies for adult anger disorders. In H. Kassinove (Ed.), *Anger disorders: Definition, diagnosis and treatment* (pp. 109–130). Washington, DC: Taylor & Francis.

Tangney, J. & Dearing, R. (2002). *Shame and guilt.* New York: Guilford.

Tavris, C. (1989). *Anger: The misunderstood emotion.* New York: Simon and Schuster.

Teicher, M. (2002, March). The neurobiology of child abuse. *Scientific American,* 68–75.

Thich Nhat Hahn (2001). *Anger: Wisdom for cooling the flames.* New York: Berkeley.

Thomas, M. (2007). Treatment of family violence: A systemic perspective. In J. Hamel & T. Nichols (Eds.), *Family interventions in domestic violence* (pp. 417–436). New York: Springer.

Tivis, L., Parsons, O., & Nixon, S. (1998). Anger in an inpatient sample of chronic alcoholics. *Alcoholism: Clinical and Experimental Research,* 22(4), 902–907.

Tracy, J., Robins, R., & Tangney, J. (Eds.) (2007). *The self-conscious emotions.* New York: Guilford.

Tucker, N., Stith, S., Howell, L., McCollum, E., & Rosen, K. (2000). Meta-dialogues in domestic violence-focused couples treatment. *Journal of Systemic Therapies,* 19(4), 73–89.

Vetere, A. & Cooper, J. (2001). Working systemically with family violence: Risk, responsibility and collaboration. *Journal of Family Therapy,* 23, 378–396.

Vetere, A. & Cooper, J. (2007). Couple violence and couple safety: A systemic and attachment-oriented approach to working with complexity and uncertainty. In J. Hamel & T. Nichols (Eds.), *Family interventions in domestic violence* (pp. 381–396). New York: Springer.

Volavka, J. (2002). *Neurobiology of violence* (second edition). Washington, DC: American Psychiatric Publishing.

Walfish, S. (1990). Anxiety and anger among abusers of different substances. *Drug and Alcohol Dependence,* 25(3), 253–256.

REFERENCES

Whitaker, D.J., Murphy, C.M., Eckhardt, C.I., Hodges, A.E., & Cowart, M. (2013). Effectiveness of primary prevention efforts for intimate partner violence. *Partner Abuse*, 4(2), 175–195.

White, G. & Mullen, P. (1989). *Jealousy: Theory, research, and clinical strategies.* New York: Guilford Press.

White, W. (2004). Substance use and violence: Understanding the nuances of the relationship. *The Addiction Professional*, 2(1), 13–19.

Wilson, S. (2001). Attachment disorders: Review and current status. *Journal of Psychology*, 135(1), 37–52.

INDEX

Note: 'f' after a page number indicates a figure, 't' after a page number indicates a table.

abandonment crisis 48
abandonment rage 53, 55–6, 61
abusers. *See* domestic violence offenders
acetylcholine 5
action phase: the brain during 147; case study 167–8; moderation principle 147; repetition principle 147, 148; substitution principle 147–8
action tendencies, of anger 7
activation phase: and anger invitations 142; the brain during 143–4; case study 167–8; prevention strategies 144
ACT theory 116
ADD. *See* attention deficit disorder (ADD)
addiction. *See* alcoholism and substance abuse
adolescents. *See* teens
adrenal gland 28, 29f
affect 6
affective approach: "anger thermometer" 133; choosing, as modality 120; and criticism 136–7; exposure techniques 133; goals of 131, 133; as intervention focus 118–19, 199; questions to increase self-awareness 132, 134; relaxation training 119, 133
aggression. *See* physical aggression
Ainsworth, Mary 32
alcoholism and substance abuse: and anger/aggression 83–7, 85t; and

assessment 76; case study 89; and individual counseling 201; and offender typologies 102; as psychological condition associated with anger 67t; treatment strategies for 83–7
American Cool (Stearns) 117
amygdala: and activation phase 143; and conscious vs. unconscious anger response 20–1; and cortisol 28–9, 29f; and depression 31; and emotions 6, 10; and "low road" brain communication system 30; and memory 10, 20; and preparation phase 146; and rage 52; and RAGE response 9; and splitting 154–5
anger: action tendencies of 7; vs. aggression 121; anger management approach 116; and attachment needs 36; behavioral sequences linked to 8; brain regulation of, as similar to fear 31; as commingled with other issues 200–2; conscious vs. unconscious aspects of 20–1; diagnosing 65–6; and dismissive attachment style 47–8; and domestic violence 96–7; in families 210–16; and fearful attachment style 49; and left hemisphere of brain 19; long-term effect of, on the brain 3; mindfulness approach 116; periaqueductal grey (PAG) region as central to 9; and pleasure 19; and preoccupied attachment style

48; psychological conditions associated with 67t, 75; purpose of 7, 9, 17, 19; vs. rage 50–1, 62; reductionist approach 116; as response to danger/fear 4, 10–11, 19–20, 31; safety as inhibitor for 19–20, 27; and secure attachment style 47; sedating effect of 83; societal ambivalence toward 117; ventilationist approach 115–16, 131–2. *See also* emotions; fear; physical aggression; rage; survival orientation

anger, repressed 218, 225

anger, self-directed: self-attack 233f, 236–7; self-blame 233f, 235–6; self-destructive behavior 237; self-neglect 232–4; self-sabotage 234–5; and shame 232–3

anger, suppressed: Anger Directed Inward Quiz 221–2, 226; anger patterns 219–20; behavior patterns 222–3; case study 228–9; and children 224–5; definition of 218; and domestic violence 220–1, 223; guidelines for treating 225–8; health problems caused by 223; as ignored in traditional treatment 238; and passive aggression 219; reasons for 218–19, 224–5; vs. repressed 225; "stuff and blow" explosions 220, 223. *See also* passive aggression

Anger/Aggression Intake Questionnaire 68–76, 87

anger/aggression logs 125, 172

anger and aggression model: action (phase four) 147–8; activation (phase one) 142–4; anger episode 143f; case study 167–8; deactivation (phase six) 153–67; feedback (phase five) 148–53; modulation (phase two) 144–6; overview of 142; preparation (phase three) 146–7. *See also* specific phases

Anger Directed Inward Quiz 221–2, 226

Anger Disorders Scale 66, 68, 219

anger episodes, as unit of analysis 77

anger invitations: in activation phase 142–3; in case study 193; and

cognitive interventions 127; management of 117–18; triggering events as 77

anger management: effectiveness of 137; as field separate from domestic violence offender treatment xi; goals of 117–18, 198; intervention methods in 199; myths of 131–2; as treatment approach 116. *See also* treatment strategies and interventions

Anger Pie 149–50, 149f, 172

anger styles: anger turned inward 80; avoidance 79; chronic 81; deliberate 80–1; distrust-based (paranoia) 81; excitatory 80; explosive 80–1; habitual 81; hidden 79–80; moral anger 81; passive aggression 79–80; resentment/hate 81; shame-based anger 80; sudden 80

Anger Styles Questionnaire 77–81, 90

"angry brain": causes of 4–6; and cognitive distortion 21–2; healing 24–5; and neural networks 4; and pessimism/negativity 22; use of term 4. *See also* the brain

antisocial personality disorder 67t, 101, 102

anxiety disorders 67t

anxious/ambivalent attachment style 33

anxious/avoidant attachment style 33

arborization 14, 17, 18f, 185

assertiveness training 116

assessment: and alcoholism/ substance abuse 76; Anger/Aggression Intake Questionnaire 68–76, 87; Anger Directed Inward Quiz 221–2, 226; Anger Disorders Scale 66, 68, 219; Anger Styles Questionnaire 77–81, 90; Buss-Durkee Hostility Inventory 65; case study 87–90; challenges of 65–6; Conflict Tactics Scale 106–7; Controlling Abusive Tactics Questionnaire (CAT-2) 107; Danger Assessment 107; and gender-inclusive treatment model 103; importance of 106; Minnesota Multiphasic Personality Inventory 65; Novaco Anger Inventory 65; Relationship Dominance Questionnaire 107–10; Safe at

Home Questionnaire 110, 184; State-Trait Anger Expression Inventory—II 66–8; Structured Interview for Anger Disorders 68; tools for 106–7, 110–11; and treatment 82. *See also* specific instruments; treatment strategies

attachment: adult vs. parental/infant 34; and anger response 36; definition of 32, 34; as epigenetic phenomenon 35–6; key characteristics of 32–4; and vagal regulation 45–6

attachment difficulties: and associated behaviors/cognitions 67t; and domestic violence 97; insecure, and abandonment rage 61; and jealousy 39–40; and offender typologies 101; as specialized area 199–200

attachment styles: of adults 34–5; of children 33–4; of domestic violence offenders 36–8; and self-esteem 38. *See also* specific styles

attachment theory 32–6, 207–8

attention deficit disorder (ADD) 27, 67t

avoidance 79

axons 14, 15f

Babcock, J.C. 97

Bartholomew, K. 34, 36, 37, 208

Beck, Aaron 127

Begley, T. 223

behavioral approach: anger/aggression logs 125; choosing, as modality 120; commitment to change 123–4; fair fighting 126; giving praise 126; goals for 121; habitual behavior 121–2; as intervention focus 118–26, 199; substitution principle 121; time outs 119, 124–5

Berecz, J. 163

Berman, W. 34

bipolar disorder (manic phase) 67t

Biven, L. 19, 35

blaming 214, 235. *See also* self-blame

Bloomquist, M. 145

borderline personality disorder 67t, 101, 199

borderline personality organization 49

Bowen, E. 180

Bowlby, John 32

the brain: during action phase 147; during activation phase 143–4; and adolescence 145; amygdala 6; and attachment 33; communication system of 30; complexity of 8; effects of chronic anger on 3; effects of trauma on 28–30; and emotions 6–8; and empathy 24, 151–2; and impulse control 10; left vs. right hemispheres 19; limbic system 8–11; during modulation phase 144; periaqueductal grey (PAG) region 6; during preparation phase 146; processes underlying change in 14, 15–16f, 17; and rage 51–2; and RAGE response 9; survival orientation of, when stressed 28–30, 29f. *See also* "angry brain"; specific components

brain-change model: case study 192–4; and client oppositionality 184; rationale for 182–4; as treatment approach 185–91

brain damage: as cause of "angry brain" 5–6; and rage 52

brain dysfunctions 27

"bus of your life" analogy 148–9

Buss-Durkee Hostility Inventory 65

Campbell, J. 107

Capaldi, D.M. 95

CAT-2. *See* Controlling Abusive Tactics Questionnaire (CAT-2)

caudate nucleus 146, 153

change: holistic 21; possibility of, and neuroplasticity 11; processes underlying, for brain 14, 15–16f, 17. *See also* brain-change model; neuroplasticity

"chase and run" pattern 38

child care 180

children: and angry families 210–16; and attachment 32–4; and corporal punishment 215; and hostile attributional bias 145; and suppressed anger 224–5; as witnesses of violence 104. *See also* teens

Ciaramicoli, A. 151, 161

client oppositionality: and brain-change model 184; and neuroplasticity 184; overcoming

22–3; overview of 183–4; and trust 184

cognitive approach: challenging "hot thoughts" 129–30; choosing, as modality 120; confronting denial 129; disputation techniques 119, 130–1, 235; as intervention focus 118–19, 199; key principles of 127–8; questions to increase self-awareness 128–9; rational-emotive therapy 127; for self-sabotage 235

cognitive behavioral therapy 105

cognitive distortion 21–2

cognitive therapy 116

Cohen, S. 205

Coleman, P. 164

commissions 155

conduct disorder 66

Conflict Tactics Scale 106–7

conscious awareness, and anger response 20–1

Controlling Abusive Tactics Questionnaire (CAT-2) 107

Cooper, J. 205

corporal punishment 215

corpus collosum 30

cortisol 10, 28–9, 31, 143, 144

couples counseling: and attachment 44, 46–7; benefits of 204–5; dangers of 203–4, 206, 208; guidelines for 208, 210; objections to 207, 208; reasons to consider 206–7, 208–10; and safety 205, 210; systems model 205–8

Cowan, C. 37–8

Cowan, P. 37–8

Cozolino, Lou 9, 24, 30, 45–6, 151

criticism 136–7, 152, 214. See also praise

CTS2 107

cultural diversity 181–2

cultural training 4–5

curiosity 152

Damasio, A. 6–7, 9

Dance of Anger (Lerner) 218

danger, anger as response to 4, 10–11, 19–20, 31

Danger Assessment 107

deactivation phase: case study 167–8; forgiveness in 156–67; and hatred 154–6; and resentment 153, 154, 155–6. See also forgiveness

defensiveness 214–15

Deffenbacher, J. 65

dendrites 14, 16f, 18f

denial 129

depression 31, 102, 200–1

Desmarais, S.L. 94

Diagnostic Statistical Manual of the American Psychiatric Association (APA, 2014) 65

DiGiuseppe, R. 38, 68, 137, 159, 219, 220

dismissive attachment style 35, 37, 47–8, 101

disorganized/disoriented attachment style 34

disputation techniques 119, 130–1, 235

dissociative identity disorder 67t, 199–200

distrust 49. See also trust

Doidge, N. 153

domestic violence: as aggression 96; and anger 96–7; and attachment difficulties 97; as bidirectional 94; definitions of 91–3; and moral rage 62; and passive aggression 220; Power and Control model 58, 97–9; prevalence of 93–4; risk factors for 95–6; and suppressed anger 220–1, 223; Wisconsin law regarding 92. See also physical aggression

domestic violence offenders: attachment styles of 36–8; cultural diversity of 181–2; gender of 93, 94; levels of 171; motivations of 94–5; oppositionality of 22–3, 183–4; typologies of 99–103; use of term xi; women as 179–82. See also treatment programs

dopamine 5, 83

dorsolateral prefrontal cortex 10, 147

Dozier, R. 154

drug abuse. See alcoholism and substance abuse

Duluth model. See Power and Control model

Dutton, D. 34, 49, 97, 100, 208

dysthymic disorder 67t

Eckhardt, C. 105, 179
effectiveness 105, 137, 179
Ellis, Albert 116, 127, 130
EMDR. *See* Eye Movement Desensitization Reprocessing (EMDR)
emotions: and amygdala 6, 10; background 6; and the brain 6–8; definition of 6; evolution of 8; vs. feelings 6–7; primary 6; primitive origins of 51; purpose of 7–8, 17; social 6–7, 177. *See also* anger
empathy: and the brain 151–2; cognitive 151; definition of 24, 151; educational handout on 173–4; emotional 151; and forgiveness 160–1, 162, 167; techniques for improving 152–3
empathy training 62, 150–3
Enright, R. 157, 159, 161, 163–4
epigenesis 5
epinephrine 31
estrogen 5
ethnic minorities 181–2
excitatory/activating processes 28
existential/spiritual approach: choosing, as modality 120; forgiveness training 119; as intervention focus 118–19, 199; mindfulness meditation 119; as neglected in anger management 135; questions to increase self-awareness 135–6
exposure techniques 133
expressive violence 96–7
Eye Movement Desensitization Reprocessing (EMDR) 25

facial expressions 7, 152
fair fighting 126
family of origin dynamics 4–5, 175, 203, 224–5
family therapy 211–16
fear: anger as response to 4, 19–20, 31; behavioral sequences linked to 8; brain regulation of, as similar to anger 31; and cortisol 28. *See also* anger
fearful attachment style 35, 37, 49
feedback phase: Anger Pie 149–50, 149f; "bus of your life" analogy 148–9; case study 167–8; empathy training 150–3; and listening skills 150; sources of feedback 148
feelings: vs. emotions 6–7; evoked by RAGE response 19; societal ambivalence toward 117
fight-or-flight response 30, 45
Fitzgibbons, R. 159, 161, 163–4
Five A's 60–1
Flanigan, B. 164
forgiveness 154; benefits of 159, 165; conditions for 160; definitions of 157–8; and empathy 160–1, 162, 167; vs. reconciliation 157; and reframing 161–2, 167; stages and processes of 163–4; techniques for 165–7
forgiveness training 119
formative attention 39
Freedman, S. 157, 159
freeze system 44–5
Freidman, D. 204

gamma-amino butyric acid (GABA) 5, 25, 28
gangs 5
gender: and attachment styles of offenders 37–8; and domestic violence 93, 94. *See also* men; women
gender-inclusive treatment model 103–4
Gender-Inclusive Treatment of Intimate Partner Abuse (Hamel) 110
genetics: and attachment 35–6; as cause of "angry brain" 5
gestalt therapy 116, 167, 218, 228
gift-giving 166
glutamate 5, 28
Gottman, J. 83, 96, 100
Graham-Kevan, N. 102
Groetsch, M. 99–100
group treatment. *See* treatment groups
guilt 160, 177, 224, 226, 228–9
"gut feelings" 7–8

habitual behavior 121–2, 127, 186. *See also* "use it or lose it" principle
Hamel, John 95, 103, 104, 110, 179, 180, 205–6
Hargrave, T. 164
hatred 154–6, 199–200
Hauck, P. 128

helplessness 58–9
Henderson, A. 34, 208
hippocampus 29f; and cortisol 144; and deactivation phase 153; definition of 10; effects of trauma on 28–9, 30; and modulation phase 144; and rage 52
Holmes, J. 36
Holtzworth-Munroe, A. 205
hormones 5, 28
hostile attributional bias 145
"hot thoughts" 129–30
hypothalamus: and cortisol 10; and deactivation phase 153; and rage 52; and RAGE response 9

illegal immigrants 182
immune system 30
impotent rage 53, 55, 58–9, 135
impulse control 10
individual counseling 196–203; and alcoholism and substance abuse 201; case study 202–3; guidelines for 201–2; for seriously impaired individuals 199–200; and trust 200
infidelity 43–4, 202–3
inhibitory/sedating processes 28
instrumental violence 96–7
intermittent explosive disorder 67t
internal working models 33
interventions. See treatment strategies and interventions
"intimacy-anger" 49
inventories. See assessment

Jacobsen, N. 83, 96, 100
jealousy: and attachment 39–40; attachment-related treatment strategies 42–4; case study 40–2, 202–3; continuum of 38–9; coping strategies 42; definition of 38; vs. envy 38; and infidelity 43–4, 202–3; and relationship drift 39
Johnson, S. 208
Jordan, C. 95
journaling 165. See also anger/aggression logs

Kaminer, D. 157
Karen, Robert 224–5
Kassinove, H. 96, 127, 133
Kuhn, Thomas 97

language barriers 182
law enforcement 171
Lazarus, R. 127
LeDoux, Joseph 6–7, 9, 28, 30
Lerner, Harriet 218
lesbian/gay/bisexual/transsexual (LGBT) individuals 181–2
letter-writing 165–6
limbic irritability 31
limbic system: and conscious vs. unconscious anger response 20–1; definition of 10; overview of 8–11; and rage 52; and splitting 154–5; and values-based moral rage 61
listening skills 150
log books. See anger/aggression logs
long-term potentiation (LTP) 14, 16f, 17, 185

major depressive disorder 67t
MAOA gene 5
Martin, R. 223
maternal attachment. See attachment
McCullough, M. 151, 157
Medeiros, R. 94
medication 46, 75–6
memory: and amygdala 10, 20; and emotions 7; and hippocampus 28; persistence of traumatic 30
men: as domestic violence offenders 94; and gender-inclusive treatment model 103–4; and Power and Control model 98. See also gender
midbrain periaqueductal grey (PAG) region 10
middle-class values 148
Miller, Michael 85
mindfulness meditation 46, 116, 119, 147
Minnesota Multiphasic Personality Inventory 65
minorities 181–2
mirror neurons 24, 151–2
modalities, choosing 120
moderation principle 147
modulation phase: the brain during 144; case study 167–8; and emotional awareness 146; time outs 144–5
moral anger 81
moral rage 53, 56, 61–2
motivation: of domestic violence offenders 94–5; research on 184

Mullen, P. 42
multiple sclerosis 14
myelination 14, 15f, 17, 185

negativity 22
Neidig, P. 204
Neihoff, D. 5
neural networks: and "angry brain"
    4; definition of 11; integrating 25;
    "neurons that fire together wire
    together" principle" 11, 12f, 23,
    186; "use it or lose it" principle 11,
    13f, 23–4, 122, 148
neuroception 44
neurochemical function, faulty 5
neuroflexibility 17
neurons: and brain change 14, 17;
    "mirror" 24; purpose of 11
neuroplasticity 11–17; and brain-
    change treatment model 185–91;
    and client oppositionality 184;
    definition of 11; and possibility of
    change 11; processes underlying 14,
    15–16f, 17; techniques for
    encouraging 23–4. See also change
neurotransmitters: acetylcholine 5;
    dopamine 5, 83; gamma-amino
    butyric acid (GABA) 5, 25, 28;
    glutamate 5, 28; norepinephrine 5,
    14, 31; serotonin 5, 14, 27, 83, 176
Niehoff, D. 9, 31, 49
Nodes of Ranvier 15f
Noller, P. 38, 208, 209
norepinephrine 5, 14, 31
North, J. 161
Novaco, R. 115
Novaco Anger Inventory 65

offenders. See domestic violence
    offenders
O'Leary, K.D. 205
omissions 155
open-ended questions 152
oppositional defiant disorder 66
oppositionality. See client
    oppositionality
orbitofrontal cortex 10, 146, 152
outrage. See moral rage
oxytocin 45

PAG region. See midbrain
    periaqueductal grey (PAG) region;
    periaqueductal grey (PAG) region

Panksepp, J. 7, 9, 19, 25, 35, 51
paradigms 97–8
paranoia/paranoid schizophrenia 67t,
    102
Parrot, W.G. 39
Partner Abuse 179
Partner Abuse State of Knowledge
    (PASK) 94, 179
passive aggression 49, 79–80, 219,
    220, 229–32, 234. See also anger,
    suppressed
periaqueductal grey (PAG) region: and
    emotions 6; and rage 51, 52; and
    RAGE response 9
perpetrators. See domestic violence
    offenders
pessimism 22
physical aggression: affective 9; vs.
    anger 121; and attention deficit
    disorder (ADD) 27; and brain
    dysfunctions 27; causes of 9; as
    commingled with other issues
    200–2; domestic violence as 96;
    inter-male 9; predatory 9; and
    serotonin 27; types of 9. See also
    anger; domestic violence
physiological systems: freeze system
    44–5; social engagement system 45;
    sympathetic-adrenal system 45
Pittman, Frank 39, 44, 48
pleasure 19
Plutchik, R. 8
polyvagal theory 44–6
Porges, Stephen 44
positive visualization 166
post-traumatic stress disorder 67t
post-traumatic stress disorder (PTSD):
    and offender typologies 102; and
    sensitization model 28; as
    specialized area 199
Potter-Efron, Patricia 77, 107, 166
Potter-Efron, Ronald 107, 117
Power and Control model: of
    domestic violence 97–9; dominance
    wheel 98; effectiveness of 105; and
    impotent rage 58
praise: in case study 194; and family
    therapy 216; giving 126, 148. See
    also criticism
prayer 166
premenstrual dysphoric syndrome 67t
preoccupied attachment style 35, 37,
    48

preparation phase: the brain during 146; case study 167–8; and gap between impulse and action 146–7; and mindfulness meditation 147
pride 177, 224
primary prevention programs 105
Principles of Neuroscience, 5th edition (Kandel et al) 8–9
psychological conditions, associated with anger 67t, 75
PTSD. *See* post-traumatic stress disorder (PTSD)

Rachal, K.C. 151, 157
rage: abandonment 53, 55–6, 61; vs. anger 50–1, 62; and the brain 51–2; and brain damage 52; definition of 50; impotent 53, 55, 58–9, 135; moral 53, 56, 61–2; near vs. partial 52; and PAG region 51, 52; shame-based 53, 55, 59–61; sudden vs. seething 52, 53–4; survival 53, 54, 58; treatment strategies for 57–8, 59, 60–1, 62; types of 52–3, 58–62. *See also* anger; specific types
Rage Questionnaire 53–6
RAGE response 9, 19
Ratey, J. 9
rational-emotive therapy 116, 127
Readiness to Change program 105
Reasons for Violence Scale 95
reconciliation 157
reductionist approach 116
reframing 161–2, 167
Relationship Dominance Questionnaire 107–10
relationship drift 39, 44, 48
relaxation training 46, 119, 133
religion 154
repetition principle 147, 148
resentment 153, 154, 155–6
Rique, J. 157
risk factors 95–6
Roberts, N. 38, 208, 209
role play 167, 227
romantic jealousy. *See* jealousy

Safe at Home Questionnaire 110, 184
safety: as anger inhibitor 19–20, 27; and attachment 32, 34; and cognitive distortion 22; and couples counseling 205, 210; and polyvagal theory 45; and survival rage 58

Sapolsky, R. 9
Saunders, D. 99
Schnell, S. 145
Schore, A. 146
secure attachment style 33, 34–5, 37–8, 47
self-attack 233f, 236–7
self-blame 233f, 235–6
self-care 177, 234
self-destructive behavior 199–200, 233f, 237. *See also* anger, self-directed
self-disclosure 153
self-esteem 38, 43, 158
self-mutilation 236
self-neglect 232–4, 233f
self-sabotage 233f, 234–5
sensitization model 28
serotonin 5, 14, 27, 83, 176
shame: core messages of 60; and forgiveness 160; and self-blame 235; and self-destructiveness 237; and self-directed anger 232–3; and self-sabotage 234; as social emotion 177
shame-based anger 80
shame-based rage 53, 55, 59–61
shortfalls 155
Siegel, D. 51
Sims, A. 208
Smedes, L. 164
Smith, J. 133
social engagement system 45
Sperling, M. 34
Spielberger, Charles 66, 219, 237
splitting 154–5, 157, 165, 167, 237
state anger 67
State-Trait Anger Expression Inventory—II (STAXI-2) 66–8, 89, 219, 237
STAXI-2. *See* State-Trait Anger Expression Inventory—II (STAXI-2)
Stearns, P. 117
Straus, M. 94
stress 28, 30
Structured Interview for Anger Disorders 68
"stuff and blow" explosions 220, 223, 231
substance abuse. *See* alcoholism and substance abuse
substitution principle 121, 147–8

suicidal ideation 237
survival orientation: and the brain 28–30, 29f; as maladaptive 31–2
survival rage 53, 54, 58
sympathetic-adrenal system 45
synaptic gap 14
systems model 205–6, 207–8, 211, 215–16

Tafrate, R. 38, 68, 96, 115, 127, 133, 137, 159, 219, 220
Tavris, C. 132
teens: bias toward negativity 145; brain development of 145; primary prevention programs for 105. *See also* children
temporal parietal junction 152
temporal pole 152
testosterone 5
thalamus 10, 30, 146
therapist-client relationship 105, 179
therapists, and victim notification 110–11
time outs 25, 119, 124–5, 144–5
trait anger 68
trauma: effect of, on hippocampus 29; long-term effects of, on the brain 28–30; memories of, as persistent 30
treatment groups: check-ins 170; initial questionnaire for 178–9; therapeutic alternatives to 196–216; and trust 170; for women 179–82
Treatment Planning Form 82–3
treatment programs: brain-change model 185–91; educational, for minimal offenders 171–3; extended, for severe offenders 174–9; and levels of intervention 171
treatment strategies and interventions: affective approach 118–19, 131–4, 199; for alcoholism/substance abuse 83–7; Anger/Aggression Intake Questionnaire 74–6; anger and aggression model 142–69; vs. anger management xi; anger management approach 116; based on offender typologies 101–2;

behavioral approach 118–26, 199; brain-change model 182–91; case study 138–41; choosing modalities 120; cognitive approach 118–19, 126–31, 199; couples counseling 203–11; for developing sense of safety 46–7; effectiveness of 137; evidence-based models for 104–6; existential/spiritual approach 118–19, 134–7, 199; family therapy 211–16; gender-inclusive treatment model 103–4; goals of 117–18, 198; group treatment 170–95; individual counseling for 196–203; intervention methods in 199; for jealousy concerns 42–4; mindfulness approach 116; overview of 115–18; for passive aggression 231–2; primary prevention programs 105; for rage 57–8, 59, 60–1, 62; reductionist approach 116; specialized area in 199–200; for suppressed anger 225–8; systems model 205–6, 207–8; ventilationist approach 115–16, 131–2. *See also* anger and aggression model; assessment; specific modalities
trust: and client oppositionality 184; in group treatment 170; and individual counseling 200
Tucker, N. 204
typologies, of domestic violence offenders 99–103

"use it or lose it" principle 11, 13f, 23–4, 122, 148, 186. *See also* neuroplasticity

vagal nerve 44, 45. *See also* polyvagal theory
vagal regulation 45, 46
values, and moral rage 61–2
ventilationist approach 115–16, 131–2
Vetere, A. 205
victim notification 110–11
victim witness handout 173–4
violence: expressive vs. instrumental 96–7. *See also* domestic violence; physical aggression; trauma

visual cortex 30
visualization exercise 166

Whitaker, D.J. 105
White, G. 42
White, W. 84
Wilson, S. 32
Wisconsin, domestic violence law 92

women: blaming of 207; and child care 180; as domestic violence offenders 94; domestic violence risk factors for 95; and gender-inclusive treatment model 103–4; treatment groups for 179–82. *See also* gender
Worthington, E. 151, 157

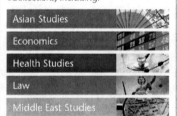
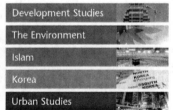

CPSIA information can be obtained
at www.ICGtesting.com
Printed in the USA
LVOW10s2308300117
522683LV00007B/106/P